Advance Praise for
Thomas Jefferson—Revolutionary

"Perhaps no figure has cast a longer shadow across the American political landscape than Thomas Jefferson; and the political thought and legacy of few figures have been the subject of more debate. In his engaging examination of Jefferson's public life, Kevin Gutzman takes his readers on a rip-roaring ride through the contests and controversies of the founding era and early republic, inviting readers along the way to challenge conventional interpretations of history and reconsider first principles. Brimming with keen insights, *Thomas Jefferson—Revolutionary* focuses on Jefferson's often radical views on federalism, the rights of conscience, race, slavery, and public education, casting light on the great political controversies that have long roiled the republic."

—Daniel L. Dreisbach, professor in the Department of Justice, Law & Criminology, American University, and author of *Thomas Jefferson and the Wall of Separation Between Church and State*

"No statesman of the United States' founding years has suffered a more precipitous decline in his reputation than Thomas Jefferson. He has been one of the principal victims of our era's small-minded rage against the very idea that imperfect men can still be heroes. It is time for a spirited corrective to this folly, and Kevin Gutzman has provided one in this book, reminding us of Jefferson's astounding range of accomplishments, and his steadfast confidence in the dignity and unrealized potential in the minds and hearts of ordinary people. Whenever we search for the core of what is greatest in the American democratic experiment, we find the towering figure of Jefferson, and the abundant evidence of his influence."

—Wilfred M. McClay, G. T. and Libby Blankenship Chair in the History of Liberty, University of Oklahoma

"When Jefferson wrote the inscription for his tombstone, he ignored the many offices he'd held and instead listed as his signature achievements the Declaration of Independence, the Virginia Statute for Religious Freedom, and the University of Virginia. Kevin Gutzman's important new book connects the dots between these and other contributions to make a compelling case that Jefferson was neither an enigma nor a paradox. Instead, he was an American Revolutionary with a consistent and coherent agenda to make America a land of liberty and opportunity the likes of which the world had never seen."

—Robert M. S. McDonald, professor of history,
United States Military Academy,
author of *Confounding Father:*
Thomas Jefferson's Image in His Own Time

THOMAS
JEFFERSON
Revolutionary

ALSO BY KEVIN R. C. GUTZMAN

James Madison and the Making of America

The Politically Incorrect Guide to the Constitution

Who Killed the Constitution?:
The Federal Government versus American Liberty from
World War I to Barack Obama
(coauthored with Thomas E. Woods Jr.)

Virginia's American Revolution:
From Dominion to Republic, 1776–1840

THOMAS
JEFFERSON
Revolutionary

A RADICAL'S STRUGGLE
TO REMAKE AMERICA

Kevin R. C. Gutzman

ST. MARTIN'S PRESS
NEW YORK

THOMAS JEFFERSON—REVOLUTIONARY. Copyright 2017 by Kevin R. C. Gutzman. All rights reserved. Printed in the United States of America. For information, address St. Martin's Press, 175 Fifth Avenue, New York, N.Y. 10010.

www.stmartins.com

Library of Congress Cataloging-in-Publication Data

Names: Gutzman, Kevin Raeder, 1963– author.
Title: Thomas Jefferson, revolutionary : a radical's struggle to remake
    America / Kevin R. C. Gutzman.
Description: New York : St. Martin's Press, 2017.
Identifiers: LCCN 2016038745| ISBN 9781250010803 (hardcover) | ISBN
    9781250010810 (e-book)
    Includes bibliographical references and index.
Subjects: LCSH: Jefferson, Thomas, 1743–1826—Philosophy. |
    Revolutionaries—United States—Biography. | Presidents—United
    States—Biography. | United States—Politics and government—1775–1783. |
    United States—Politics and government—1783–1809. | BISAC: BIOGRAPHY &
    AUTOBIOGRAPHY / Historical. | HISTORY / United States / 19th Century. |
    HISTORY / United States / Revolutionary Period (1775–1800).
Classification: LCC B885.Z7 G87 2017 | DDC 973.4/6092 [B]—dc23
LC record available at https://lccn.loc.gov/2016038745

Our books may be purchased in bulk for promotional, educational, or business use. Please contact your local bookseller or the Macmillan Corporate and Premium Sales Department at 1-800-221-7945, extension 5442, or by e-mail at MacmillanSpecialMarkets@macmillan.com.

First Edition: January 2017

10 9 8 7 6 5 4 3 2 1

To Marika—
Carpe diem!

Contents

Note from the Author

Jefferson lived and worked in an age before standardization of grammar and spelling. Rather than substitute our taste and rules for his, I have generally left his prose as I found it. I would not correct Shakespeare or the Authorized Version, either.

THOMAS JEFFERSON

Revolutionary

Introduction

Thomas Jefferson's influence on American political history outstrips that of any other figure. Only Franklin Roosevelt rivaled President Jefferson's dominance of the federal government, and Jefferson was more than the supreme politician of the revolutionary era: he was its symbol, even in his own day.

George Washington became the symbol of the Continental Army and of American patriotism, even American nationhood, but Jefferson stood for the principles with which the American Revolution was synonymous: the equality of man, liberty of conscience, and republican self-government. His diplomatic masterstroke, the Louisiana Purchase, and its implementing initiative, the Voyage of Discovery (aka the Lewis and Clark Expedition), made America a continental republic.

That America would be a continental colossus seems a logical outcome of what Jefferson and his contemporaries did. They set the stage for American economic, cultural, military, and legal influence to reach into every corner of the globe. Yet, let us resist the impulse to think that what came after resulted inevitably from what happened in Jefferson's day. While he expected much of what we know, other aspects of contemporary life would thrill, shock, exasperate, disappoint, invigorate, amaze, or horrify him.

Historians commonly find it surprising that when Jefferson sketched his grave marker, he omitted that he had been governor of Virginia, secretary of state, vice president, and president. In our day, holding such offices is taken as a great accomplishment in itself. Jefferson had a different understanding. He once talked a prominent American scientist out of forsaking science for politics, arguing that America had only one Ben Franklin and only one man like his correspondent, and it would be a shame for such people to leave science. After all, any reasonably bright man could be a politician.

Jefferson did more than merely hold offices, however. The marks of his statesmanship are with us all over America, every day. Those coins in your pocket, representing various numbers of hundredths of a dollar, reflect Jefferson's proposal of a decimal-based coinage—the world's first. All over the world, other countries have followed the American example on this score; in living memory, even the United Kingdom finally yielded to the American example.

So too the upper house of your state legislature is likely called a "senate," as is the upper house of the US Congress, after Jefferson's 1776 proposal for Virginia's upper house. Student of ancient history that he was, he thought it obvious that the colonial "council" had to go.

While Jefferson served as American minister to France in the 1780s, lawmakers back home in Richmond (which the General Assembly had designated to replace Williamsburg as the state capital at Jefferson's suggestion) thought to build a new state capitol. Jefferson insisted they not just throw up a Georgian rectangular building, but instead use the pattern of a Roman temple in the South of France which he had learned to love. Greco-Roman architecture, it seemed to Jefferson, combined concern with beauty with proportion, form, and stateliness in just the way that would encourage republican citizens to comport themselves in a republican fashion. Persuaded, the General Assembly let Jefferson himself draw up the building's architectural plans. Somewhat expanded to accommodate modern government, Jefferson's Virginia capitol sits on the bank of the James River even now.

When he became secretary of state in 1790, Jefferson unexpectedly found himself in a position to help shape the layout of the federal capital and the architecture of its first government buildings. Like Virginia's, they would have classical architectural elements. Today, the same is true of many state government public buildings as well.

The Virginia capitol serves as the seat of the Old Dominion's republican government, the government of an independent state since May 15, 1776. The rest of the original thirteen joined Virginia in independence on July 4, and they did so by adopting a declaration "&c." written chiefly by Jefferson. Jefferson described that document at the time as laying out his political creed. Much of American political history since his day concerns the ways and extent to which Americans should understand Jefferson's creed as our common creed. Jefferson struggled with those questions virtually to his last day. He chose to claim authorship of the Declaration of Independence as his own feat on the aforementioned gravestone. In doing so, he claimed the associated authority for himself as well.

Jefferson hoped to see America adopt a lasting federal union. A commonplace among nationalist historians and commentators says that the US Constitution is better for his absence from the country at the time of its drafting and ratification, as well as the drafting of its first ten and twenty-seventh amendments. How his presence in Philadelphia in the summer of 1787 and/or in New York in 1789 would have affected those events will forever be unknown, but some light is shed upon the matter by Jefferson's work in drafting state constitutions for his home state in 1776.

Jefferson's draft constitutions began with a preamble laying out the philosophical and historical grounds of the Old Dominion's break with King George III. That section mirrored the first two sections of the Declaration of Independence, which he was drafting at the same time. It also featured population apportionment of both houses of the state legislature, which Jefferson hoped to see replace the geographic apportionment Virginia had borrowed from English practice. The omission of this practice by the Virginia Convention led Jefferson to favor revision of Virginia's state constitution for the rest of his life.

As a state legislator, Jefferson led the way in abolition of the feudal land tenures, primogeniture and entail, which had perpetuated a very small aristocracy's ownership of approximately two-thirds of the land in today's Virginia throughout the colonial period. In their place, Jefferson persuaded the General Assembly to establish the principle that all children, including females, would inherit equally in cases in which the deceased did not leave a will. Jefferson thought that equalized land ownership would buttress the egalitarian republic he wanted Virginia to become. Jefferson considered his land reforms as basic to his program, and their effects indeed pervaded Virginia society even in his own lifetime.

With that in mind, Jefferson included a constitutional provision that any "person" (again not specifically male) who did not own fifty acres of land and had not owned that amount should be given that allotment out of the public lands. Additionally, he would have extended the suffrage beyond those meeting the colonial property qualifications to all taxpayers.

Jefferson from his teens had been up to speed with the latest currents in European thought. Among the European ideas that appealed to him was Cesare Beccaria's notion that punishments ought to be proportionate to crimes. Where English law in the 1770s provided death as the penalty for virtually any crime, Beccaria held that the most severe punishment should be for the worst crimes and that the severity of the punishment ought to decline as the crime became less significant. Jefferson proposed a Bill to Apportion Crimes and Punishments in 1779, but it ultimately ran aground on the House of Delegates' insistence that horse thieves suffer death. In time, however, Jefferson's position would prevail—in Virginia and elsewhere.

Many of these reforms were successful at a stroke. Some won passage only significantly later, but did not absorb much of Jefferson's energy. Our attention will be devoted hereafter to the major legislative and constitutional efforts that ran through his career: in behalf of federalism, freedom of conscience, colonization of blacks abroad, assimilation of Indians into American society, and public education. Each will be the subject of one chapter.

By "federalism," I understand the relationship between the central government and the constituent parts of a federal union. We will see in chapter 1 that although it was more prominent in his thought at some times than at others, Jefferson's insistence on a particular understanding of this relationship ran through his entire political and intellectual career, from 1774 to 1825. On a proper federal arrangement, all else depended, and respect for each man's equal right to self-government mandated that the federal government accept Jefferson's position regarding federalism.

Freedom of conscience is, after independence, likely the chief concept with which Jefferson's name is associated. His devotion to it led him to include a related provision in his draft constitution and, that effort having been rejected, to draft a bill to establish the principle on the firmest statutory basis. His presidency, coming after his bill's passage by the Virginia General Assembly, gave him the opportunity to make perhaps the most famous American statement about freedom of conscience. That statement has been misconstrued. This issue is the topic of chapter 2.

Jefferson struggled through his political life with the question of slavery and the related issue of race. He claimed, though some historians have denied, that he worked for abolition from his earliest days in the House of Burgesses—Virginia's lower legislative chamber during the colonial era.

He early conceived of colonization as a necessary twin of abolition. Blacks and whites in Virginia would always hate each other, according to Jefferson, and yet blacks must be given their freedom in the end. He thought blacks inferior, which meant that he could not conceive of a biracial society anyway. He insisted that only by sending all blacks out of Virginia—indeed, out of America—could a race war be avoided. Chapter 3 tells this story.

On the other hand, Jefferson judged American Indians the equals of whites. Jefferson held that the reason they seemed backward was that they did not know better than to live as they lived. Whites could teach them. Americans could benefit from converting Indians to European-style farmers, as well, for most of their land would thereby be made available to whites. Should Indians prove too slow in converting to white ways for whites' taste, they could be nudged along through economic manipulation. This saga is recounted in chapter 4.

Jefferson rightly claims the premier place among American proponents of republican government and democratic equality. However, he denied that simply remaking governments from monarchical to republican could be the end of the story. Rather, common Virginians must be educated if they were going to use their newfound power responsibly—or even happily. He proposed to the House of Delegates in the 1770s that public schooling be provided to all free children. Among other things, his vision extended to a new university. Logically, the story of his birthing that institution is the subject of our last chapter, chapter 5.

Thomas Jefferson's hopes and fears go far toward explaining the course of American political history. Many of his competing impulses ultimately came to be claimed by competing political parties, as indeed they still are today. Some of his specific positions, however, are alien to today's American scene. Underlying the stories told in all five chapters of this book, a bedrock of belief in human equality of a particular kind shaped virtually his entire political career, and much of his other work. We can see that belief play out in each chapter, though not always in a way we might expect. Thomas Jefferson's intellectual life serves as a prime illustration of the fact that, as novelist L. P. Hartley said, "The past is a foreign country: they do things differently there." If not for that, the past would be far less fascinating—not to mention by turns less inspirational and less tragic.

Chapter 1

~~~~~~~~~~~~~~~~~

Federalism

Thomas Jefferson's name is most commonly associated in American popular culture with what we now call "democracy," which Jefferson's friend and collaborator James Madison called "republicanism": government by elected officials. Abundant evidence supports that Jefferson placed a high priority on this principle.

It was not the only one. Even more important was freedom of conscience, the great American contribution to world freedom. Closely related to republicanism and freedom of conscience, in Jefferson's mind and practice, was a third: federalism.

This idea commonly goes by the name "states' rights" these days. Its opponents have conflated it with power in state governments, and some of those opponents have been so influential that many of federalism's friends are prone to see it that way too.[1] As Jefferson and the like-minded understood it, however, it meant limitation on federal power. Insofar as the US government did not have power, they believed, that power remained in the states as distinct, preexisting political communities.

Whether those communities gave particular powers to the state governments was up to them.

Their promise that the federal government would rest on this principle was a key component of the Federalists' success in persuading the states to ratify the Constitution in 1787–1790. In fact, it was *the* key component. Not just outliers, but leading Federalists in at least eight states made it the bottom line in their argument that the Constitution was not a threat to the revolutionary legacy. To join the new union under the new Constitution would not amount to surrender of the insistence on local self-government—"no taxation without representation," and since representation of the colonies in Parliament was impossible, taxation only by their provincial assemblies—that underlay the colonists' contention that Parliament was trying to deprive them of their political inheritance as Englishmen.[2] New York's Alexander Hamilton and Virginian James Madison said so in *The Federalist*. Governor Edmund Randolph said so, repeatedly, in the Virginia Ratification Convention.[3] A delegate from Jefferson's Albemarle County and close Madison collaborator, George Nicholas, echoed Randolph.[4] William Cushing of Massachusetts said the same, as did South Carolina's Charles Cotesworth Pinckney. Pennsylvania's James Wilson outlined this argument in the most widely disseminated Federalist case for the Constitution, his famous State House Yard Speech.[5]

Thomas Jefferson believed them. In fact, since he held that the Constitution's meaning was to be found in its friends' explanation of it during the ratification campaign, the fact that these and other prominent Federalists sold it this way—while no significant Federalist said they were wrong—closed the question for him.[6] Like it or not, the Constitution gave the federal government only the enumerated powers.

This is not to say that federalism was a be-all, end-all principle for Jefferson. On the one hand, he sometimes insisted on the common identity of an American people. That is certainly the most plausible reading of the first sentence of the Declaration of Independence, for example. Predictably, he spoke as an American in his roles as secretary of state and president. On the other hand, he held that to arrive at the optimal political organization, Virginians must "divide and subdivide": their counties were not the smallest political unit he wanted, but instead he hoped to see them adopt the idea of "ward republics." There, even common citizens might conduct their everyday civic affairs in company with their immediate neighbors. There, an average man could be the "political animal" to which Aristotle referred.

Yet, it was the states that were the chief resource of Jeffersonian constitutional thought. It was upon them that he relied for protection against overweening central authority, first British and then American. It was in Virginia that he endeavored to realize his chief revolutionary reforms. It was perforce in state-level politics that he would endeavor to sell his fellow citizens on the idea of ward republics.

Jefferson did certainly like the federal principle. In fact, this feature of the Constitution pleased him greatly. As Federalists had taught him to do, he considered it ever after as the Constitution's leading feature. For him, that made the Constitution a fulfillment of the revolution. He had after all first become prominently involved in the imperial crisis precisely over the question of federalism.

That came in response to the Townshend Acts.[7] The House of Burgesses, the lower house of Virginia's colonial legislature and the Western Hemisphere's first representative assembly, on May 16, 1769, adopted four resolutions: that only the Burgesses had the right to tax Virginians; that intercolonial cooperation in resistance was lawful; that all trials for crimes committed in Virginia must be held in Virginia before Virginia juries; and that George III be petitioned to intervene with Parliament on the colonists' behalf. The Burgesses also adopted a "humble address" to George III.[8]

When the royal governor dissolved the House, Jefferson joined the Burgesses' leadership, including his cousin Speaker Peyton Randolph, in signing a nonimportation agreement: the Association. Signatories would boycott British goods taxed by Parliament for revenue purposes. While some northern ports had taken similar steps, this was the first time a colonial port had taken what one of the leading Jefferson scholars called "an act of rebellion." Other colonies followed Virginia's example, and the effect on British business prompted Parliament to repeal all but the tax on tea. Among the other significant effects of this chain of events was that it persuaded Jefferson of economic coercion's utility. He had not, however, become a prominent opponent of British policy.

That happened in 1774. Jefferson, barely past age thirty, had sat for a few years in the House of Burgesses, the lower house of the colony's legislature. Although connected by blood to the speaker, the attorney general, and other leading political figures (his mother was a Randolph), he had not made much of an impression. Absent the dispute with Britain that marked the period 1765–1776, his name would likely have been forgotten.

In response to Parliament's hostile measures against Massachusetts, the House of Burgesses called for a Continental Congress to commence in 1774. Jefferson, by now a moderately senior member of the House of Delegates, contemplated Virginia's role. As the largest, most prosperous, and most lucrative colony, besides Massachusetts' longtime coadjutor in leadership of the resistance, it would be expected to take a stand. The Albemarle County delegate's proposal took the form of a pamphlet ultimately known as "A Summary View of the Rights of British America."

"Ultimately known," because Jefferson's physical indisposition kept him away from the House of Burgesses that term.[9] He therefore sent his pamphlet to Williamsburg for senior members' consideration. They decided not to adopt it as the Burgesses' official position, but did have it published under the unwieldy, therefore un-Jeffersonian, title. Perhaps the Burgesses' leadership judged Jefferson's very forceful summary of the patriot position impolitic, as they had Patrick Henry's Stamp Act Resolutions in 1765.

Thomas Jefferson struck those who interacted with him in politics as reserved, even taciturn. His friend John Adams, a short, round man whose loquacity matched the tall, thin Jefferson's reserve, said that "during the whole Time I sat with him in Congress, I never heard him utter three Sentences together."[10] On the other hand, Jefferson as penman could rile a reader with the best of them. In "A Summary View," Jefferson put his writing talents on full, public display for the first time.

"A Summary View of the Rights of British America" combined several forms of writing in one.[11] It was a polemic. It was a historical argument. It was a legal argument. It was a political argument. Most of all, it was a virtuoso display of rhetorical ability. In writing it, Jefferson had punched his own ticket to immortality: due primarily to this performance, Adams would tap Jefferson to draft the Declaration of Independence two years later.

✓"A Summary View" begins by saying that it is to be an instruction to Virginia's congressmen "to propose . . . a humble and dutiful address" to King George III. That address, it continues, has been provoked by "the legislature of one part of the empire" (Parliament), which has been infringing upon the American colonists' God-given and legal rights. Here in its first sentence we see that Jefferson will be developing the theory that Parliament, understood in Britain as sovereign over the entire British Empire, is simply the local assembly of one part of the empire. The king is going to be asked to intervene "in the language of truth . . . divested of those expressions of servility which would persuade his majesty that [the colonists were] asking favours, and not rights." The king should accept this as appropriate, because he is "no more than the chief officer of the people, appointed by the laws, and circumscribed with definite powers, to assist in working the great machine of government, erected for [the people's] use, and consequently subject to their superintendence."

The "humble and dutiful address" would not be very humble. Its version of the imperial constitution would instead be . . . revolutionary.[12]

Drawing on the teaching of his cousin and fellow burgess Richard Bland, Jefferson next somewhat fancifully recounted the settlement of the North American colonies.[13] The colonists had left the mother country in exercise of their natural right to emigrate, he said. They had established the North American colonies through their own effort and with their own money. They had entered into a legal relationship with the Crown of their free will and for their own good. Parliament had no role in the story. True, he conceded, Britain had finally—for the first time—given financial aid during the Seven Years' War, but that did not prove that Parliament rightly could legislate for the colonies. After all, Parliament had given similar aid to Portugal, and no one contended Parliament could legislate for Portugal.

Jefferson complained of the interruption of "a free trade with all parts of the world, possessed by the American colonists, as of natural right," through various acts of Parliament's legislation from time to time over more than a century. Not only that, he said, but Parliament had occasionally intruded into the colonies' internal legislation, such as by creating a North American post office—which served chiefly to establish a patronage plum.

After these five pages of introductory material, Jefferson turned to contemporary matters in the essay's remaining twelve. While there had occasionally been objectionable acts of the English-cum-British government before, he said, things had changed markedly in the years leading up to 1774. "Scarcely have our minds been able to emerge from the astonishment into which one stroke of parliamentary thunder has involved us, before another more heavy, and more alarming is fallen on us."

In 1763, Britain had emerged victorious from the first world war. Americans generally refer to that conflict as the French and Indian War. Europeans know it as the Seven Years' War. Americans used different terminology for the war because it lasted more than seven years in North America and because the adversaries of the British colonies were the French and their allied Indians.

Britain's smashing victory, won against overwhelming odds over Europe's foremost military power, had two notable legacies. First, it made the British masters of North America above the Rio Grande, and second,

it left Britain enormously in debt. The reason that Britain, far less populous than Louis XV's France and inferior in every kind of natural resource,
had won the war was that it had invented a system we still know, if not
exactly love, today: deficit finance.

The war's end left Britain with an unprecedented problem of political
economy. Traditionally, the United Kingdom—island nation that it was—
had relied on its naval superiority for protection. When a war started,
his majesty's government would raise taxes to pay for putting his army
on a war footing. When the war ended, nearly always successfully, the
soldiers would virtually all be discharged, and taxes would return to
peacetime levels.

The new national debt meant that this last step could not be taken in
1763 or the years following. Even with the discharge of the soldiers, Britain had to maintain wartime taxes to service its debt. This problem
proved especially pressing because in those days, only about 10 percent
of male Britons were eligible to vote in elections for the House of Commons. Those 10 percent were the wealthiest male commoners, the men
who met the income threshold for voting. They were also the ones who
had to keep paying wartime taxes even with the war behind them.

An obvious solution to this conundrum was to make the innovation
of taxing the North American colonists to help defray the expense. Since
those colonists had turned out to be the French and Indian War's chief
beneficiaries, with the threat of French attack from their north permanently eliminated and Francophile Indians' threat to them forever vitiated,
the idea proved especially appealing.

The measures Jefferson listed in the next section of "A Summary View"
were all very familiar to his readers.[14] He had no need of naming them,
but instead could give brief descriptions of the various attempts by
Parliament to tax the colonists and, when they proved resistant, to show
them who was boss. The short of it is that the Seven Years' War/French
and Indian War (1754–1763) had left Britain in a tangled political knot.
Where customarily military victory led immediately to reduction of

Britons' taxes to peacetime levels, the sizable debt incurred fighting this first world war made that step impossible. Taxpayers, for their part, insisted that their taxes be cut, and the substantial property qualification for voting members of the eighteenth-century House of Commons meant that taxpayers and the constituents of Parliament's lower house were essentially the same people. Politically speaking, what taxpayers wanted to happen would happen.

Jefferson referred in his pamphlet to the chief attempts by Parliament to levy taxes in North America in the years after the French and Indian War: the Sugar Act (1764), the Stamp Act (1765), and the Townshend Acts (1767). He also referred to some of the draconian measures Parliament adopted in its attempts to wring the anticipated revenue out of recalcitrant colonies: the Quartering Act (1765), the suspension of the New York Assembly (1767–1769), the Coercive (Intolerable) Acts (1774), and the Quebec Act (also 1774). Those acts had prompted the colonists to develop formal arguments against them (notably Patrick Henry's Stamp Act Resolutions, adopted by the Virginia House of Burgesses in 1765, the Stamp Act Congress's resolutions of that same year, Richard Bland's 1766 "An Inquiry into the Rights of the British Colonies," and John Dickinson's 1767–1768 *Letters from a Farmer in Pennsylvania*). They also led the colonists into continental boycotts of British goods. Besides making legal/constitutional arguments and launching boycotts, colonists used mob violence in several urban areas to coerce some people who cooperated in enforcing or even simply obeyed the British legislation.

Things changed markedly on December 16, 1773. That night, numerous men dressed as Indians, with war paint on their faces and feathers in their hair, boarded British ships in Boston Harbor, broke into chests, and dumped a fortune in tea into the water. An extremely large crowd of onlookers cheered them on.

When news of the Boston "Tea Party" reached England, Parliament had finally had enough. Within weeks, it adopted the four Coercive Acts—

dubbed by Massachusetts resistance leaders the Intolerable Acts—to compel the Bay Colony to bend the knee. First came the Boston Port Act, which closed the Port of Boston to all shipping, incoming or leaving, until the city compensated the East India Company for its tea. This extreme measure seemed to Sam Adams's relatively moderate cousin, lawyer John Adams, to violate the basic English legal principle that only those found guilty at law should be punished. Far from training its fire solely on those responsible for the Tea Party, this act blasted New England's leading city and its extensive economic hinterlands, which included virtually all of New England. John Adams became a foursquare opponent of British rule in response to the Port Act.

Yet, there was more. A few weeks later, Parliament by the Massachusetts Government Act essentially revoked Massachusetts' charter. Now town meetings would not be able to meet without the approval of the general sent to serve as governor, and he would assume the function formerly filled by the elected lower house of the General Court in selecting members of the Council. The Administration of Justice Act empowered the governor to move the trial of any government employee—say, a soldier—accused of murder in Massachusetts to some other part of the British Empire. Not a Boston jury, but perhaps an admiralty judge in Halifax, Nova Scotia, would decide whether the accused agent of King George was guilty and, if so, what punishment he received. Finally, a Quartering Act empowered British officials in certain circumstances to commandeer sleeping quarters for British troops in Massachusetts. The hated "lobsterbacks" not only would be staying on in Boston for the purpose of cowing the locals indefinitely, but now they might be imposed upon property owners.

Fortuitously, Parliament also at nearly the same time finally resolved the issue how to govern the Canadian Frenchmen conquered in 1763. Far from oppressing these devotees of hated papism, the great Protestant power according to its Quebec Act would allow them to keep their religion and their traditional form of local government. In fact, King George III would guarantee both.

From where devout New England Puritans such as Boston's Sam Adams sat, these developments formed a cohesive whole.[15] Throw in rumors that the British planned to send an Anglican bishop to North America, and it seemed clear that the Episcopalian king of England and his ministers were plotting to destroy God's province—Massachusetts—once and for all.

Hearing of this in distant Virginia, the colonial leadership decided to adopt resolutions of protest.[16] When the royal governor, Lord Dunmore, rejected the resolutions, the Burgesses passed a resolution for a day of prayer and fasting—a traditional response in anglophone jurisdictions to societal travails. Dunmore dissolved the house. The Burgesses then marched down the street from the colonial capitol to the Apollo Tavern, where they agreed upon a call for a Continental Congress. Philadelphia, at once the largest city in the colonies and somewhat centrally located, would be an obvious meeting place.

So here Jefferson was. He got to the nub of his argument: "Single acts of tyranny may be ascribed to the accidental opinion of a day," he wrote, "but a series of oppressions, begun at a distinguished period, and pursued unalterably through every change of ministers, too plainly prove a deliberate and systematical plan of reducing us to slavery."

Who were the planners Jefferson had in mind? "Not only the principles of common sense, but the common feelings of human nature, must be surrendered up before his majesty's subjects here can be persuaded to believe that they hold their political existence at the will of a British parliament." In other words, while there was a tie between Great Britain and any particular American colony, it was not through an all-powerful British legislature.

Jefferson insisted vociferously that American colonists could not be subject to an unaccountable legislature whose members they had not elected and with whom they had no influence at all. He called Parliament "a body of men, whom they never saw, in whom they never confided, and over whom they have no powers of punishment or removal." That summed up the North American position.

Suppose Americans consented to this system of parliamentary sovereignty, which was vaunted in Britain as the fruit of the glorious revolution, what would their situation become?[17] Jefferson held that if "160,000 electors in the island of Great Britain should give law to four millions in the states of America, . . . instead of being a free people, . . . we should suddenly be found the slaves, not of one, but of 160,000 tyrants." Those 160,000 electors, he continued, elected the body that had inflicted the Coercive Acts on the colony: the House of Commons, lower house of the British Parliament. Far from the rightful legislature of the entire empire, in Jefferson's understanding, Parliament was "a body of men, foreign to our constitutions, and unacknowledged by our laws."

A Briton reading this far might have thought that despite the respectful language with which Jefferson had begun the pamphlet, he (or, if he had had his way, the First Continental Congress) intended a separation of the colonies and the mother country—secessions of the thirteen colonies from the British Empire. Far from independence, however, Jefferson actually looked at this time to King George III to stake out a federal position by urging Parliament to revoke the offending acts.

If that was not enough, Jefferson next proceeded "to mark out [George's] deviations from the line of duty." Imagine the effrontery. No one addressed King George in such a way. Even to approach his person required punctilious observance of formal protocol. Yet here was Jefferson imagining a frontal and detailed rebuke of the king.

The king had a theoretical power to veto Parliament's legislation, Jefferson observed. He and his predecessors had for decades refrained from exercising this power. Now, however, "the addition of new states to the British empire has produced an addition of new, and sometimes opposite interests. It is now, therefore, the great office of his majesty, to resume the exercise of his negative power, and to prevent the passage of laws by any one legislature of the empire, which might bear injuriously on the rights and interests of another."

While following his ancestors in not vetoing Parliament's legislation, Jefferson continued, King George had vetoed American legislatures' bills—sometimes "for no conceivable reason at all." For example, he had on three occasions prevented Virginia from implementing legislation taxing slave imports so much as to render further importation of slaves economically unviable. This, Jefferson said, would have been a first step toward ending slavery. Additionally, while kings of England had long accepted their incapacity for dissolving Parliament, they continued to claim a power to dissolve the legislatures of the North American colonies.

George III, like the other Hanoverian kings George I and George II before him, retained the title of Elector of Hanover and, as prince of that significant German state, control of its armed forces. Yet, during the Seven Years' War, George II conceded that he had to have Parliament's consent before he could bring some of his German troops to England to defend the kingdom. The same reasoning should be understood, Jefferson insisted, as foreclosing George III's stationing British troops in any North American colony without the local legislature's consent. George of course had consented to soldiers' being sent to the North American colonies because Parliament wanted them there, but this violated Jefferson's conception of the relationship among the various parts of the king's empire. At last clearly stating the role of the common chief executive in his dominions, Jefferson wrote, "He possesses, indeed, the executive power of the laws in every state; but they are the laws of the particular state which he is to administer within that state, and not those of any one within the limits of another." Thus, each must decide for itself how many soldiers it wanted within its territory, and from where. Each must make its own laws for its own good, and the king must consider the good of the affected "state" and the rightfulness of that state's exercise of its authority when deciding whether to exercise his veto.

Note Jefferson's use of the word "state" in relation to the various parts of King George III's empire. This word, introduced into modern political science by the Florentine man of letters Niccolò Machiavelli in the sixteenth century, refers to sovereign entities—not Catalonia in Spain or Burgundy in France, but Spain or France. Jefferson's meaning was that Rhode Island, Pennsylvania, Georgia, and so forth stood on a par with Spain, France, and the United Kingdom, and the king should treat them as such. They were, in other words, foreign to Great Britain except for sharing a chief executive—a king—and George should use his veto power to prevent Great Britain from dominating the North American colonies on the ground of its superior power. Instead, Jefferson lamented, George had "expressly made the civil subordinate to the military" in North America.

In one last paragraph, Jefferson forcefully summarized all that had come before. He had, he said, used "that freedom of language and sentiment which becomes a free people claiming their rights." Those rights were "derived from the laws of nature, and not . . . the gift of their chief magistrate." George should understand why the Americans' (remember, this pamphlet was to serve as instructions for Virginia's delegation to the First Continental Congress) language packed such a punch: "Let those flatter who fear; it is not an American art." He should not look for servility from the North American colonists, because "kings are the servants, not the proprietors of the people." George should "no longer persevere in sacrificing the rights of one part of the empire to the inordinate desires of another; but deal out to all equal and impartial right. Let no act be passed by any one legislature," Jefferson counseled, "which may infringe on the rights and liberties of another."

Lest George miss the full significance of Jefferson's—America's— lecture, Jefferson stated his threat more clearly. George was king of each of the dominions separately, "holding the balance of a great, if a well poised empire," and his due attention to the principles upon which America insisted could result in "the preservation of that harmony which alone c[ould] continue both to Great Britain and America the reciprocal advantages of their connection. It is neither our wish, nor our interest, to separate from her." Americans would bear their part of the burden of continued ties—if the British would be just. Forcing them to rely on Britain for markets for American goods that the British did not want or goods that the British did not produce, let alone taxing and regulating American property and activities within the American colonies, did not satisfy that condition. "The God who gave us life gave us liberty at the same time; the hand of force may destroy, but cannot disjoin them." Americans hoped George would heed their "last . . . determined resolution."

The revolution's beginning on April 19, 1775, left unclear what outcome the colonists would accept. Certainly independence had not yet become their goal. Jefferson, for one, remained content to be a British subject. He required that King George III subscribe to his theory of federalism, however.

Lord Dunmore, ignoring these events, convened the General Assembly.[18] Presented with Prime Minister Lord North's "Conciliatory Proposal," the Burgesses gave Jefferson the task of answering. North thought to end the recurrent disputes between the mother country and the colonies over taxation by leaving it to the colonists to tax themselves their share of the cost of the empire's defense and the cost of their own civil government. Jefferson held that North's proposal "only changes the form of oppression. . . . It is not merely the mode of raising but the freedom of granting our money for which we have contended." The House rejected its committee's draft response in favor of Jefferson's, and then it named him to the new Continental Congress in place of his cousin, the Congress's former president, Peyton Randolph.

Jefferson immediately found himself given similar tasks by his fellow congressmen.[19] First he and Pennsylvania's John Dickinson wrote the "Declaration of the Causes and Necessity of Taking Up Arms," and then—

apparently happy with both that joint effort and Jefferson's Virginia version—Congress had him write its reply to Lord North's Conciliatory Proposal.[20]

Jefferson thundered "that the colonies of America are entitled to the sole . . . privilege of giving . . . their own money," including deciding for what purpose and how much they would pay. It was "a high breach of this privilege" for Parliament, a "body of men, extraneous to their constitutions," to dictate these matters to the colonies. For the colonies to give Parliament their money without retaining any oversight power, and thus enable Parliament to use the money to support standing armies to intimidate them or to pay "the venal and corrupt" to "undermin[e] their civil rights," "is to propose that they shall . . . put it in the power of others to render their gifts, ruinous, in proportion as they are liberal."

If the colonies complied with the British demand, they would buy themselves only a temporary reprieve, because "no experience has shown that a gift of perpetual revenue secures a perpetual return of duty or of kind disposition." That was why Parliament granted the Crown its funds only on an annual basis. Parliament also would not have accepted such a demand when accompanied by stationing of fleets and armies in its territory, as they had been stationed in the colonies. Besides that, trying to tax the colonies by intimidation had been proven unnecessary by the colonies' willing contribution of men and money to the common effort in the French and Indian War.

Talk of making the colonists begin to contribute to the British treasury, Jefferson continued, overlooked an important point: that Britain's Navigation Acts controlled American trade for the benefit of Great Britain. "If we are to contribute equally with the other parts of the empire," he wrote, "let us equally with them enjoy free commerce with all the world." Until they did, it would be unjust for the Americans to have to pay the same taxes as the Britons who benefited from free trade had to pay.

Jefferson drove home the federalism point: "We conceive that the British Parliament has no right to intermeddle with our provisions for the support of civil government, or administration of justice. The provisions we have made are such as please ourselves, and are agreeable to our own circumstances." As to British aims, "we do not mean that our people shall be burthened with oppressive taxes to provide sinecures for the idle or the wicked, under colour of providing for a civil list." In summary, "while Parliament pursue their plan of civil government within their own jurisdiction, we also hope to pursue ours without molestation." "A Summary View" had become Congress's position. Until Parliament accepted it, the Congress would hold that "nothing but our own exertions may defeat the ministerial sentence of death or abject submission."

George's August 23, 1775, proclamation that the colonies were in rebellion meant that George would never concede the point. Jefferson and others ultimately desired independence. When the ruling Virginia Convention established the Old Dominion's permanent republican status on May 15, 1776, Williamsburg denizens celebrated independence.[21] Down from atop the colonial capitol came the Union Jack, symbol of British authority, and up went a "continental union flag." On June 29, 1776, Patrick Henry took the oath of office as Virginia's first republican governor. Now it became imperative that, as the Convention had instructed them to do, Virginia's congressmen persuade the Second Continental Congress to join them in declaring independence. To remain the sole independent state would be insupportable.

Acting on the Convention's instructions, Congressman Jefferson's colleague Richard Henry Lee stood up in Congress to urge the other colonies to act.[22] Scion of one of Virginia's most prominent families, Lee had for years been one of the most devoted patriot leaders. In the House of Burgesses, his polished, formal rhetoric and cool leadership style made a kind of counterpoint to Patrick Henry's fiery oratory. Lee appeared dressed in fine fashion, a silken scarf wrapped around one hand to obscure the results of the hunting accident that had mangled it. Henry, for his part, appealed to listeners' emotions in the manner of prominent evangelical preachers. When he wanted to be humorous, he was prone to pick up the wig from atop his head, spin it around, and plop it back down as he spoke. When he wanted to persuade, he could sway any jury, and in a parliamentary body, he could make the heavens shake.[23] Lee and Henry led the two great phalanxes of burgesses. With Henry away in Williamsburg waiting to become governor, it fell to Lee in Philadelphia to stand and move that Congress declare "that these colonies are, and of right ought to be, free and independent states."

Jefferson would have preferred to be in Williamsburg too. He did not have his eye on the governorship or any particular office in the new state government. Instead, he aspired to greater fame: that of a lawgiver.[24] Historically, lawgivers—authors of constitutions—were considered the greatest of politicians. However significant Pericles or Themistocles may have been, both always operated in the shadow of Athens' lawgiver, Solon. He had formed Athens' constitution. The Spartan Lycurgus won similar repute by crafting Sparta's constitution.

Congressman Jefferson wanted to help write Virginia's—America's; indeed, the world's—first republican constitution written by the people's representatives. As he put it, "In truth it is the whole object of the present controversy; for should a bad government be instituted for us in future it had been as well to have accepted at first the bad one offered to us from beyond the water without the risk and expence of contest."[25]

Jefferson's departure from Philadelphia would have left the Virginia delegation without a quorum, however. Since each state had one vote, a state delegation without a quorum would have no vote at all. Jefferson therefore asked to be relieved. No relief came. Frustrated, Jefferson turned to writing a constitution anyway.[26] He could send it to Williamsburg and have some friendly member of the Convention submit it for that body's consideration. In the end, the Convention used Jefferson's preamble, which laid out the argument for supplanting George III as Virginia's king, along with a few minor elements such as calling the upper house the "Senate."

So Jefferson had to content himself with drafting the Declaration of Independence. One might have thought it would just repeat the language of Lee's Resolution, which had actually come from the Virginia Convention: "these colonies are, and of right ought to be, free and independent states." Declarations merely announced what was true, they did not actually do anything, and so Jefferson could be excused for aspiring to the status of Virginian Solon instead of the one he actually obtained.[27] Yet, Jefferson made more of the task. In a letter written soon after the Declaration's drafting, he referred to his handiwork as "my political creed in the form of a 'Declaration &c.' "[28] What we call the Declaration of Independence is not simply a declaration of independence.

Jefferson found himself one of five men appointed to a committee for the purpose. The chairman, John Adams, selected Jefferson to draft it. Had he known what great repute its author would earn, Adams doubtless would have kept the job for himself. Impressed with the gravity of other tasks then on his plate, he handed it off to Jefferson—who had the advantages of being Virginian, eloquent, and less disliked in Congress than Adams.

One could point to Jefferson's authorship of the Declaration as an illustration of the truth that politicians always try to do more, or other, than they are charged with doing. He—in fact, even Congress—had no commission to write a "political creed." The Virginia delegates had been told simply to declare independence, some other states' delegates had instructions to declare independence if other states did, and some states had no instructions on this question at all. Arguably only the declaration, not the "&c.," had any democratic legitimacy.

As adopted by Congress, the Declaration of Independence had four sections: the philosophical section, the bill of particulars against King George III, the denial of inattention to the family ties to the British people, and—shortest of all—the actual declaration of independence.[29] After "A Summary View of the Rights of British America," the contents of the Declaration are unsurprising.

Where "A Summary View" said that George III's family had become monarchs of the North American colonies by the free will of the original colonists, the Declaration of Independence laid out a general right of a people to create its own government. While Jefferson in 1774 had intimated to George that he could be replaced if he did not begin to fulfill the conditions on which he had come to be the colonists' king, the Declaration said that "it is the right of the people to alter or abolish" any government which "becomes destructive of" the people's ends in creating it. People generally did not immediately remove rulers who abused them, Jefferson observed. "But when a long train of abuses & usurpations begun at a distinguished period and pursuing invariably the same object, evinces a design to reduce them under absolute despotism, it is their right, it is their duty to throw off such government, & to provide new guards for their future security." King George had provoked them to this step via "a history of unremitting injuries & usurpations, among which appears no solitary fact to contradict the uniform tenor of the rest."

Then followed the list of George's supposed offenses. In general, they fell under the category "Steps Taken to Enforce Parliament's Policy in North America." This point is made explicit where Jefferson charges him with "combin[ing] with others to subject us to a jurisdiction foreign to our constitutions & unacknowledged by our laws, giving his assent to their acts of pretended legislation." This paragraph ends with a reference to Parliament's claim in the Declaratory Act (1766) of a "power to legislate for [the colonies] in all cases whatsoever."

Historians generally have credited Congress with improving Jefferson's draft in the editing process. For instance, Congress removed Jefferson's absurd passage blaming George III for slavery in North America, which certainly would have weakened the states' case considerably. However, other redlining weakened Jefferson's composition. Among passages weakened by the editors was Jefferson's statement that "We have warned them [the British people] from time to time of attempts by their legislature to extend *a* jurisdiction over *these our states*." Instead of the four italicized words, Congress chose to put "us" at the end of the sentence. We have no explanation for this decision, which obscures Jefferson's federal message.

More strikingly undermining Jefferson's intention was Congress's decision to remove a long passage essentially restating the Bland-Jefferson thesis found in "A Summary View." Jefferson had written, "[our immigration and settlement] were effected at the expense of our own blood & treasure, unassisted by the wealth or the strength of Great Britain . . . in constituting indeed our several forms of government, we had adopted one common king, thereby laying a foundation for perpetual league & amity with [our British brethren]: but . . . submission to their parliament was no part of our constitution, nor even an idea." Congress's excision of this passage left Americans formerly having relied solely on Britons' "native justice and magnanimity," along with blood ties.

Most important in illustrating Jefferson's theory of federalism, however, is the operative, final section. Rather than claim independence for "America" or for one people, it used the Virginia Convention's (Richard Henry Lee's) phrase, calling them "free & independent states." In adopting a declaration culminating in this nomenclature, Congress accepted the account of the new states' relations to one another on which Jefferson had insisted in "A Summary View," the screed that first brought him to the attention of politically aware people outside Virginia.

Jefferson left Philadelphia in the wake of the Fourth of July. On arrival back in Virginia, he was elected one of Albemarle County's two members of the new House of Delegates. His stint in that office, 1776–1779, included his taking the leading role on the Committee of Revisors. Along with Edmund Pendleton and George Wythe, he authored a package of proposed legislation whose purpose was to republicanize the Old Dominion's laws. We will return to this topic in later chapters.

Under the Virginia Constitution of 1776, the legislature elected the governor. Jefferson's election to three consecutive one-year terms as governor should be understood, then, as a mark of the great esteem among Virginia's political elite he had earned by taking the lead as a revisor and through his other legislative achievements. While his role as a revisor was the high point of his statesmanship, his governorship proved so unsuccessful that one House of Delegates member filed an impeachment resolution. After speaking against it from the House floor, Jefferson received a unanimous resolution of appreciation for his service. Still, his heart broken, he retired from politics for a while. During this period, his young wife died, apparently insisting on her deathbed that he vow never to remarry: she had been raised by a stepmother, the story goes, and wanted to ensure her children did not suffer the same fate.

Her death so devastated Jefferson that some thought he would die. His friend Congressman James Madison maneuvered to draw him back into public life by giving him a place on the American commission that was negotiating the Treaty of Paris (1783), but the treaty was concluded before Jefferson could embark for Europe. Nonetheless, Jefferson went to France as American minister (that is, ambassador) from 1784 to 1789. Thus, he did not participate directly in the drafting of the Articles of Confederation, the US Constitution, or the federal Bill of Rights. He did weigh in on the general issue of federal reform, however. His comments underscored his federal vision for American politics.

Before they were finally ratified in 1781, the Articles of Confederation already faced severe criticism. Proponents of further centralization of government authority calling themselves Federalists contended that an adequate government must be able to tax and to raise an army, instead of asking the state governments to do so on its behalf. Jefferson's correspondence with leading Federalists, notably James Madison, prompted him to ponder the questions of how much authority the central government should have and how it should be organized.

In 1786, Jefferson supported efforts to confer power over commerce with foreign nations upon the Confederation Congress.[30] For him, this would be consistent with the general need to divvy powers up between the state and federal governments so that "with respect to everything external we be one nation only, firmly hooped together." "Interior government," he said, "is that which each state should keep to itself." Omission to join in giving power over foreign affairs to the Confederation government would impress Europeans with America's weakness, he thought, and "insult & war are the consequences of a want of respectability in the national character." Besides that, the states' control over their own relations with foreign countries would forever embroil them in foreign quarrels—a tendency Jefferson wanted to avoid.

Later in 1786, Jefferson wrote to Madison on the same question. He still had the same vision: "To make us one nation as to foreign concerns, and keep us distinct in domestic ones, gives the outline of the proper division of power between the general and particular governments." Here he echoed the Declaration of Independence, with its reference to the former colonies as "states" (and thus as sovereigns), as well as "A Summary View," with its insistence that each dominion in the British Empire had a local legislature to legislate for it and govern in cooperation with the common king.

Madison ultimately disagreed. By year's end, he and a few like-minded men succeeded in organizing the Annapolis Convention to address the Confederation Congress's lack of power over foreign trade.[31] When attendees judged the Annapolis Convention's attendance inadequate for their purposes, they sent out a call for another attempt the following year in Philadelphia. This time, the program would extend beyond commercial regulation to proposing remedies to all of the Articles of Confederation's shortcomings.

From his vantage point, Madison believed he saw "the crisis of republican government." Particularly worrisome was Shays' Rebellion, a 1786 Massachusetts tax revolt. Besides that, in his "Vices of the Political System of the United States" (1786), Madison catalogued numerous other shortcomings of the state and federal constitutions, including that the states tended to ignore the Confederation's requisitions of men and money, tended to encroach on each other's territory, and tended to oppress their own minorities.

In response to his evaluation, Madison went to the Philadelphia Convention with an extremely ambitious nationalizing program—one well beyond Jefferson's conception of the requisite delegation of authority to the center. Madison intended completely to remake the system, subordinating the states to the center except insofar as the states could be "subordinately useful." Madison proposed that the "national legislature" be able to veto all state legislative bills, and he justified this idea partly by reference to the greater tendency toward just policy-making to be expected from a national, rather than a local, legislature. This idea, which can be found in his correspondence of 1786–1788, the "Vices," and his speeches both in the Philadelphia Convention and in the Virginia Ratification Convention, took its most famous form in *The Federalist* No. 10.[32] It put Madison on the opposite end of the federalism spectrum from Jefferson. Historians generally understate, when they don't simply ignore, Madison's divergence from Jefferson at this point.

Far from thinking American republicanism endangered by the consequences of the Articles of Confederation's woeful inadequacy, Jefferson wrote to another prominent Virginia politician during the Philadelphia Convention that "with all the defects of our constitutions, whether general or particular, the comparison of our governments with those of Europe, are like a comparison of heaven & hell." Yet, he did believe reform necessary, particularly because he agreed with the principle of the separation of powers in the Virginia Declaration of Rights.[33]

Jefferson therefore welcomed Madison's and others' success in bringing about the Philadelphia Convention. What with George Washington, Benjamin Franklin, Madison, John Rutledge, John Dickinson, George Wythe, George Mason, and numerous other of the most esteemed men and accomplished patriots in America among its members, it seemed to him "an assembly of demigods."[34] Decrying the Convention's initial decision to close the doors and swear members to secrecy, Jefferson held that "I have no doubt that all their measures will be good and wise."

The Convention concluded its deliberations eighteen days after Jefferson wrote that sanguine forecast. It would be thirty-seven days before Madison finally sent him a letter describing the course of the deliberations, explaining what he saw as the proposed constitution's chief shortcomings, and enclosing a copy of the document. By that time, Jefferson had already received it from other hands.

Jefferson's initial reaction would not have pleased Madison. Writing to the American official in Britain from whom he had received it, Jefferson said, "There are very good articles in it: & very bad. I do not know which preponderate."[35] The Dutch example showed him that a chief magistrate should not have so long a term as the proposed president's, while the Polish example "should have forever excluded the idea of one continuable for life." This letter also merits our attention for its evaluation of Shays' Rebellion. Although that event had prompted prominent politicians like Washington into thinking that something must be done to strengthen the central government immediately, Jefferson sloughed it off. If a country is to remain republican, he posited, its people must retain the attentiveness to their liberties demonstrated by Shays' rebels. Their motives, Jefferson insisted, "were founded in ignorance, not wickedness. God forbid we should ever be 20 years without such a rebellion." For the people simply to accept the misgovernment to which the rebels had believed they were being subjected would be "a lethargy, the forerunner of death to the public liberty." So "let them take arms. The remedy is to set them right as to facts, pardon & pacify them."

While Jefferson's solution to such a problem was to inform the people better, Federalists' was to grant the central government sufficient power to cow future popular resistance. "What country," Jefferson asked, "can preserve it's liberties if their rulers are not warned from time to time that their people preserve the spirit of resistance?" Excessively concerned with the Shays' precedent, the Philadelphia Convention's delegates "are setting up a kite to keep the hen-yard in order." He hoped the proposed charter would be amended to weaken the presidency prior to ratification.

That same day Jefferson wrote to his friend John Adams that "I confess there are things in [our new constitution] which stagger all my dispositions to subscribe to what such an assembly has proposed."[36] After expatiating on the likelihood that, as in the case of Poland, an elective chief magistracy would make foreign bribery a prominent element of the American political scene, Jefferson exclaimed that "Indeed I think all the good of this new constitution might have been couched in three or four new articles to be added to the good, old, and venerable fabrick, which should have been preserved even as a religious relique." Clearly Jefferson had not yet received Adams's note asking whether Jefferson had yet seen the Philadelphia Convention's proposal and asking, "What think you of a Declaration of Rights? Should not such a thing have preceded the model?"[37]

When he finally received Madison's very lengthy missive, Jefferson knew precisely what he intended to say.[38] Ever the diplomat, and knowing what great labor Madison had expended in preparing for and participating in the Convention, Jefferson couched his reaction in diplomatic terms. He said he liked numerous elements of the document, such as the creation of three new branches of government, the congressional taxing power, and the direct election of representatives. He liked the veto power and the override provision, the compromise over congressional apportionment, and numerous other things. But he had reservations: "First the omission of a bill of rights providing clearly & without the aid of sophisms for freedom of religion, freedom of the press, protection against standing armies, restriction against monopolies, the eternal and unremitting force of the habeas corpus laws, and trials by jury." James Wilson of Pennsylvania, a prominent and active Philadelphia Convention delegate, had opened the ratification campaign with a speech at the statehouse in Philadelphia describing the proposed constitution. Antifederalists erred in lamenting the absence of a bill of rights from the document, said Wilson, because unlike state governments—which had all powers not expressly denied them—the new government would have only the powers enumerated. Jefferson made short shrift of this assertion, which was "opposed by strong inferences from the body of the instrument, as well as from the omission of the clause of our present confederation which had declared that in express terms [Article II]." "Let me add"—Jefferson warmed to his argument—"that a bill of rights is what the people are entitled to against every government on earth, general or particular, & what no just government should refuse, or rest on inferences."

Jefferson also complained about the absence of term limits, particularly for the president. After explaining why he thought that officer would come to hold his position for life and that elections would be as corrupt as those for kings of Poland, Jefferson said he had not decided whether he favored ratification in hope of future amendment or a new convention to perfect the Philadelphia conclave's product prior to ratification.

Here Jefferson also confided in his friend that he evaluated the situation facing the country differently because of his underlying attitudes. "I own I am not a friend to a very energetic government," Jefferson wrote. "It is always oppressive." Madison might be concerned over recent developments, but Jefferson insisted that Shays' Rebellion had "given more alarm than I think it should have done." One rebellion in thirteen states in eleven years came to one per state every 143 years, which would be far better than the record of any significant European state.

Faced with a closely divided state ratification convention and the possibility of a stunning defeat for the Federalist movement, Massachusetts Federalists hit upon a strategy: they promised that if their fellows voted to ratify the proposed constitution, they would seek amendments in the First Congress. Madison, prodded not only by Jefferson but by fellow Virginia Philadelphia Convention delegates Edmund Randolph and George Mason, besides the Baptists among his own Orange County constituents, decided to make the same argument as Bay State Federalists had made. In the First Federal Congress, Representative Madison did indeed push for amendments, and as a result Congress sent twelve proposed amendments to the states for their ratification.[39] In time, however, Madison would oppose Jefferson's last hopeful point: that the people would amend the new constitution "whenever they shall find it work wrong."

The Constitution's ratification by a ninth state in 1788 put it across the Article VII threshold, and thus it would be implemented in 1789 by the eleven states that had ratified it by then. Jefferson soon found himself in the new position of secretary of state. Theoretically, he became the senior member of President George Washington's cabinet when he wrote to Washington accepting the post on Valentine's Day, 1790.[40]

By then Congress had already been prompted by Madison to propose amendments to the states. The Preamble attached to Congress's proposal frankly said that the amendments' purpose was to allay the fears of those who had complained during the ratification struggle that the Constitution did not clearly enough mark the limits of Congress's powers.[41] Congress had opted for a coherent program despite Madison's repeated attempts to coax his colleagues into including a provision empowering federal courts to intervene in state policy-making in case local authorities infringed on religious liberty, the right to trial by jury, or the freedom of the press. In other words, Madison had attempted to sacrifice Congress's federal program at the altar of his own post-revolutionary idea, most famously developed in *Federalist* No. 10, that national majorities were more trustworthy than local ones. Like the Philadelphia Convention, Congress rejected this idea, opting for a suite of amendments all of which reinforced the Constitution's federal element. Ten of its twelve proposals—the Bill of Rights—would be ratified in 1791. Another of them became the Twenty-seventh Amendment in 1992.

Besides drafting proposed amendments, the First Congress also busied itself with the task of creating the federal government's executive and judicial branches. When George Washington raised his hand off the Bible upon taking the presidential oath of office, there was precisely one person in the executive branch: Washington. Congress passed legislation in 1789 creating the State, Treasury, and War Departments and the three-tiered federal judicial branch that has existed ever since. Besides providing for a secretary of the treasury and a treasurer, the bill creating the Department of the Treasury also called upon the secretary to submit a report outlining a new federal tax system.

At Madison's suggestion, Washington finally settled upon Alexander Hamilton as his treasury secretary.[42] Although descended from a Scottish laird, Hamilton had been born out of wedlock—not in North America, but on the Caribbean island of Nevis. Recognized as brilliant at an early age, Hamilton was sent to New York for an education at King's College. His low background did not keep him from striking up lasting friendships with the bluest of New York blue bloods, including John Jay and Gouverneur Morris, both of whom would be important political and social allies.

Leaving college for a junior officer's post in the Continental Army, the short, dashing Hamilton impressed senior leaders almost immediately. He was both brave and smart. In the end, Hamilton found his way onto General George Washington's staff, where he was a dynamo of activity. Perhaps it was not Hamilton who persuaded Washington to adopt the Fabian (defensive) grand strategy that ultimately won the war, but Hamilton certainly conceived of it early on, and he was never shy about letting his opinions be known.[43] Hamilton was the kind of fellow who always considered himself the smartest guy in the room, and although Morris, Jefferson, and Madison were enormously intelligent, he possibly was. By all accounts, despite his stature, women found him strikingly handsome as well.

Characteristically, Hamilton left Washington's staff in a fit of pique over a supposed slight. Back in New York, where he had made a very favorable marital match, he ascended to notable political and professional heights. Not only did he serve in Congress and prosper at the bar, but he founded the *New York Post* and the Bank of New York, both of which are still prominent New York institutions today. He joined with Madison and others in leadership of the 1780s Federalist movement, but his New York colleagues' early departure, an extended absence, and his own rather pointedly monarchist proclivities, set out at length in a day-long June 18, 1787 speech, consigned him to a marginal role in the Philadelphia Convention. That impolitic speech summarized Hamilton's political persona perfectly. Cocksure, the youngest of the founding fathers could have stood to learn a thing or two. After taking the lead in securing New York State's ratification of the Constitution, he would get his chance.

Upon his appointment as secretary of the treasury, Hamilton submitted numerous proposals to Congress. It should fund its debt and assume responsibility for the state governments' debts, which it should pay at face value.[44] It should charter a national bank, after the British model.[45] It should grant various kinds of subsidies and privileges to favored manufacturers.[46]

As Congress worked its way through Hamilton's program, Virginia leveled a mighty blast against it.[47] Patrick Henry, still the reigning eminence in the General Assembly, joined with 1788 Federalist Henry "Light-horse Harry" Lee in proposing a resolution decrying Congress's assumption of state debts. That act, they insisted, was "repugnant to the Constitution, as it goes to the exercise of power not *expressly* granted to the General Government." Their emphasis on the word "expressly" echoed vows made by Governor Edmund Randolph and Madison's close collaborator George Nicholas in the Virginia Ratification Convention of 1788. The governor, the most loquacious of Federalists (proponents of ratification) in that convention, had repeatedly insisted that Congress would under the Constitution have only the powers "expressly" granted. The Convention had ratified very narrowly. Henry, ratification's chief opponent, intended to hold the new government to Randolph and Nicholas's standard. His resolution passed the House of Delegates on the day it was introduced—November 3, 1790.

We have no direct evidence that the temper of Virginia politics affected his position, but Madison, long Hamilton's coadjutor, surprised him by leading congressional opposition to the Bank Bill.[48] The Virginian, though also among the youngest of the founding fathers and also extremely bright, shared little else with Hamilton. While Hamilton strutted, Madison stood off in a corner, mulling. Hamilton had been an authentic war hero, but Madison had made his mark in legislative chambers during the war. While Hamilton came of disreputable parentage and from a foreign land, James Madison Jr. was the oldest son of Orange County's richest resident. Certainly Madison was not the type to unburden himself of an ill-considered oration he confessed no one would welcome. What Madison said, he hoped would sway his audience. In a long speech in the House of Representatives, the Virginian insisted on the Bank Bill's unconstitutionality. Congress, said Madison, possessed only the enumerated powers. Its enumerated powers did not include one to charter a corporation, let alone a bank corporation; in fact, he remembered the Philadelphia Convention's decision to deny Congress that power. The argument of Bank Bill proponents that the General Welfare Clause, which Madison described as a kind of preamble to the enumeration of powers in the balance of its section of the Constitution, gave Congress power to charter a bank must be facetious: if it did, there was no need for the enumeration of powers that immediately followed it, because a legislature that could pass any bill purportedly in furtherance of the general welfare could pass any law at all. The Necessary and Proper Clause at the conclusion of the enumeration of powers did not apply either, because chartering a bank was not necessary to coining money, regulating trade with the Indians, raising an army, establishing post roads, declaring war, or any of the other enumerated congressional powers. Congress passed the bill anyway, but that was not the end of the matter.

Since Madison had been among proponents of chartering a bank in the old Confederation Congress, Hamilton had expected his support.[49] Stunned by his opposition, Hamilton wrote that if he had known Madison would oppose him, he would never have accepted the office of secretary of the treasury. President Washington, hearing of Madison's performance, put off signing the bill. He turned to his cabinet for advice.

Besides Jefferson and Hamilton, the other members of the first cabinet were Secretary of War Henry Knox and Attorney General Edmund Randolph. The portly Knox, sole nonlawyer of the four, had done yeoman's service in the revolution. His masterstroke of seizing Fort Ticonderoga, complete with its numerous cannons, early in the war made him a favorite of Washington's. Not only did he serve as chief of artillery through the balance of the conflict, but he always had Washington's ear. He was among those who wrote the retired general in 1786 with extremely worried takes on Shays' Rebellion. In the cabinet, he virtually always went along with Hamilton.

Randolph's experience bore more directly on the issue. Son of Virginia's last colonial attorney general, Randolph served for ten years as its first republican one before becoming governor just prior to the Philadelphia Convention.[50] Tall, handsome, and polished, besides a scion of his state's most prominent political family (and thus yet another Jefferson cousin), he was the obvious choice to present the Virginia Plan (known throughout the assemblage as "Randolph's Resolutions") to the Philadelphia Convention.

Although he played one of the handful of leading roles in Philadelphia, Randolph in the end refused to sign the draft constitution. He gave several reasons, among them that the limits of federal authority were not clearly enough defined and that there was no bill of rights. His letter to the House of Delegates' speaker became a centerpiece of the Virginia antifederalist movement. When the Richmond Ratification Convention assembled in June 1788, however, Madison's persistent urging bore fruit: Randolph early announced that he now favored ratification. Since eight states had already ratified, Randolph said, it was too late to amend the Constitution before ratifying it. Those eight would not reconsider merely because Virginia insisted upon it. For him, the issue had come down to union or disunion.

As in Philadelphia, Governor Randolph played a leading role in Richmond. In fact, he spoke more than any other Federalist delegate, repeatedly refuting Patrick Henry's urgent, eloquent, impassioned, mesmerizing arguments against ratification. In the end, Randolph told the Convention that the Congress would have only the powers "expressly" granted. He said this over and over. A young lawyer-delegate named John Marshall, new to the highest levels of Virginia politics, heard every word.[51] For good measure, the third most loquacious Federalist delegate, Madison's friend and close ally George Nicholas of Jefferson's Albemarle County, assured delegates in the Convention's last major speech that Virginia in ratifying the Constitution would be one of thirteen parties to a compact, and its understanding of the Constitution at the time of ratification would bind the other parties.[52] Congress, Nicholas joined Governor Randolph in saying, would have only the powers "expressly granted."[53] John Marshall heard this too.

Washington held multiple cabinet meetings on the Bank Bill. Jefferson and Randolph lined up on the side of the argument Madison had delivered in the House: that the bill was unconstitutional. Knox joined the bill's author, Hamilton, in arguing for its constitutionality. Finally, Washington asked each of the four to prepare him a written memorandum on the subject.

Jefferson's and Hamilton's views remain today the classic statements of federal (Jefferson's) and national (Hamilton's) constitutionalism. Apparently Washington read Jefferson's first, then presented it to Hamilton for a response.

Jefferson began by describing the Bank Bill's provisions, then saying that he understood the underlying principle of the Constitution to be that "all powers not delegated to the United States, by the Constitution, nor prohibited by it to the States, are reserved to the States or to the people."[54] (Here he quoted the Tenth Amendment, which at the time lay before the state legislatures for their ratification.) Power to pass the bill had not been delegated to the United States, he insisted. It did not fall under the power to tax for the purpose of paying debts, because the bill neither paid debts nor taxed. It did not fall under the power to borrow money, because the bill neither borrowed nor ensured there would be borrowing. It did not fall under the Commerce Clause, for it did not regulate commerce. Jefferson understood regulating commerce to mean "prescrib[ing] regulations for buying and selling," which the Bank Bill did not do. If it did that, he continued, the bill "would be void" due to its equal effects on internal and external commerce of the states. "For the power given to Congress by the Constitution," Jefferson continued, "does not extend to the internal regulation of the commerce of a State, (that is to say of the commerce between citizen and citizen,) which remain exclusively with its own legislature; but to its external commerce only, that is to say, its commerce with another State, or with foreign nations or with the Indian tribes."

No other enumerated power gave Congress ground for passing this bill either, he concluded.

Besides the enumerated powers, the General Welfare Clause and the Necessary and Proper Clause had also been invoked by the bill's proponents. Jefferson disposed of those clauses deftly as well. First, the General Welfare Clause said that Congress had power "to lay taxes for *the purpose* of providing for the general welfare [emphasis Jefferson's]." The reference to the general welfare, he insisted, was bound to the power to tax. It did not create a separate power "to do any act they please, which might be for the good of the Union," which Jefferson thought the preceding and following enumerations of powers rendered entirely obvious. To read the General Welfare Clause any other way would make the enumerations "completely useless. It would reduce the whole instrument to a single phrase, that of instituting a Congress with power to do whatever would be for the good of the United States; and as they would be the sole judges of the good or evil, it would be also a power to do whatever evil they please."

Jefferson, skilled lawyer that he was, noted that one of the most basic rules of construction cut strongly in the direction of his argument. It was "where a phrase will bear either of two meanings, to give it that which will allow some meaning to the other parts of the instrument, and not that which would render all the others useless." Besides that, the Philadelphia Convention had considered and rejected a proposal to empower Congress to create corporations. The rejection, he noted, was based partly on the fact that with such a power, Congress would be able to create a bank.

As for the Necessary and Proper Clause, Jefferson noted that it said that the Congress could "make all laws *necessary* and proper for carrying into execution the enumerated powers. But they can all be carried into execution without a bank. A bank therefore is not *necessary*, and consequently not authorized by this phrase [emphasis Jefferson's]." The Bank Bill's proponents had argued for the great convenience of having a bank, which might aid in exercising powers enumerated in the Constitution, but Jefferson would have none of the idea that "necessary" could be twisted into "convenient."

Jefferson concluded his memorandum with a brief statement on the president's veto power, which he called "the shield provided by the constitution to protect against the invasions of the legislature: 1. The right of the Executive. 2. Of the Judiciary. 3. Of the States and State legislatures." To his mind, the Bank Bill presented "the case of a right remaining exclusively with the States"—that of chartering a corporation. Congress's attempt to take this right to itself violated the Constitution, and Washington should veto the bill.

Washington did not agree. Instead, perhaps on the basis of Hamilton's argument that Congress could adopt whatever kind of legislation it judged helpful in supervising the national economy, he signed the Bank Bill.[55] (Though historians commonly assume that Hamilton persuaded Washington, Washington never explained his decision.) This event helped prod Jefferson and Representative Madison to organize opposition to Hamilton. The two soon found themselves at the head of a like-minded phalanx of congressmen generally dissatisfied with the vector of Hamilton's policies—particularly as the division of powers between federal and state governments (federalism) was concerned.

It was here that Jefferson's memorandum had its main significance. His chief point was that the Constitution rested on the principle of limited delegation of power to the US government. He rebuffed the classic nationalist arguments for unlimited congressional power. He closed with the assertion that the presidential veto power was to be used to protect the federal executive, the federal judiciary, and the states against congressional usurpations. Where today people are prone to speak of the separation of powers among the federal branches as the chief structural protection of their liberties in the US Constitution, Jefferson not only called the division of powers between the states and the US government— the Tenth Amendment principle—the Constitution's basis, but said that the president should consider it as one of the two principles he must protect with his veto power.

Secretary of State Jefferson had occasion to consider the matter of the US Constitution and national banks from the state perspective nearly two years later. The issue came up in a letter to Madison written on October 1, 1792.[56] Governor Henry Lee, a Richmond Convention Federalist whose attitude regarding federal power underwent substantial revision during the controversy over federal assumption of state debts, proposed to thwart the Bank of the United States by having the General Assembly charter Virginia state banks. Jefferson adjudged this proposal "not only inadequate, but objectionable highly." He confided in the congressman that Lee's idea "rather recognises than prevents the planting among them a source of poison and corruption to sap their catholicism, and to annihilate that power, which is now one, by dividing it into two which shall counterbalance each other."

Rather than tamely accepting the federal government's invasion of Virginia's sovereignty, Jefferson counseled, the Commonwealth's leaders should resist it. Anyone who cooperated in the federal bank system in Virginia, "whether by signing notes, issuing or passing them, acting as director, cashier or in any other office relating to it," should be tried in a state court and executed for high treason. If North Carolina could be persuaded to follow the Old Dominion in adopting this policy, he reasoned, other states likely would follow. Despite Secretary of State Jefferson's statement that "I really wish that this or nothing should be done," the General Assembly passed Lee's bill to create two state banks.

Another of Hamilton's pet proposals offered Jefferson an opportunity to assert his limited-government position the next year.[57] Hamilton's 1792 Report on Manufactures proposed various kinds of assistance—tax breaks, straight subsidies, protective tariffs, and exemptions from tariffs—for American manufacturers. Jefferson and his friend Madison objected to Hamilton's claims concerning the General Welfare Clause in this document. To Jefferson, the General Welfare Clause was not a separate grant of power, but a statement about the proper use of the taxing power. Hamilton's claim that the General Welfare Clause authorized Congress to do whatever might be said to be for the public good was a "sham limitation," Jefferson insisted. Washington never had to decide this question, because Congress did not adopt Hamilton's proposals.

Jefferson did not abandon the idea of using state actions as means for defending Virginia's reserved Tenth Amendment rights after the bank fight, either. The matter came up again in 1797. Justice James Iredell, who had been a leading—perhaps the leading—North Carolina Federalist during the ratification campaign and a moderate member of that party, urged a Richmond federal grand jury to root out "differences of opinion," which otherwise might "corrode into enmity."[58] The grand jury responded by issuing a presentment against Jefferson's own congressman, Samuel J. Cabell. His offense: having criticized President

John Adams's foreign policy in a circular letter (what today we would call "junk mail") to his constituents.

Vice President Jefferson, outraged, drafted a petition for his fellow Cabell constituents to submit to the General Assembly.[59] He claimed that Virginia's 1776 Constitution, like the unwritten constitution of Great Britain, rested in the end on the freedom of communication between legislators and constituents. The grand jurors in the Cabell matter, having endeavored to deprive Virginians of this fundamental right, ought to be impeached and barred from holding such offices by the General Assembly.

Jefferson's draft petition brought this matter arising in the federal court under the cognizance of the Virginia legislature by reference to an express provision of the 1776 Constitution. The portion empowering the General Assembly to impeach directed that power at "the Governor, when he is out of office, and *others* offending against the state, either by maladministration, corruption, *or other means* by which the safety [of the state may be endangered] [emphasis Jefferson's]." Jefferson thought the grand jurors fell under that final category. "We denounce to you a great crime," the petition said, "wicked in its purpose, and mortal in its consequences unless prevented, committed by citizens of this commonwealth against the body of their country." The version of the petition finally entered into the journal of the House of Delegates, while it called for the jurors' impeachment, omitted the paragraph in which Jefferson had defended the appropriateness of this response to the problem.[60]

The enraged vice president explained his thinking in correspondence with his political ally Governor James Monroe.[61] Yes, Jefferson conceded, the idea that the General Assembly lacked jurisdiction over misbehaving federal grand jurors had occurred to him. Yet, he came down on the side of state authority.

Jefferson classed the "right of free correspondence" as a natural right. As it had not been the gift of the federal Constitution, a congressional statute, or a treaty, it remained under the authority of the state governments: "The courts of this commonwealth . . . still retain all their judiciary congisances not expressly alienated by the federal constitution." (Note the word "expressly," which Governor Edmund Randolph and George Nicholas had used repeatedly in describing the US government's powers to the Richmond Ratification Convention.)

Besides, Jefferson reasoned, where a question of the line between federal and state authority was a close one, the side that ceded the issue would lose. "The system of the General government is to sieze all doubtful ground," he noted. "We must join in the scramble or get nothing." (Although at that point he was vice president, Jefferson's use of the first-person plural placed him among Virginians against federal officials.) In this situation, the petitioners did not have ultimate authority anyway. They should play their part in getting the matter before Virginia's courts, who would have the ultimate power to decide.

Jefferson drew a distinction between an attempt to vindicate Congressman Cabell's rights and what Jefferson had in mind:

> Observe that it is not the breach of Mr. Cabell's privilege which we mean to punish: that might lie with Congress. It is the wrong done to the citizens of our district. Congress has no authority to punish that wrong. They can only take cognisance of it in vindication of their member.

Only the General Assembly could defend the rights of Cabell's constituents in this case.

In the end, Cabell was never indicted, and the House of Delegates passed a resolution upbraiding the grand jurors without calling for their impeachment.[62]

The general issue of the relationship between the states and the federal government was pushed strongly to the fore the following year during what came to be known as the Alien and Sedition Acts Crisis of 1798. Centering on the passage and enforcement of those three laws, the crisis actually lasted from President John Adams's signing them on Bastille Day, July 14, 1798, to the expiration of two of the acts and President Thomas Jefferson's pardoning of those convicted under them in early 1801.[63]

Federalists of the 1790s, and Republicans for that matter, never conceded the legitimacy of party contest. Party, aka "faction," drew the scorn of all and sundry, even as virtually every significant politician aligned himself with a party. Madison had made the classic theoretical argument against faction in *The Federalist* No. 10, but Jefferson—typically—put the common view more memorably:

> I never submitted the whole system of my opinions to the creed of any party of men whatever in religion, in philosophy, in politics, or in any thing else where I was capable of thinking for myself. Such an addiction is the last degradation of a free and moral agent. If I could not go to heaven but with a party, I would not go there at all.[64]

From Federalists' perspective, the Republicans' consistent opposition to administration measures seemed illegitimate. Anti-constitutional. Seditious. Un-American.

Criminal.

The persistent tendency of immigrants to join the Republican legions upon arriving in America struck leading Federalist figures in Congress, on the federal courts, and in the executive branch as simply intolerable. What to do? Fortunately, the common law provided antecedents for a remedy. Perhaps the Richmond grand jury had never indicted Congressman Cabell, but federal judges armed with a seditious libel statute would have no reason for forbearance.

Adams did not sign the Alien and Sedition Acts into law on Bastille Day by happenstance. Commemoration of major events in the French Revolution helped bind Jeffersonians together in the late 1790s, and so Adams knew full well that choosing that day for that act was sticking his thumb in the Republicans' eye.[65]

First, Congress passed a law—the Alien Act—extending the time in residence required before an immigrant could become an American citizen to the longest ever required in American history: fourteen years.[66] Next, Congress passed the Alien Enemies Act, which empowered the president to expel enemy aliens in time of hostilities.

More controversial still, the Sedition Act made it a crime to say anything that tended to bring the federal government into ill repute. Far from rhetorical, this law ultimately underlay dozens of prosecutions and numerous convictions, including those of several prominent Republican journalists and even of a Republican congressman from Vermont. The congressman's offense closely resembled Representative Cabell's of 1797: he criticized President Adams.

With all three branches of the federal government arrayed against them—the judiciary vociferously—Republicans decided on the only response available: to have the Virginia General Assembly and some other state legislature issue formal protests.[67] The results were the Virginia and Kentucky Resolutions of 1798.[68]

While Madison had considered the late 1780s as "the crisis of republican government," Jefferson saw that in the late 1790s. Possibly for the only time, he feared that Americans would accept a king and lords in lieu of the US Constitution. The Alien and Sedition Acts, in this reading, were "merely an experiment on the American mind, to see how far it will bear an avowed violation of the constitution." The Alien Act's targeting of Swiss-born Pennsylvania Republican Albert Gallatin struck him as an egregious abuse of congressional power, and Jefferson thought it entirely possible that he, the vice president of the United States, would become the target of a Sedition Act prosecution. He implored Madison to verify that the seals to his letters were arriving unbroken, for Federalist postmasters to open and read his letters would not be beyond them.

The best safeguard against such developments, as Jefferson had said the previous year, was "that the states retain as complete authority as possible over their own citizens."[69] He held that the Constitution had been adopted with this principle foremost in citizens' minds. The first of the nine Kentucky Resolutions makes this claim clear. It says, "That the several states composing the United States of America are not united on the principle of unlimited submission to their General Government." Here we see the Tenth Amendment principle which Jefferson had highlighted in the cabinet debate over Hamilton's Bank Bill seven years before.

Jefferson took it further, calling the Constitution "a compact" and saying that under it, the states "constituted a General Government for special purposes,—delegated to that government certain definite powers, reserving, each State to itself, the residuary mass of right to their own self-government." Here Jefferson had summarized the position he had taken in "A Summary View" and refracted it through the understanding of ratification's significance conveyed to the Richmond Convention by Governor Edmund Randolph, George Nicholas, and James Madison— an understanding made explicit by the Tenth Amendment.

Where Nicholas had told the Richmond Convention of 1788 that Virginia could reclaim the powers it was granting in case the new government abused them, Jefferson said "that whensoever the General Government assumes undelegated powers, its acts are unauthoritative, void, and of no force." So far as he was concerned, a law like the federal Sedition Act could be treated—should be treated—as if it simply did not exist.

Who would decide whether the federal government had abused its powers? Jefferson did not even pause. "The government created by this compact," he said, "was not made the exclusive or final judge of the extent of the power delegated to itself; since that would have made its discretion, and not the Constitution, the measure of its powers." So much for judicial supremacy, the twenty-first-century answer to this kind of question. For Jefferson, "as in all other cases of compact among powers having no common judge, *each party has an equal right to judge for itself*, as well of infractions as of the mode and measure of redress [emphasis added]." Madison, writing for Virginia, put it even more emphatically, saying in that state's third resolution that "the states have the right, and are in duty bound, to interpose for the redress of grievances."[70] What Jefferson envisioned Kentucky's calling its "right," Madison conceived of as being Virginia's "duty."

Jefferson's second resolution considered the constitutionality of two new congressional statutes establishing federal crimes. Since it was "true as a general principle" and "one of the amendments to the Constitution [had] also declared" that "the powers not delegated to the United States by the Constitution, nor prohibited by it to the States, are reserved to the States respectively, or to the people"—here Jefferson had simply quoted the Tenth Amendment in full—the statutes were unconstitutional. In other words, they were "altogether void, and of no force."

The third resolution repeated the language of the Tenth Amendment before weighing congressional legislation restricting the freedoms of religion, speech, and the press against it. "All lawful powers respecting the same," Jefferson said, "did of right remain, and were reserved to the States or the people . . . thus was manifested their determination to retain to themselves the right of judging how far the licentiousness of speech and of the press may be abridged without lessening their useful freedom, and how far those abuses which cannot be separated from their use should be tolerated, rather than their use be destroyed."

As was characteristic of Republican disputants in the 1780s and '90s, Jefferson tied violation of the freedoms of speech and the press to threats against the freedom of religion. Federal constitutional protection for those three rights was to be found "in the same sentence, and under the same words . . . insomuch, that whatever violated either throws down the sanctuary which covers the others, and . . . libels, falsehood, and defamation, equally with heresy and false religion, are withheld from the cognizance of federal tribunals." The Sedition Act, he insisted, "is not law, but is altogether void, and of no force." The fourth resolution made the same argument in relation to the Alien Friends Act, as when it came to such people, Jefferson insisted, "no power . . . has been delegated to the United States." Besides that, he noted in the fifth resolution, the 1808

Clause of Article I, Section 9, of the Constitution expressly reserved power over migration of alien friends into the individual states until 1808 to the states.

The sixth resolution scored the Alien Act for giving the president power to imprison aliens without resort to the judicial branch, which violated both Article III's delegation of the judicial power to federal judges (besides vesting this power in an official who already had the executive power and part of the legislative power) and the Fifth Amendment's Due Process Clause. It also ran afoul of the Sixth Amendment's guarantees of the rights to public trial by jury, to be informed of the charges, to confront witnesses, to compulsory process, and to counsel.

The seventh resolution said that the federal government's various acts under a Hamiltonian construction of the General Welfare and Necessary and Proper Clauses went "to the destruction of all limits prescribed to their power by the Constitution." Both clauses, according to Jefferson, were "meant by the instrument to be subsidiary only to the execution of limited powers" and "ought not to be so construed as themselves to give unlimited powers." When the time came, the people should see to the "revisal and correction" of the Constitution to ensure that the Federalists' abuses along these lines (assumption of state debts, the Bank Law, etc.) ceased.

Having thus made publicly what in 1791 had been his private argument about the proper method of constitutional construction, Jefferson turned in his eighth resolution to the steps properly to be taken by Kentucky and its fellow members of the federal union to remedy the problem. Kentucky, it said, "continues in the same esteem of their [meaning the other states'] friendship and union which it has manifested from that moment at which a common danger first suggested a common union." (Jefferson here seems to have imposed upon Kentucky the history of Virginia, as he had done to all of the other colonies in "A Summary View" twenty-four years previously and the Declaration of Independence two years after that.) The present problems had not brought the end of Kentucky's filial affection for the other states. Rather, "it considers union, *for specified national purposes, and particularly to those specified in their late federal compact*, to be friendly to the peace, happiness and prosperity of all the States [emphasis added]." In other words, Jefferson remained committed, as he had been since 1774, to a federal vision in which individual states retained primary authority over their own affairs. The federal government should be understood as possessing only the few powers the states had granted it through the enumerations found in the Constitution.

To Jefferson, identifying powers properly federal posed no significant difficulty. Kentucky yearned for preservation of the union under the Constitution "according to the plain intent and meaning in which it was understood and acceded to by the several parties." To treat the question in some other way—to allow the federal government to exercise other powers "without regard to the special delegations and reservations solemnly agreed to in that compact"—would inure to the marked injury of the union's members. It would not be "for the peace, happiness or prosperity of these States."

As in 1774, Jefferson in 1798 used highly pugnacious language. He envisioned the Kentucky legislature saying, "This commonwealth is determined, as it doubts not its co-States are, to submit to undelegated, and consequently unlimited powers in no man, or body of men on earth." In case of abuse of delegated powers, elections provided the remedy; where the federal government arrogated powers not granted, however, "a nullification of the act is the rightful remedy."

Jefferson explained that "every State has a natural right in cases not within the compact . . . to nullify of their own authority all assumptions of power by others within their limits." Rather than exercise this right, however, Kentucky chose to communicate with its sister states to see whether they would join in opposition. Further acts such as the Alien and Sedition Acts, he concluded, "necessarily drive these States into revolution and blood, and will furnish new calumnies against republican government, and new pretexts for those who wish it to be believed that man cannot be governed but by a rod of iron." The current system amounted to "a tyranny" under the president. Therefore, "let no more be heard of confidence in man, but bind him down from mischief by the chains of the Constitution." The states must join in protesting the federal government's claim of power to bind the states "in all cases whatsoever." The echo of the Declaratory Act of 1766, in which Parliament claimed power to legislate for the colonies "in all cases whatsoever," cannot have been lost on Jefferson's audience. The states had a natural right to declare federal legislation "void, and of no force" "in cases not made federal" and take steps to prevent its enforcement "within their respective territories." For that reason, the ninth resolution looked to communication with other states' officials.

The most influential account of those resolutions appeared in an academic history journal in 1948.[71] It concluded that the goal motivating "Jefferson and Madison" to invent the doctrines laid out in the Virginia and Kentucky Resolutions was to defend the freedoms of speech and of the press. In endeavoring to explain the resolutions' purpose, that article's authors omitted any attention to the Virginia House of Delegates' debates about them. In asserting that the compact theory of the Constitution was new, they omitted any discussion of Federalists' accounts of the Constitution during the ratification campaign and of Virginians' discussion of these questions before and since.

Why would two prominent scholars have overlooked literally the most obvious sources? The answer appeared in an extraordinary editorial note preceding the article. There the *William and Mary Quarterly*'s editor said that he was happy to publish this article, because it supported President Harry Truman in his ongoing dispute with a fellow Democrat, Senator Harry F. Byrd Jr. of Virginia, over the nature of the US Constitution and the states' place within the federal system. In other words, because they disliked the facts concerning the Jeffersonian Republicans' understanding of the nature of the federal union, the authors and the editor simply pretended those facts did not exist. This article's account of the Virginia and Kentucky Resolutions dominated scholarly accounts of the era, such as Dumas Malone's six-volume Jefferson biography and Merrill Peterson's one-volume version, for several decades thereafter.[72]

The Virginia and Kentucky Resolutions drew harshly negative responses from states to the Old Dominion's north. Scholars have always said that no other state accepted Virginia's and Kentucky's call on other states to endorse their opinion concerning the offending legislation. The latest scholarship shows that this is not so, however: Georgia and Tennessee adopted resolutions holding it unconstitutional.[73] Apparently Virginia and Kentucky were not the outliers they have long been held to have been, their resolutions were not extreme at all, and there is no mystery that although their principles had been rejected by Federalists in 1798, Virginia Republicans' leaders became president and secretary of state in 1801.

Jefferson told Madison that Kentucky and Virginia should reply to the criticisms by saying that although they had a right to take action against such federal attempts against the Constitution as the Alien and Sedition Acts, their love of the union would keep them from being precipitate in defense of "those rights of self government the securing of which was the object of that compact."[74] Jefferson and Madison outlined a new draft set of resolutions for Kentucky and drafted a legislative report for the Virginia House of Delegates, respectively, to clarify those states' positions and refute Federalist attacks upon them.[75] In the midst of these events, Jefferson wrote to his cousin and former cabinet ally Edmund Randolph that Virginia had been a "nation" already in the period "before the revolution."[76] His view of Virginia's, and thus America's, constitutional history remained clear, if only errant Federalists would open their eyes and see the truth. Yet, persuading Federalist politicians had never been the Jeffersonian leadership's aim.

Jefferson had his hopes set on winning the 1800 election. This led to his insistence that the Kentucky and Virginia responses to northern criticism be couched in expressions of affection for the union. Unlike some of his top political allies, Jefferson held that the problems Republicans faced were not systemic. He blamed them on the bad policies and principles of Hamiltonian Federalists. Remove those men from office and influence and repeal their policies, and things would be fine. So Jefferson believed. The goal must be to win the next election.[77]

And win they did. Now all of the Jeffersonians' dreams would come true.[78]

Jefferson made this expectation clear in his First Inaugural Address.[79] While virtually all presidential inaugural addresses are unreadable, Jefferson's first is a classic of the genre—poetically written, optimistic, and substantial. In it, he clearly forecast what the Virginia dynasty and its congressional allies would do in control of the federal government's elected branches over the following quarter of a century. Central to this great speech—one of only two public speeches Jefferson gave (his Second Inaugural Address was the other)—was his commitment to federalism.

Fundamental to his thinking, federalism for Jefferson underlay the constitutional vision America's revolution had been fought to vindicate. Yes, politicians had argued over the question in the 1790s, but only the peculiar combination of Washington's unique prestige and Hamilton's inexplicable sway over him accounted for that. As Jefferson saw it, Americans had "been led hood-winked from their principles, by a most extraordinary combination of circumstances."[80] Now, what he would in time call "the Revolution of 1800" had swept Hamiltonianism away.[81] He said in his address that "we have called by different names brethren of the same principle. We are all Republicans, we are all Federalists." So few were the true opponents of the American constitutional system that they could "stand undisturbed as monuments of the safety with which error of opinion may be tolerated where reason is left free to combat it." These assurances were no mere public pose intended as party propaganda: Jefferson used very similar language to a French friend several months later.[82]

In his First Inaugural Address, Jefferson called on Congress to act on this understanding. Rather than prop up a significant military establishment with onerous taxes, he would rely on the militia (that is, the states) as the first line of America's defense. This would be safe, for American men—uniquely—would fly to the colors in case of a foreign threat. "Let us, then," he urged, "with courage and confidence pursue our own Federal and Republican principles, our attachment to union and representative government." Blessed as Americans were, with a huge ocean separating their country from European quarrels, with land enough "for our descendants to the thousandth and thousandth generation," with "a due sense of our equal right . . . to the acquisitions of our own industry," with a benign religion inculcating social virtues, they needed only "a wise and frugal Government . . . to close the circle of [their] felicities."

The Constitution provided for such a government, essentially banning Hamiltonianism, through the principle of enumeration of powers, which Federalists had assured people was inherent in the unamended Constitution, and through the Tenth Amendment, which made that principle explicit. While he promised "the preservation of the General Government in its whole constitutional vigor, as the sheet anchor of our peace at home and safety abroad," he also pledged "the support of the State governments in all their rights, as the most competent administrations for our domestic concerns and the surest bulwarks against antirepublican tendencies." If he had not thought so before, the Alien and Sedition Acts Crisis of 1798–1801 would have impressed this conviction upon his mind. As it was, Jefferson saw his revolutionary commitment vindicated.

Jefferson's Republican allies in Congress quickly turned to paring back the Federalist establishment insofar as it was possible, hurriedly legislating the end of the president's authority to expand the army and navy and disdaining to reinstate the Alien and Sedition Acts. Jefferson used his pardon power to free and reimburse everyone sentenced under the Sedition Act and happily signed the associated legislation, including repeal of the Judiciary Act of 1801. On taking office, he found commissions for new judges appointed by President John Adams to fill posts created by the Judiciary Act of 1801 awaiting delivery in the State Department, and he decided against delivering them; the purpose of the judges' appointments, he believed, was to attempt to thwart his administration, and so to that extent illegitimately contrary to the result of the election that had already put him in line to succeed Adams.[83] Among the judges not commissioned as a result was a cousin of his—and brother of his other cousin, Chief Justice John Marshall.

Jefferson's chief disappointment in regard to federalism in his presidential years would be the Senate's acquittal of Justice Samuel Chase, who richly deserved conviction at his impeachment trial. Chase had taken the lead in enforcing the Sedition Act, even vowing a man's conviction and harsh sentence before he had been indicted and intervening to prevent defense counsel from presenting their full case for the accused.[84] Jefferson decided upon learning of Chase's acquittal that impeachment, which Alexander Hamilton had promised in *The Federalist* would be a solution to judicial usurpation, was "not even a scare-crow."[85] The lack of an effective check on the judiciary in case of usurpation would haunt Jefferson in retirement—as it has disastrously influenced subsequent events.

The bruising political battles of the 1790s had driven a wide wedge between Jefferson and Federalists formerly his friends. Chief among those were President John Adams and his wife Abigail. From early in 1797 through his own administration and much of his successor's, Jefferson essentially did not communicate with them. A temporary interruption of this pattern came in 1804. Abigail Adams, hearing of the death of Jefferson's younger daughter, wrote the grieving president to commiserate. Jefferson replied that he had long awaited an opportunity to resuscitate the friendship. Along the way, however, he complained about Adams's attempt to install anti-Jeffersonian judges in the wake of his 1800 electoral defeat.

Mrs. Adams, long her husband's closest political confidante, would have nothing of it. She wrote back in an aggrieved tone to upbraid the president for supporting one anti-Adams journalist and pardoning another. Besides insisting that he had been more sinned against than sinning in the partisan wars of the 1790s, and had neither sicced a journalist on President Adams nor thought Adams had sicced one on him, Jefferson defended his pardons of those convicted under the Sedition Act.[86] That law, he held, was "a nullity as absolute and as palpable as if Congress had ordered us to fall down and worship a golden image."

Abigail again replied, this time noting that Jefferson's replacement of her son with someone else in a minor administrative post in the judicial branch had been a personal slight. Jefferson answered that he had not known her son held such a post, to which he would happily have reappointed him instead of the other Federalists he had put in the same posts in Boston.[87] To Adams's claim that it was up to the judges, not the president, to decide whether the Sedition Act was constitutional, Jefferson replied that the judges had to enforce the laws they considered constitutional, and the president was obliged to pardon people he believed had been unjustly punished under laws he considered unconstitutional.

Jefferson next made a statement strongly underscoring his federal principles. It is worth quoting in its entirety:

Nor does the opinion of the unconstitutionality and consequent nullity of that law remove all restraint from the overwhelming torrent of slander which is confounding all vice and virtue, all truth & falsehood in the US. The power to do that is fully possessed by the several state-legislatures. It was reserved to them, & was denied to the general government, by the constitution according to our construction of it. While we deny that Congress have a right to controul the freedom of the press, we have ever asserted the right of the states, and their exclusive right, to do so. They have accordingly, all of them, made provisions for punishing slander, which those who have time and inclination resort to for the vindication of their characters. In general the state laws appear to have made the presses responsible for slander as far as is consistent with their useful freedom. In those states where they do not admit even the truth of allegations to protect the printer, they have gone too far.

Where his friend Madison had endeavored in the first federal Congress to have that body send the states a proposed constitutional amendment providing for federal enforcement of the principle of freedom of the press against the states, thus disempowering the states to adopt sedition acts, Jefferson held a different position. As he saw it, the First Amendment was a federalism provision. Its purpose was to leave such matters as punishing slander, whether ordinary or seditious, to the state governments. They alone, in the federal system, had the right "to controul the freedom of the press." To date, he said, they were doing a good job of it.

Alas, unpersuaded, Abigail Adams rejoined her husband as a former friend of Thomas Jefferson. The three of them would endure that situation for nearly another decade.[88] During that decade, President Jefferson—true to his reading of the US Constitution, if not to his more general principles—favored state prosecutions of his own critics for seditious libel.[89]

By the time of this correspondence with Abigail Adams, Jefferson had already fallen into the crowning accomplishment of his presidency: the Louisiana Purchase. Sent to France to buy New Orleans from the French Republic, Jefferson's men were shocked to be offered all of the Louisiana Territory. Doing their best not to seem too enthused at the prospect, they accepted the offer.[90] Secretary of State James Madison was elated at the news. New England Federalists were not. Nor was Jefferson.

To the New England Federalists, the Louisiana Purchase held out the prospect of permanent submersion into a sea of Jeffersonian states. Already a minority section controlling a minority party, New England now looked likely to be forever denied control over the federal government in case the treaty with France were ratified by the Senate. Jefferson, for his part, believed that the treaty should be preceded by an amendment authorizing the federal government to agree to it.

In time, Jefferson decided that raison d'état required him to approve the treaty without the amendment and hope that the people would live with the consequences. So good a bargain must not be lost. The New Englanders, for their part, tossed out whatever contrary arguments came to mind. At one point, they suggested trading Spain the Louisiana Territory for the Floridas—today's state of Florida, plus the coastal areas of Alabama, Mississippi, and Louisiana east of the Mississippi River.[91] Not to take this step, they guessed, could mean that eventually the Mississippi region would separate from the Atlantic states. For his part, Jefferson rejected the idea of surrendering control of any of the Mississippi's tributaries to any foreign power. He would, however, accept those new states' decision as to how to respond to problems between them and the old states—even if they chose disunion. "If it should become the great interest of those nations [notice that word] to separate from this, if their happiness should depend on it so strongly as to induce them to go through that convulsion, why should the Atlantic States dread it?"

For Jefferson, the United States were not an awe-inspiring extent of territory colored the same color on a map, nor were they a huge region to compare to France, Spain, or Russia. They were instead "nations" freely leagued for their mutual benefit. In case of a division, he continued, "why should we, [the Atlantic states'] present inhabitants, take side in such a question?" "The future inhabitants of the Atlantic & Missipi States will be our sons. We leave them in distinct but bordering establishments." (He meant that they would live in different, though neighboring, states.) "We think we see their happiness in their union, & we wish it." Here is the important part: "Events may prove it otherwise; and *if they see their interest in separation, why should we take side with our Atlantic rather than our Missipi descendants* [emphasis added]?" Should the western states choose to leave the union, "it is the elder and the younger son differing. God bless them both, & keep them in union, if it be for their good, but separate them, if it be better." Far from a passing opinion, this was one that Jefferson expressed again, in almost identical language, more than five months later.[92]

Jefferson as president also repeatedly encountered the question of the division of powers between the central and state governments in regard to what in his day were called "internal improvements," which we would now call "infrastructure." Even the oldest portions of the country had few high-quality roads. The western sections were almost entirely unimproved. One solution might be to have the federal government undertake a program of roadbuilding. Jefferson called in two of his eight annual state of the union addresses for Congress to begin to fund roadbuilding.[93]

A problem presented itself, of course: that the Constitution did not authorize Congress to pass any such law. However, it also provided a remedy: Article V, the amendment provision. Jefferson therefore proposed that Congress send the states an amendment giving Congress this power for the states to ratify. In both his Sixth Annual Message and his Eighth Annual Message, Jefferson immediately followed his invocation of the desirability of federal roadbuilding with reference to the possibility of amending the Constitution to make up any defect in Congress's authority to do things like this. Although he wanted Congress to apply what would, as soon as the debt accrued during the revolution had been repaid, be its surplus revenue to purposes such as this one, he held that amendment was necessary to make such expenditures constitutional. His closest political ally, Madison, would in his last presidential act veto a congressional roadbuilding program due to the omission to amend the Constitution first.[94]

President Jefferson also encountered the federalism issue in relation to government's relationship to religion. Perhaps the most famous statement on the question of church-state relations issued from Jefferson's pen on January 1, 1802. It was then that he sent his famous Letter to the Danbury Baptist Association.[95] In this he told the association that he considered "with sovereign reverence that act of the whole American people which declared that *their* legislature should 'make no law respecting an establishment of religion, or prohibiting the free exercise thereof,' thus building a wall of separation between Church & State."

Various practitioners of law-office history have held that this statement reflected a general Jeffersonian, and thus American, hostility to any connection between church and state. They have erred in overlooking the federal principle in Jefferson's thought.[96] Not only was Bill No. 82 but one of several religion-related bills drafted by Jefferson as part of the revisal of Virginia law, but he addressed this very question in a memorable passage of his Second Inaugural Address. Looking back on his first term as chief executive, he recalled that "in matters of religion, I have considered that its free exercise is placed by the constitution independent of the powers of the general government. I have therefore undertaken, on no occasion, to prescribe the religious exercises suited to it; but have left them, as the constitution found them, under the direction and discipline of state or church authorities acknowledged by the several religious societies."[97]

This reading of the Religion Clauses of the First Amendment echoes his explanation to Abigail Adams three years before of his understanding of the Press Clause. In fact, Jefferson wrote an analogous letter on the question of the federal system and jurisdiction over religion questions.[98] Jefferson was asked early in 1808 whether a request that he recommend a day of prayer and fasting would be congenial to him. The reverend who asked him conceded that there might be constitutional or other objections to such a request.

Jefferson responded by explaining that not only the Establishment Clause but also the Tenth Amendment banned the federal government "from intermedling with religious institutions, their doctrines, discipline, or exercises." "Certainly," he said, "no power to prescribe any religious exercise, or to assume authority in religious discipline, has been delegated to the general government. It must then rest with the states, as far as it can be in any human authority." Unlike his predecessors, Jefferson never issued any such recommendations or proclamations.

. . .

In his post-1809 political retirement, Jefferson became a kind of "great lama of the mountain" (as John Marshall put), the veritable "Sage of Monticello" (to admirers).[99] Americans, and not just Americans, sought his opinions on all kinds of matters. Among them were manuscripts written by a French nobleman and sometime French senator, the comte Destutt de Tracy.

Tracy ultimately sent Jefferson two manuscripts, one on ideology and one on political economy.[100] Jefferson translated one of Tracy's works and saw to the circulation of both. Along the way, he also corresponded with Tracy, whose commitment to republicanism Jefferson of course shared.

Jefferson wrote to Tracy about the latter's work in political science on January 26, 1811.[101] He began with praise for the work overall, then took exception to Tracy's argument for a plural executive. Having disposed of this argument, Jefferson turned to the American arrangement guaranteeing citizens' liberty: "the true barriers of our liberty in this country are our State governments; and the wisest conservative power ever contrived by man, is that of which our Revolution and present government found us possessed." He knew whereof he spoke, having made his entry upon the continental stage thirty-seven years before as author of an essay pointing to the colonies' status as Americans' first political communities—the claim underlying his Declaration of Independence.

The seventeen states of 1811, according to Jefferson, could never be gulled by a single demagogue. They could not be forced to obey him either. "The republican government of France was lost without a struggle," he said, "because the party of '*un et indivisible*' ['one and indivisible'] had prevailed," leaving no provincial governments to stand against the center, which easily assumed all of the force of the state. It could not happen here.

On the other hand, Jefferson said, America's federal organization, complete with fully articulated state governments, might lead to attempts at

secession "from local and occasional [meaning ephemeral] discontents."
The secessionists would be unable "to face the sound parts of so extensive an Union," and if in a majority, they could correct the policies of the
central government by the regular republican process. They might likely
be stifled in their efforts by the tendency of our politics toward the development of plural parties in each state, he concluded.

The views Jefferson expressed concerning temporary secessionism
springing from fleeting sentiments in his letter to Tracy differed from his
position in case a state came to a definitive conclusion that it wanted to
leave the union, however. America, so far as he was concerned in 1816,
might ultimately have to decide whether it would be content with a chiefly
agricultural domestic economy and peaceful foreign relations, on the one
hand, or would bear frequent wars in the name of international commerce,
on the other.[102] The latter course had dragged England down into enormous debt. Such debt, in turn, drove common laborers into long days of
labor—all to support, as Jefferson saw it, the speculations of a rapacious
few. He had other hopes for America. "If any State in the Union will declare that it prefers separation with the first alternative, to a continuance
in union without it," he concluded, "I have no hesitation in saying, 'let us
separate.' I would rather the States should withdraw, which are for unlimited commerce and war, and confederate with those alone which are
for peace and agriculture."

For Jefferson in 1816, then, states had a clear right to leave the union.
Whether to remain in federal relations depended on the states' convenience. His unspoken assumptions in these regards remained essentially
unchanged since "A Summary View."

As Jefferson pondered the federal union in 1816, he also reached a
new insight. Not only should authority generally be exercised at the
most local practical level in the federal system, but the same was true
in Virginia. Where practicable, not the Old Dominion or even its
county subdivisions, but "ward republics" ought to hold sway.[103] As
Jefferson explained,

the way to have good and safe government, is not to trust it all to one; but to divide it among the many, distributing to every one exactly the functions he is competent to. Let the National government be entrusted with the defence of the nation, and it's foreign & federal relations; the State governments with the civil rights, laws, police & administration of what concerns the state generally; the Counties with the local concerns of the counties; and each Ward direct the interests within itself. It is by dividing and subdividing these republics from the great National one down thro' all it's subordinations, until it ends in the administration of every man's farm and affairs by himself; by placing under every one what his own eye may superintend, that all will be done for the best. . . . I do believe that if the Almighty has not decreed that Man shall never be free, (and it is blasphemy to believe it) that the secret will be found to be in the making himself the depository of the powers respecting himself, so far as he is competent to them, and delegating only what is beyond his competence by a synthetical process, to higher & higher orders of functionaries, so as to trust fewer and fewer powers, in proportion as the trustees become more and more oligarchical. The elementary republics of the wards, the county republics, the State republics, and the republic of the Union, would form a gradation of authorities, standing each on the basis of law, holding every one it's delegated share of powers, and constituting truly a system of fundamental balances and checks for the government. Where every man is a sharer in the direction of his ward-republic, or of some of the higher ones, and feels that he is a participator in the government of affairs not merely at an election, one day in the year, but every day; when there shall not be a man in the state who will not be a member of some one of it's councils, great or small, he will let the heart be torn out of his body sooner than his power be wrested from him by a Caesar or a Bonaparte.

Jefferson had developed a profoundly democratic republican vision just as the opposite impulse was about to win permanent victories in constitutional law and politics. That development would pain him greatly to the end of his mortal days.

Questions of federalism repeatedly came to Jefferson's attention during the 1810s and '20s. Not only did the sections' markedly different responses to Congress's declaration of war in 1812 propel them there, but so did the performance of the US Supreme Court, the Panic of 1819, and the Missouri Crisis. The chief justice, Jefferson's cousin and old antagonist John Marshall, repeatedly authored opinions in Jefferson's twilight years violating the key Jeffersonian principle of federalism or states' rights.[104]

All the while, what Jefferson had anticipated as a respite from his long political labors turned out to be anything but. His hope as a young man that he might eventually return from political labors to the beautiful, charming wife who shared his love of musical performance and at least some of his literary taste had been disappointed by her early death and his vow to her that he would never remarry. Thereafter, he persistently tried to recruit friends such as James Madison and James Monroe to come live at or near Monticello and create a retirees' community with him. This hope also came to nothing. Instead, one of his two children to survive into adulthood predeceased him.[105]

In addition, another close political ally, sometime Virginia governor and US senator Wilson Cary Nicholas, dragged Jefferson down toward financial ruin. Cosigning a large note on behalf of Nicholas must have struck Jefferson as only a slight risk at the time. What were the chances that a former Richmond bank president, a man who had steadfastly supported Jefferson's administration in Congress and whose progeny had intermarried with Jefferson's, a scion of one of Virginia's greatest political dynasties, would leave him holding the bag? Nicholas's bankruptcy meant that what might have been a comfortable old age for the Sage of Monticello degenerated into a time of constant worry about his and his family's future.[106]

Jefferson tended to blame his misfortunes on others—particularly banks. The party propaganda of the 1790s, according to which bankers' behavior all redounded to their own selfish benefit and the truly productive members of society suffered in the process, had at least one sincere exponent. So too did Jefferson's Bank Bill argument in George Washington's cabinet and the Kentucky Resolutions of 1798 and 1799. That man was Thomas Jefferson. Thus, when John Marshall's Supreme Court handed down a string of nationalist decisions in Jefferson's last years, when the Old Dominion's economy was rocked by the Panic of 1819, and when the Missouri Crisis threatened to rend the United States in twain, Jefferson had a ready template for explaining these events.

The year 1811 saw the expiration of Alexander Hamilton's bank law and, with it, of the First Bank of the United States' federal charter. President Madison, persuaded by Secretary of State Albert Gallatin, favored rechartering the bank, but he essentially kept mum on the issue while it was decided by Congress. The bank died.

The War of 1812 changed matters, at least for Madison.[107] Unable to fall back upon the Bank of the United States for help, Madison and Gallatin faced great difficulty in financing the war. Therefore, within months of the war's conclusion, the administration urged Congress to pass a new bank law. Over the objections of a few Jeffersonian sticklers, it did. The Second Bank of the United States (BUS) was up and running in no time.

Washington Jeffersonians' abandonment of the argument that Congress lacked power to charter a bank did not mean that all Republicans agreed. Some states passed laws meant to keep the Second Bank of the United States from operating within their territory. Among them, historical pride of place went to Maryland.

Maryland's anti-bank law would become the subject of the Supreme Court's most important case. Under the Maryland statute, the state's branch of the BUS faced a tax of $15,000.[108] In those days, that was real money. The cashier (branch president), William McCulloch, refused to pay. He soon found himself in court.

The issues before the Supreme Court in *McCulloch v. Maryland* (1819) were whether the law chartering the BUS was constitutional and whether Maryland had a right to tax the BUS.[109] Marshall easily disposed of the second question, saying "the power to tax involves the power to destroy," and that since Maryland had no right to destroy instrumentalities of federal policy, it had no power to tax the BUS. That part was easy. The chief issue was the BUS charter's constitutionality.

Marshall began by noting that there had been another law chartering a Bank of the United States. It had stood for years, and other court cases had been decided on the assumption that the bank's charter was constitutional. Numerous Congresses had come and gone without disputing this idea. "The original act was permitted to expire," Marshall wrote, "but a short experience of the embarrassments to which the refusal to revive it exposed the Government convinced those who were most prejudiced against the measure of its necessity, and induced the passage of the present law." All of these facts together, Marshall continued, would make it difficult to conclude that the present bank's charter was "a bold and plain usurpation to which the Constitution gave no countenance."

Next, the chief justice turned to the Virginian reading of the Constitution—to Jefferson's theory of federalism. As he told it, the Jeffersonian position had been taken in oral argument before the Supreme Court by "the counsel for the State of Maryland," Luther Martin. It will be of some interest in considering the rest of Marshall's, and the court's, opinion to note a few facts about Martin.[110] First, he was the attorney general of Maryland. Second, although he was agreed by all to be an able advocate, he also had a reputation in a day far more indulgent in spirituous liquors than our own for imbibing to excess. Third, and most important, he had been a significant, though not a leading, participant in the Philadelphia Convention of 1787, which wrote the Constitution.

As Marshall put it, "the counsel for the State of Maryland have deemed it of some importance . . . to consider [the Constitution] not as emanating from the people, but as the act of sovereign and independent States."

This distinction is an odd one in light of Article VII of the Constitution, which says that, "The Ratification of the Conventions of nine States, shall be sufficient for the Establishment of this Constitution between the States so ratifying the Same." The conventions to which this article refers are the type of constituent conventions that had been used in some states, most famously Massachusetts, to ratify revolutionary constitutions. Such a convention *was* the people of the state in question, the theory held.[111] Why then would Marshall distinguish between the two?

Marshall proceeded to concede that the people "act in their states," but then he denied that the acts they took were acts of their state governments. If responsive to Martin's argument, this statement demonstrated chiefly that Martin had botched his case: the Jeffersonian position was not that the state governments had granted the federal government power by ratifying the Constitution, but that the sovereign peoples of the states had done so.[112] Marshall knew this perfectly well, as he had been in the minority of the Virginia House of Delegates when that body adopted the Virginia Report of 1800, drafted by Madison in defense of the Virginia Resolutions of 1798. Madison had in that document explained that when Republicans insisted the states were sovereign, they did not mean the territory of a state or the government of a state was sovereign, but that the sovereign people of each state was. This is the sense in which the word "state" is used in Article VII, as well.

Perhaps Martin had misstated the Jeffersonian position. Marshall responded by misstating the facts. So far as he had it, the choice was between one American people acting in thirteen separate states because that was where they lived, on one hand, and thirteen state governments being sovereign, on the other. Responding to an assertion that having created sovereign states, the people had no more power to grant, Marshall said Americans generally accepted that the people could reclaim and reallocate the powers they had granted to governments. "Much more might the legitimacy of the General Government be doubted had it been created by the States [meaning state governments]," he asserted.

Having confused the issue of the states' role in creating the federal government—which one might have thought that Article VII made perfectly clear—Marshall next turned to the extent of that government's power. "This government," he continued, "is acknowledged by all to be one of enumerated powers. . . . That it can exercise only the powers granted to it, would seem too apparent" to need to be defended. Like Hamilton before him, the chief justice immediately rushed to say that granting this premise did not resolve anything.

Yes, he conceded, the power "of establishing a bank or creating a corporation" was absent from the Constitution. Still, he noted, there was nothing in the Constitution echoing Article II of the Articles of Confederation. That provision of the first federal constitution said Congress would have only the powers "expressly delegated." "Even the 10th amendment" did not include the word "expressly." From this he inferred that whether a particular power had been granted would "depend on a fair construction of the whole instrument." Recall that Governor Edmund Randolph and George Nicholas, two of the Federalists' three leaders, had told the Virginia Convention of 1788 that Congress would have only the powers "expressly" granted by the Constitution. Thus, Marshall's opinion was that the Tenth Amendment had actually given Congress additional powers: omission of the word "expressly" from that amendment negated the Randolph-Nicholas principle of the unamended document.

Still in a Hamiltonian vein, Marshall turned to the Necessary and Proper and Due Process Clauses. The "necessary" in the Necessary and Proper Clause, Marshall intoned, did not mean "necessary," but had a more capacious content. In common parlance, "we find that it frequently imports no more than that one thing is convenient, or useful, or essential to another." Necessary means could include "any means calculated to produce the end." The bill incorporating the Bank of the United States could have been seen as "necessary" in that sense. Congress had understood it in that way in numerous other instances. Even without the Necessary and Proper Clause, "Congress would have some choice of means." What then could have been the point of adding the clause? Marshall said that it made "any means adapted to the end" constitutional. In general, any law that was "adapted to" a constitutional end and "not prohibited" was constitutional. The bank law fell into that category, and so was constitutional.

Virginia's chief judge, Spencer Roane of the court of appeals, could not stomach this performance. He did not have to. Instead, he took to the Virginia newspapers with repeated blasts at Marshall and his Supreme Court.[113]

Roane, son-in-law of leading Virginia revolutionary and antifederalist Patrick Henry, had butted heads with the Marshall Court before. Three years before *McCulloch*, Justice Joseph Story wrote on behalf of the court (Marshall had recused himself, pleading conflict of interest) that the Virginia court of appeals must obey the Supreme Court's formal command to send along its papers in the case of *Martin v. Hunter's Lessee* (1816). While constitutional law and history classes commonly say that Story's opinion decided the question of the relationship between federal and state courts in favor of Story's claim to Supreme Court supremacy, the Virginia court of appeals (now known as the Virginia Supreme Court) ignored the order. Roane and his colleagues insisted that the federal and state court systems were parallel, not parts of a single pyramid.[114]

Roane was ready for the Supreme Court's very broad claim of congressional authority, then. *McCulloch* can be seen as analogous to *Martin* in claiming almost limitless legislative authority for the federal government just as *Martin* had staked a claim to federal courts' superiority to state courts. Roane saw it that way.

Roane blasted *McCulloch* in a series of highly persuasive attacks. Essentially, he laid out the position taken by Edmund Randolph in Richmond in 1788's ratification convention, echoed by Henry and Lee in their 1790 legislative resolution and Madison in the House debate on Hamilton's bank bill, and developed in detail in the Virginia and Kentucky Resolutions of 1798, the Kentucky Resolutions of 1799, and the Virginia

Report of 1800: that the federal government had only the enumerated powers. All claims to more were usurpation.

Marshall responded with a series of newspaper columns of his own. Apparently unable to find a Virginia paper to publish them, he placed them in one out of state. R. Kent Newmyer, Marshall's most perceptive biographer, judges Marshall's argument very effective. However, he misses important evidence.

Marshall's chief contention was that *McCulloch* was consistent with the undisputed doctrine of enumerated powers. Roane had highlighted that allowing Congress to use distantly related means amounted to eliminating the principle of enumeration. In the chief paragraph of his description of Roane's argument, Newmyer says, "Like the Anti-Federalists before him and John C. Calhoun afterward, Roane rested his case for state sovereignty on the fact that ratification took place in specially called state conventions whose members were elected by the people of each state. From that, he deduced that the Constitution was simply a contract created by sovereign states as the primary contracting parties; the national government was nothing but 'an alliance, or a league' of sovereign states . . . who would be the final judges of the constitutionality of congressional acts."[115]

Fortunately for Roane's argument, and unfortunately for Newmyer's, the image of each ratifying state as a party to a compact with the others and with ultimate authority over the Constitution's meaning did not originate with antifederalists. Rather, it was laid out in detail by a leading Federalist in the Richmond Ratification Convention of 1788, George Nicholas.

Pleased with himself, Roane sent copies to Jefferson and Madison. Presented with the *McCulloch* opinion, Madison recoiled. Yes, he had signed the bill chartering the Second Bank of the United States, but only on the basis of the most Jesuitical reasoning. Perhaps he had argued that Hamilton's Bank Bill of 1790 was unconstitutional, President Madison said, but congressional majorities had disagreed and President Washington had signed the bill into law. Other presidents and numerous Congresses had gone about their business accepting the bank's existence. He had to yield to their wisdom. A quarter of a century later, he accepted the verdict of history regarding bank bills, although he would not apply the constitutional reasoning they had used to other questions.[116]

John Marshall, on the other hand, had done exactly that. This troubled Madison greatly. Marshall's reading gave Congress power "to which no practical limit can be assigned."[117] "It was anticipated, I believe, by few if any of the friends of the Constitution," Madison averred, "that a rule of construction would be introduced, as broad and as pliant as what has occurred. Those who recollect, and still more, those who shared in what passed in the State Conventions, thro' which the people ratified the Constitution, with respect to the extent of the powers vested in Congress, can not easily be persuaded that the avowal of such a rule would not have prevented its ratification." Here lay the gravest theoretical problem with Marshall's opinion: it directly contradicted an essential element of the states' understanding of the Constitution when they ratified it.

Following a train of thought very similar to that of his Bonus Bill Veto Message of 1817 (and of Alexander Hamilton's *The Federalist* No. 1), Madison said, "It has been the misfortune, if not the reproach of other nations, that their Governments have not been freely and deliberately established by themselves. It has been the boast of ours that such has been its source, and that it can be altered by the same authority only which established it. It is a further boast that a regular mode of making proper alterations, has been providently inserted in the Constitution itself." In case the powers of Congress proved inadequate, in other words, they could be extended by amendment. Nowadays, people commonly say that federal courts ought as well to change their position concerning the Constitution's meaning when a worthy new concept presents itself. Madison disagreed, calling it "anxiously to be wished therefore that no innovations may take place in other modes; one of which would be a constructive assumption of powers never meant to be granted." Article V, the amendment

article, not Article III, the judicial article, provided the constitutional solution to perceived errors in the allocation of power between the states
and the federal government. Marshall's approach—to say that the Constitution gave Congress powers that it did not—thwarted the people's will.

Roane wrote to Jefferson on the same issue, again enclosing a copy of
his anti-*McCulloch* articles.[118] "The friends of liberty in our Country
[Virginia] continue to regard you with veneration and gratitude, for your
great & eminent services," he told Jefferson, "and your opinion on such
a question as this, would [be] considered as a great authority." This meant
that if Jefferson wrote him a cogent letter critical of the Supreme Court,
Roane would show it to other prominent Virginia officials.

Jefferson told Roane that he did not want to be drawn into a public
dispute.[119] Still, his response to Roane's columns could not have been any
more enthusiastic. He had read the columns as they had appeared in the
paper, the lama of the mountain reported, and "I subscribe to every tittle
of them."

What had Roane said? As "Hampden," he had written three editorials. Generally, they established as clearly as one might have hoped that
Jefferson's, not Marshall's, position had been the one on which at least
Virginia and, if *The Federalist* was to be credited, New York, had ratified. When it came to the central question—whether Congress had had
constitutional power to charter the Second Bank of the United States
because the Necessary and Proper Clause allowed Congress to choose
any means to constitutional ends—Roane cited Madison's Virginia Report
of 1800 in support of the claim that "congress under the terms 'necessary and proper,' have only all *incidental* powers necessary and proper,
&c. and . . . the only enquiry is whether the power is properly an *incident*
to an express power and *necessary* to its execution, and . . . if it is not,
congress cannot exercise it."[120] Not only did this reading pervade the
constitutional drafting and ratification processes, he asserted, but it "is
absolutely necessary to *consist* with the idea of defined or particular powers [emphasis in original]." He summarized, "Again it is said, that none

but the express powers and those *fairly incident* to them were granted by the constitution." Recall Jefferson's statement that he agreed with "every tittle" of Roane's series.

The Marshall Court's behavior could not be classified as anything other than counterrevolutionary, Jefferson lamented.[121] Roane's editorials "contain the true principles of the revolution of 1800. For that was as real a revolution in the principles of our government as that of 76. was in it's form." Through the electoral processes established by the Constitution and the state legislatures, "the nation declared it's will by dismissing functionaries of one principle, and electing those of another, in the two branches, executive and legislative, submitted to their election." In a well-constituted republic, that should have resolved the problem of Hamiltonians' efforts to remake American government and society along British lines, but it had not. "Over the judiciary department," Jefferson noted, "the constitution had deprived them of their controul." From its redoubt, the Supreme Court "therefore has continued the reprobated system." One might have expected the three Republican presidents' appointees to change the Supreme Court's direction, but no: "altho' new matter has been occasionally incorporated into the old yet the leaven of the old mass seems to assimilate to itself the new." Jefferson did not know how to explain this phenomenon, which he bitterly lamented.[122]

Marshall and his colleagues constantly negated the electoral systems' results, Jefferson noted. "After 20. years confirmation of the federated system by the voice of the nation declared thro' the medium of elections, we find the judiciary on every occasion still driving us into consolidation." By "consolidation," Jefferson meant what we would call "centralization"— the opposite of the Jeffersonian principle of federalism, which he here called "the federated system."

Jefferson took issue with the view of the judges' role laid out by Publius in *The Federalist*. If the judges were to decide upon the Constitution's meaning not only in regard to their own performance of their duties but also in regard to the other branches' performance in office, the

Constitution's establishment of three independent, coordinate branches would be transformed into a system of three branches all bound to obey the rules laid out by the judicial branch. Jefferson noted that in withholding commissions of Adams's judicial appointees in 1801, pardoning men convicted under the Sedition Act, withholding the Monroe-Pinkney Treaty, and taking other such steps, Jefferson had as president acted on the principle that each branch must read the Constitution for itself.

What difference did that make? For Jefferson, it was determinative. By Marshall's theory, not only was one branch made supreme, but it was "that one too which is unelected by, and independent of, the nation. For experience has already shewn that the impeachment it has provided is not even a scare-crow," hardly adequate to the task of preventing judicial usurpation. The judges, led by Marshall, stealthily issued pronouncements "not belonging to the case often, but sought for out of it, as if to rally the public opinion beforehand to their views, and to indicate the line they are to walk in." In theory, such behavior merited impeachment. In practice, these performances "have been so quietly passed over as never to have excited animadversion, even in a speech of any one of the body entrusted with impeachment [the House of Representatives]."

In the end, "the constitution, on this hypothesis, is a mere thing of wax in the hands of the judiciary which they may twist and shape in to any form they please." Unfortunately, the form they consistently chose was the Hamiltonian, nationalist one. At last Jefferson answered Roane's other query: whether Roane might make the older man's opinions known. No, Jefferson said, they must remain secret lest they undercut public support for the great project of his old age. He did not want any backlash to reduce legislative support for the University of Virginia.

The year of *McCulloch*, 1819, also marked the commencement of a congressional roil which Jefferson insisted centered on the issue of federalism. It arose out of the need for Congress to dispose of an application for membership in the union from residents of the Territory of Missouri.

Due to its latitude, Missouri counted many Virginians, some even distant cousins of Jefferson's, among its initial settlers.[123] When they moved to Missouri, they naturally took slaves with them. When they submitted a state constitution to Congress and requested admission to the union, that constitution predictably contemplated the continuation of slavery in the state.[124] Speaker Henry Clay of Kentucky, master politician that he was, seems to have expected no controversy over the application when he scheduled it for committee consideration. To Clay's surprise, a New York Republican otherwise unremarked in history proposed amending the Missouri statehood bill to put Missouri slavery on a train toward ultimate extinction, and suddenly Congress entered into a state of . . . bedlam.

Congress was stuck on Missouri for years. Jefferson, from afar, looked on in despair.[125] The year 1819 had begun with notice of the bankruptcy of Wilson Cary Nicholas, a former Virginia governor, US senator, and Richmond bank president whose progeny had intermarried with Jefferson's and for whom Jefferson had cosigned a loan.[126] From January 1819 to his death, Jefferson would live under the cloud of impending financial ruin.[127] That ruin would have befallen anyone else in Jefferson's circumstances, but Jefferson's creditors waited until his death to lower the boom on his daughter and his slaves. Not only did this problem rear its head in 1819, the year of the Supreme Court's monumental anti-Jeffersonian decision in *McCulloch v. Maryland*, but the Missouri Crisis commenced then as well.

Jefferson considered the Missouri Crisis as an attempt by northern Federalists to resuscitate Hamiltonianism on the basis of an end to the revolutionary union. It was a rule-or-ruin gambit: since they had been forever defeated on the basis of the old issues of banks, tariffs, federal government direction of the economy, social hierarchy, and militarism, they would make an issue of the great factor distinguishing North from South: slavery.[128]

Some called the issue at stake in the Missouri Crisis a moral one,

Jefferson said, but it was not. Spreading slave population across more territory would not enslave anyone who would otherwise have been free, he insisted. In fact, doing so likely would facilitate steps toward freeing them, because whites were more apt to emancipate where slaves were few than where they predominated. What raising the issue of closing Missouri to slavery would do, however, was divide the country between fourteen northern and ten southern states. Thus, agitators of the question hoped to elevate themselves to power.

Jefferson's greatest biographer downplayed Jefferson's concern over the matter of slavery in the Missouri Crisis. The historian's attitude is hard to square with Jefferson's statement that "with this geographical minority [the South] it is a question of existence. For if Congress once goes out of the Constitution to arrogate a right of regulating the condition of the inhabitants of the states, it's majority may, and probably will next declare that the condition of all men within the US. shall be that of freedom. In which case all the whites South of the Patomak and Ohio must evacuate their states."

Jefferson's views reflected the consensus among his state's ruling class. Virtually all dependent upon slavery, virtually all defended it. When the Missouri Crisis first developed in 1819, Virginia still housed about a third of America's one and a half million slaves.[129] Although by that point Virginia had become a slave exporter, its white men feared that blacks' superior fecundity meant that eventually Virginia would be a majority-black state like South Carolina. The alternative was diffusion—exporting slave population across the North American continent. Though the experience of the War of 1812, when slaves who had the chance were more apt to escape than to wreak physical vengeance, ought to have dispelled the notion, Virginians remained in the grip of the idea that they had "the wolf by the ears" and "could neither hold him nor safely let him go."[130] Jefferson's splenetic response to the Missouri Crisis, then, reflected the fears of his society generally.[131]

Still, Jefferson's understanding of Missourians' constitutional situation during the Missouri contest, seldom if ever noted, is perhaps the most interesting point in his extensive and fascinating correspondence on the general topic. Missouri Territory, recall, had been carved out of the Louisiana Purchase Territory. Its residents, other than slaves and Indians, had drawn up a constitution. They had sent it to Congress with a request that they be admitted to the union as a member. Typically, scholars refer to that last step as an application for statehood. As Jefferson saw things, however, Missouri was already a state: it had a territory and a republican constitution. The issue was whether it would be accepted into the United States with the constitution it had drafted. "If rejected unconditionally," Jefferson warned, "Missouri assumes independant self-government, and Congress, after pouting awhile, must recieve them on the footing of the original states."[132]

Notice: Congress could not make Missouri a state, because it already was one. Congress could only admit it to, or exclude it from, the union. In his eyes, Missouri would hold the whip hand in the event Congress refused it membership in the union.

Jefferson's reference to "the footing of the original states" went to the gravamen of his insistence Missourians must not capitulate. Each of the original states, as he recounted it, had decided for itself whether to have chattel slavery. Some had decided to have it. Some had decided not to have it. Under the constitutional conception of federalism made explicit by the Tenth Amendment (and absent the prohibition later imposed via the Thirteenth Amendment), that had been their right.

To Massachusetts congressman John Holmes, Jefferson said that he had been slumbering, confident that the present administration would carry America safely forward.[133] News of the Missouri Controversy, however, "like a fire bell in the night, awakened and filled me with terror. I considered it at once as the knell of the Union." In our day, with less congested housing patterns, the silence imparted by window glass, and professional firemen equipped with advanced technology, the image of the clanging of the fire bell may not be so evocative as in Jefferson's time. He was born, after all, less than a century after the Great Fire of London and died less than a century before the Great Chicago Fire. Still, his metaphor packs a punch. Similarly, church bells ringing the mournful pattern of a funeral—a knell—are not familiar now, but we can understand one of his meanings.

The second, perhaps more pressing, concerned slave rebellions. Virginia masters in general were always on a hair-trigger lookout for slave rebellion, which the authorities would warn them was under way by sounding a fire bell, day or night—night being more frightening.[134]

Still more striking is the ancient image Jefferson borrowed for the most arresting passage in his gigantic surviving correspondence. "We have the wolf by the ear," he pleaded, "and we can neither hold him, nor safely let him go. justice is in one scale, and self-preservation in the other." Here he hoped Holmes would accept the prudential argument that emancipation could not be undertaken at once, for the result would be—as Jefferson had said in *Notes on the State of Virginia*—a horrible race war. For a man of the Enlightenment, avoiding that outcome ("self-preservation") was the only consideration deserving a higher rank than justice.

Besides, Jefferson confided hopefully, "of one thing I am certain, that as the passage of slaves from one state to another would not make a slave of a single human being who would not be so without it, so their diffusion over a greater surface would make them individually happier and proportionally facilitate the accomplishment of their emancipation; by dividing the burthen on a greater number of co-adjutors." Allowing the old states to send some of their slaves to Missouri would slacken resistance to ultimate elimination of the institution from those first states, and at no cost.

Jefferson concluded this passage with his constitutional argument, saying, "An abstinence too from this act of power [that is, congressional imposition of a slavery policy on Missouri—which, note, Jefferson considered as flowing from "power," not concern for justice or any such higher good] would remove the jealousy excited by the undertaking of Congress;

to regulate the condition of the different descriptions of men composing a state. This certainly is the exclusive right of every state, which nothing in the constitution has taken from them and given to the general government." The power to make slavery policy for a state, Jefferson insisted, had not been given to Congress by the Constitution; therefore, it remained in the states' hands. Lest his Yankee correspondent forget that slavery was not an exclusively southern institution, Jefferson concluded by asking, "Could congress, for example say that the Non-freemen of Connecticut, shall be freemen, or that they shall not emigrate into any other state?" If not, he implied, Congress had no such power in relation to Missouri either. Federalism meant not only that Congress had a few enumerated powers, but that all of the states had the same rights. There were no inferior states. Jefferson had helped to enshrine that principle in the Northwest Ordinance of 1787, and he insisted on it now, more than three decades later.[135] Missouri had every reason to expect the same freedom to make its own slavery policies as was enjoyed by Connecticut.

Jefferson considered this principle so integral to the revolution's legacy that abandoning it would mean abandoning the revolution. He closed the letter to Holmes on that note, saying that it seemed the younger generation had determined to give up what its fathers had won through rivers of blood. His only consolation lay in the certainty that he would not live to see it. This "treason against the hopes of the world" was compounded for him by the likelihood that the slaves' condition had a better chance of amelioration in the union than without it. Fortuitously, as in most political arguments, Jefferson concluded with a claim that granting him his way would have no negative consequences, and in fact would make everything work out right. That was Jefferson's reflex. He seems to have been candid in it.

As Jefferson worried about the contest in Congress, he had company among the old Republican leadership. John Taylor of Caroline, the prolific 1790s anti-Hamiltonian pamphleteer, Virginia House of Delegates sponsor of the Virginia Resolutions, and occasional US senator, in the 1810s and '20s published a number of interesting books. Pride of place must go to *Tyranny Unmasked*, the 1822 book in which he decried the political phenomenon economists call "rent-seeking," and which the rest of us call "crony capitalism."[136] At once cogent and clearheaded, Taylor's analysis showed how powerful citizens and power-hungry officials had combined and would combine to flout the Constitution—particularly the principle of federalism—in pursuit of their own selfish interests. Taylor's 1823 *New Views of the Constitution of the United States* also merits careful attention, as it was the first account of the Philadelphia Convention to make use of its official journal and the extensive notes of New York antifederalist Robert Yates, one of the delegates.[137]

What drew Jefferson's attention during the Missouri Crisis, however, was Taylor's blast at John Marshall, *Construction Construed, and Constitutions Vindicated*.[138] That book's chief contention was that the Marshall Court's nationalizing decisions threatened liberty, particularly in conjunction with Congress's post–War of 1812 decision to retain protective tariffs whose effect was to transfer southern wealth to the rest of the country.[139] Taylor considered federalism to be, in the words of a recent scholarly study, "the only guarantee of American republicanism."[140] Thus, he leveled *Construction Construed* at *McCulloch v. Maryland*.

Upon receiving Taylor's book from leading Richmond newspaperman Thomas Ritchie, Jefferson said he certainly would profit from reading it. "That the present volume is . . . orthodox," Jefferson allowed, "I know before reading it, because I know that Col° Taylor and myself have rarely, if ever, differed in any political principle of importance. Every act of his life, & every word he ever wrote satisfies me of this." (Jefferson actually had disagreed with Taylor's slavery-related writings, as we will see.[141])

Early in 1821, the Supreme Court announced its decision in *Cohens v. Virginia*. Marshall and his confreres there acted to negate most of the effect of the Eleventh Amendment. That constitutional provision, adopted in response to the Jay Court's usurpatious decision in *Chisholm v. Geor-*

gia (1793), stood for the idea that state governments had not by ratifying the Constitution submitted themselves to federal courts' jurisdiction. Because *Chisholm* was a case in which a citizen of one state sued the government of another state in federal court, the Eleventh Amendment said that a citizen of one state could not sue the government of another state in federal court. Marshall's decision in *Cohens* said the Eleventh Amendment would be read narrowly. It did not mean that federal courts could not exercise jurisdiction over state governments without their consent, but only that a citizen of one state could not sue another state in federal court. A citizen of one state could still appeal a judgment in favor of another state to a federal court.

Jefferson finished reading *Construction Construed, and Constitutions Vindicated* by February 14, 1821. He then wrote to Taylor with his evaluation. He could hardly have been more enthusiastic: "I recieved some time ago . . . ," he said, "a copy of your late work on the constitution of the US." Although he had passed along his thanks for the book at the time, "I am glad to avail myself of this opportunity of doing it directly and with the more pleasure after having read the book, and acquired a knolege of it's value. I have no hesitation in saying that it carries us back to the genuine principles of the constitution more demonstratively than any work published since the date of that instrument." Turning to specifics, Jefferson gushed that it demolished the Supreme Court's decisions in both *McCulloch* and *Cohens*: "it pulverises the sophistries of the Judges on bank taxation, and of the 5. lawyers on lotteries." Jefferson held *Cohens* an especially lame performance, saying, "this last act of venality (for it cannot be of judgment) makes me ashamed that I was ever a lawyer." At a time when US senators were still elected by state legislatures and when Virginia tradition held that the Old Dominion's must either obey the General Assembly's formal instructions—embodied in legislative resolutions—or resign, he confided that "I have suggested to a friend in the legislature that that body should send a copy of your book to every one of our Representatives & Senators in Congress as a standing instruction and with a declaration that it contains the catholic faith which whosoever doth not keep whole & undefiled without doubt he shall perish everlastingly."[142] (Jefferson routinely alluded to Christian creeds to underscore his most significant political points, as here.)

Among the arguments Taylor made against Marshall's famous opinion was that reliance on precedents as having established a practice's constitutionality smacked of the English doctrine of parliamentary sovereignty. It was inappropriate also because the harmful tendency of a practice might become evident just at the time that the practice had become a precedent. Besides, "under the federal constitution, the argument has moreover a fraudulent aspect, because its provisions for amendment have taught the people to believe, that there are no other modes by which the constitution can be altered; and lulled them into security against precedents." Rather than have this practice of elevating precedents into constitutional provisions without the people's noticing, "It would have been better to have declared, that all laws which should live to a certain age should be engrafted into the constitution, because it would have kept the people attentive." Taylor averred that it was entirely unlikely the people would have agreed to amend the Constitution to empower Congress "to create banks, to bestow bounties, to grant exclusive privileges, to make roads and canals, to annex conditions to the admission of new states to the union, and to prohibit the state governments from taxing the persons or property it should invest with exclusive privileges." Absent such amendment, he concluded, the people could logically have assumed that whatever a law could do, another law could undo.[143] Taylor's arguments against the rest of Marshall's opinion were equally logical and persuasive—and yet in the end, as we know, unavailing.

The "everlasting" fate Jefferson wanted the General Assembly to threaten was banishment from the highest Virginia political circles. Federalism, Jefferson's dearest constitutional principle for nearly half a century, seemed the target of an ongoing Federalist campaign. John Marshall led the charge.[144] "The great object of my fear," the Sage of Monticello told the sympathetic Judge Roane soon after reading Taylor's tome, "is the federal judiciary. that body, like Gravity, ever acting, with noiseless foot, & unalarming advance, gaining ground step by step, and holding what it gains, is ingulphing insidiously the special governments [the state governments] into the jaws of that which feeds them [the Federal Government, which pays the federal judges]." The like-minded must be on their guard and "let the eye of vigilance never be closed."

The Missouri Crisis ended in 1821 with President James Monroe signing legislation admitting Missouri to the Union with the constitution it had proposed. The federal principle for which Jefferson had contended—that new states must be treated as equivalent to the original ones—triumphed to that extent. In joining Maine's admission to Missouri's and excluding slavery from the remaining portion of the Louisiana Purchase Territory north of Missouri's southern border, however, Congress rejected the Jeffersonian position.

Meanwhile, the Marshall Court continued along its antifederalism path. Jefferson ascribed much of the responsibility to Chief Justice Marshall. Known in Virginia as a bon vivant and hail-fellow-well-met, Marshall seemed to warp all who came into contact with him. Jefferson had warned President Madison against putting New England Republican congressman Joseph Story on the court, and so cannot have been terribly surprised when Story came to be Marshall's right-hand man. That his own appointee, William Johnson, usually joined in Marshall's opinions bothered him. That Johnson abided the chief justice's innovation of having the court issue only one opinion in virtually every case troubled Jefferson exceedingly.

Prior to Marshall's appointment, the Supreme Court had followed the English practice of having each judge present his own opinion. To derive the majority's reasoning in a particular case was a task for lawyers in later cases. Under Marshall's guidance, the court abandoned that practice in favor of the one familiar to us, issuing one opinion, usually read from the bench by the chief justice. Unlike today, when virtually every significant case the court decides results in more than one opinion, only very occasionally did anyone dissent during Marshall's long tenure.

Jefferson decried this practice, and Marshall's influence generally, in a lengthy 1820 missive to Virginia's—and probably the South's—most prominent journalist, Thomas Ritchie of the *Richmond Enquirer*.[145] In prose dripping scorn, Jefferson scrawled that "the Judiciary is the subtle corps of sappers & miners constantly working underground to undermine the foundations of our confederated fabric." Here he had the federal judges acting as a hostile army digging under the walls of the citadel of liberty, which they intended to weaken so greatly that it could not perform its vital function of protecting the people against un-republican threats beyond its walls. Their method was "construing our constitution from a coordination of a general [federal] and special [state] governments to a general & supreme [national, entirely centralized] one alone. this will lay all things at their feet, and they are too well versed in English law to forget the maxim 'boni judicis est ampliare jurisdictionem' [It is the responsibility of a good judge to enlarge his jurisdiction[146]]." If they continued to behave this way, "I will say that 'against this every man should raise his voice,' and more, should uplift his arm." Jefferson at least rhetorically contemplated not only vocal but physical resistance.

Jefferson thought the decision in the Chase impeachment explained the judges' barefaced grasping at powers reserved to the states: "having found from experience that impeachmt is an impracticable thing, a mere scare-crow," he said, "they consider themselves secure for life." Not only was impeachment no threat to them, but the judges had lit upon a practice that insulated them even from individual criticism: "they sculk from responsibility to public opinion the only remaining hold on them, under a practice, first introduced into England by Ld Mansfield. An opinion is huddled up in Conclave, perhaps by a majority of one, delivered . . . as if unanimous, and, with the silent acquiescence of lazy or timid associates, he [Marshall] sophisticates the law to his mind by the turn of his own reasoning."

Those "lazy or timid associates" had by the time Jefferson wrote this letter been appointed mainly by Republican presidents, and yet their chief continued to drive them in a Hamiltonian direction. "Frustration" is too weak a word to describe Jefferson's feeling. That the Republicans should dominate the federal elections for ten consecutive federal cycles, elevate numerous justices to the court, and see Marshall continue to write his nationalist heresies into constitutional law proved what it meant that "a judiciary independent of a king or Executive alone, is a good thing; but independance on the will of the nation is a solecism, at least in a republican government." The unaccountable judges could impose a constitution the people had never approved and, if their votes were any indication, never wanted.

Jefferson took up the issue with one of his appointees, Justice William Johnson of South Carolina.[147] The former president did not come out and say what he thought of the court, and the Republicans on it, generally, but his opinions were hard not to infer. Jefferson lamented that "I have been blamed for saying that a prevalence of the doctrines of Consolidation would one day call for reformation, or *revolution*." He responded: "I answer by asking if a single state of the Union would have agreed to the constitution had it given all powers to the General government?" Calling the justice's attention to the ratification debates of 1787–1790, he wanted to know "if the whole opposition to it did not proceed from the jealousy and fear of every state of being subjected to the other states in matters merely it's own?" He thought the question rhetorical: surely Johnson knew that the chief argument of the ratification contest had been over the question whether Congress's powers would be effectively limited under the US Constitution. So how to account for the change in the government under which Americans lived? Was there "any reason to believe the states more disposed, now than then, to acquiesce in this general surrender of all their rights and powers to a Consolidated government, one and undivided?"

Jefferson thought that the uninterrupted Jeffersonian dominance of the Congress and executive branch since the Revolution of 1800 answered these questions. Johnson had asked him whether he thought the Supreme Court had exceeded the limits of its own authority, thus infringing upon the states'. He answered that Roane had given a conclusive answer in his "Algernon Sidney" essays for the *Richmond Enquirer.* They refuted "every word which had been delivered by Judge Marshall of the extrajudicial part of his opinion; and all was extrajudicial, except the decision that the act of Congress had not purported to give to the corporation of Washington the authority claimed by their lottery law. of controuling the laws of the states within the states themselves. But, unable to claim that case, he could not let it go entirely, but went on gratuitously to prove that; notwithstanding the Xth amendment, of the constitution a state *could* be brought, as a defendant, to the bar of his court. And, again, that Congress might authorise a corporation of it's territory [the District of Columbia] to exercise legislation within a state, and paramount to the laws of that state." Roane's angry essays included a passage mocking Marshall for the inconsistency between his Richmond Ratification Convention speech insisting that states would not be susceptible if the Constitution were ratified to being hauled before federal courts and his opinion in *Cohens* claiming the opposite.[148] If Roane was mistaken, Jefferson added, "I surrender human reason as a vain and useless faculty, given to bewilder, and not to guide us. and I mention this particular case [*Cohens*], as one only of several, because it gave occasion to that thoro' examination of the constitutional limits between the General and state jurisdictions which you have asked for."

We can imagine the relish with which Jefferson conveyed these observations to a member of the Supreme Court—one whose appointment he had expected to help move Marshall from a dominant position on the court into minority status. Besides anathematizing Marshall for his legislative behavior on the bench, Jefferson went further: he laid out two guiding principles (again alluding to religious law, he called them "canons") for federal judges. First, "the capital and leading object of the Constitution was to leave with the states all authorities which respected their own citizens only, and to transfer to the US. those which respected citizens of foreign or other states: to make us several as to ourselves, but one as to all others." The exceptions, he said, were the Legal Tender Clause and the Contracts Clause.

The other "canon" Jefferson relayed was "2. on every question of construction, carry ourselves back to the time when the Constitution was adopted, recollect the spirit manifested in the debates, and instead of trying what meaning may be squeezed out of the text, or invented against it, conform to the probable one in which it was past." On the surface, this does not appear to be a federalism provision, but in light of the way that Article VII worked—making the Constitution effective among ratifying states as soon as nine had ratified, and among others only once they had ratified—it meant that the states' ultimate authority in the system, their sovereignty, controlled. Jefferson was certain, he told Johnson, that the court's decision in *Cohens* did not meet this test. After all, the statute at issue in that case concerned morality in Virginia. Jefferson could not imagine how anyone could conclude that the states had intended to surrender control of such questions within their territory to the new federal government.

Respecting federalism—the proper decentralization of powers—was the best way to ensure that the government remained republican, as Jefferson would have it. Where power remained near at hand, it could be vigilantly superintended by the people. "I believe the states can best govern our home concerns," he said, "the general government our foreign ones. I wish therefore to see maintained that wholesome distribution of powers established by the constitution for the limitation of both: & never to see all offices transferred to Washington, where further withdrawn from the eyes of the people, they may more secretly be bought and sold as at market." Where Marshall said "there must be an ultimate Arbiter some where" (and for him it was the Supreme Court), Jefferson asked why that ultimate arbiter must be the states or the federal government. For Jefferson, it was the amendment convention, called by two-thirds of the states, for which Article V of the Constitution provided. Let them decide disputes over the allocation of powers, Jefferson concluded.

Jefferson left off by urging the justice to dissent more often. Only by having the judges take responsibility for their individual opinions could the American people use what little power the Constitution gave them to hold those officials accountable. Along the way, Jefferson hoped, the judge should continue to stand both for republicanism and for federalism, "the two sheet-anchors of our Union. If driven from either, we shall be in danger of foundering." In response, Johnson explained Marshall's sway over the other judges to Jefferson. "While I was on our state-bench," he said, "I was accustomed to delivering seriatim [meaning separate] opinions in our appellate court, and was not a little surprised to find our Chief Justice in the Supreme Court delivering all the opinions in cases in which he sat, even in some instances when contrary to his own judgment and vote." However, his complaints fell on deaf ears, and he soon knew why: "Cushing was incompetent. Chase could not be got to think or write—Patterson [*sic*] was a slow man and willingly declined the trouble, and the other two judges [Bushrod Washington and Marshall] you know are commonly estimated as one judge [meaning they always agreed]."[149]

Still, Johnson at last accepted Jefferson's criticism and took his advice. He wrote to say that he would from that point on file separate opinions "on all subjects of general interest; particularly constitutional questions. On minor subjects it is of little public importance."[150] Yet, Johnson's example did not change the behavior of his associates on the court—perhaps because his candid description of them was too accurate.[151]

As the 1820s began, what with his party's ongoing electoral dominance, Jefferson might have expected political repose. Indeed, he repeatedly told his correspondents that although the issues they had in mind—slavery, federalism, public primary and secondary education, and numerous others—interested him, he wanted to devote all of his strength to the fledgling University of Virginia. Events would not let him do it.

He did succeed in getting the university up and running. However, a Hamiltonian recrudescence seemed possible, even probable, to the very end of his days. The March 4, 1825, Inaugural Address of President John Quincy Adams, son of the last Federalist president and a former Federalist himself, stoked those fears.[152] Adams's selection of American System founder Henry Clay as secretary of state, and thus presidential heir apparent, compounded the issue.

In his speech, Adams eschewed Jeffersonian principle. Jefferson cannot have enjoyed reading the new president's estimation that since the US Constitution had been implemented, "a coordinate department of the judiciary has expounded the Constitution and the laws, settling in harmonious coincidence with the legislative will numerous weighty questions of construction which the imperfection of human language had rendered unavoidable." Sounding every bit the New England Federalist he supposedly no longer was, Adams proposed that the Congress leave aside disputing about the power of Congress to fund construction of roads, canals, and bridges ("internal improvements") in the expectation that their benefits would win praise "by a practical public blessing." Here was an utter repudiation of the Bonus Bill Veto Message James Madison had authored eight years previously.

Adams expanded upon this proposal in his First Annual Message (what we would now call his First State of the Union Message).[153] Although he, like Madison and Monroe before him, followed Thomas Jefferson's example of delivering the message in writing, Adams struck out on a new but familiar path. He called for establishment of a national university in Washington, DC, the launching of American voyages of discovery, experiments to establish uniform weights and measures, more internal improvements projects, and construction of at least one "lighthouse of the skies" (that is, astronomical observatory). This last became the butt of opposition joking immediately and remained so through the rest of Adams's administration, and indeed of his public career. Also much mocked was the presidential injunction that the members of Congress not "be palsied by the will of our constituents." (One cannot imagine Thomas Jefferson saying any such thing.) Adams, like his father prone to be resentful, after his single term bent his energies to revenge upon the mainly southern politicians who had seen to it that he was not reelected. Given a seat in the House of Representatives, he would die at his desk attacking slavery.

Jefferson responded to Adams's statements with outrage. After mulling them over, he decided it was time to fall back upon a tried-and-true Virginia stratagem: having the General Assembly adopt resolutions laying out Virginia's dissenting position. And he was just the man to draft them.

Jefferson's "Draft Declaration and Protest" finds him in his very last weeks and months recurring to the same federal view that underlay his entire political career.[154] "The States in North America," he said, had "confederated to establish their independence of the government of Great Britain." "On that acquisition," they "became . . . free and independent States," each with a right to make whatever type of government "for itself" it wanted.

"They entered into a compact, (which is called the Constitution of the United States of America) by which they agreed to unite in a single government as to their relations with each other, and with foreign nations, and as to certain other articles particularly specified. They retained at the same time, each to itself, the other rights of independent government, comprehending mainly their domestic interests." Note the precision Jefferson attributed to the ratifiers with the words "certain" and "particularly specified." In his account of the Constitution's adoption, here as since he first considered the issue as Washington's secretary of state in 1791, Jefferson depicted the states as parsimoniously yielding a few well-delimited powers to the central government.

Jefferson explained that there were powers "specifically made federal, exercised over the whole" by the federal government, while "the residuary powers, retained to the other" are "exercisable exclusively over its particular State." The states remain "foreign herein, each to the others, as they were before" the Constitution. "To this construction of government and distribution of its powers," he said, "the Commonwealth of Virginia does religiously and affectionately adhere, opposing, with equal fidelity and firmness, the usurpation of either set of functionaries [the state or the federal] on the rightful powers of the other." Jefferson here once again used the religious language he consistently deployed when discussing his chief political and philosophical commitments. Notice too that he was equally committed to state as to federal compliance with the allocation of powers established by the Constitution's ratifiers (the "states" of Article VII) in ratifying it.

Next came the punch line: Jefferson referred to the federal government's long-standing habit of "assum[ing] in some cases, and claim[ing] in others, a right of enlarging its own powers by constructions, inferences, and indefinite deductions from those directly given, which this assembly does declare to be usurpations of the powers retained to the independent branches, mere interpolations into the compact, and direct infractions of it." The tendency of people like John Marshall on the bench, Henry Clay in the Congress, and John Quincy Adams in the White House to be constantly grasping at unenumerated (because ungranted) powers, Jefferson insisted, amounted to "usurpations" and "interpolations." The example Jefferson offered—the one that had prompted him to this exertion— was the federal government's claim of power to build roads across state territory. This power appeared nowhere in the Constitution, Jefferson insisted. He hurried to add that the use of the General Welfare Clause as a source of power for Congress to do anything it wanted, so long as it claimed to be acting in pursuit of the general welfare, was specious. If it had been accurate, the federal government would have had all governmental power. That clause's meaning was simply that Congress could tax to fund its exercise of the enumerated powers.

Jefferson wanted the General Assembly, in adopting these resolutions, to make clear that it did not mean to threaten secession or resistance. Virginians could and should tolerate the federal government's misdeeds for now, he said. Here he must have realized that he was acting on the principle mentioned in the Declaration of Independence's statement that "prudence, indeed, will dictate that governments long established should not be changed for light and transient causes." With luck, the other states would join in stilling the usurpatious current so evident in Washington. The undercurrent, however, was that compliance with usurpation would not continue indefinitely.

Merrill Peterson, one of the two most prominent twentieth-century Jefferson scholars, explained the "Draft Declaration" by reference to "the gloom around" Jefferson in his final year.[155] We should not understand this states' rights salvo as "the whole of" Jefferson's legacy, he said. "Only the sadder part."

Merrill Peterson erred. Federalism—the principle that all governmental power in the American system remained in the states, unless the US Constitution said otherwise—was not a subsidiary idea. Rather, it was the thread connecting Jefferson's patriotism in the imperial crisis and the revolution, his opposition to Hamiltonianism, and his ongoing faith that Virginians and other Americans could continue to prosper together in a common society.

Twentieth-century historians distorted history in making federalism less important in their accounts of Jefferson than it was to him. Peterson contributed to this tendency by omitting several of the documents referenced in this chapter from his widely influential *Thomas Jefferson: Writings*; in light of that volume's length, the omission cannot have been accidental. Prominent historians erred in, for example, making the Alien and Sedition Acts Crisis for Jefferson primarily about the First Amendment's Speech and Press Clauses, despite the fact that Jefferson's draft Kentucky Resolutions mentioned the Tenth Amendment, the federalism amendment, first.[156] In some cases, the focus of those accounts on questions other than federalism arose from expressly stated present partisanship and involved exclusion of the most obvious documentary sources.[157]

James Madison received a letter from the *Richmond Enquirer*'s editor, Thomas Ritchie, asking how to proceed in the situation.[158] Rather than pointing to Jefferson's draft resolutions, Madison opined that Virginia's General Assembly should give "instructions to her Representatives in Congs.; to oppose measures violating her constructions of the Instrument; with a preamble appealing, for the truth of her constructions, to the cotemporary expositions by those best acquainted with the intentions of the Convention, which framed the Constitution; to the Debates & proceedings of the State Conventions which ratified it; to the universal understanding that the Govt. of the Union was a limited not an unlimited one; to the inevitable tendency of the latitude of Construction in behalf of internal improvements, to break down the barriers against unlimited power; it being obvious that the ingenuity which deduces the authority for such measures, could readily find it for any others whatever."

Madison soon wrote to Jefferson that legislative instruction to congressmen was likely to be Virginia's response to the situation.[159] He added that "the question, whether the powers exist, will more & more, give way to the question, how far they ought to be granted"—that is, arguments over the extent of Congress's power probably would soon yield to a debate concerning the terms of a constitutional amendment granting Congress additional power so that it could build roads consistently with Jefferson's understanding of federalism.

Fittingly, that was the last substantive political matter Madison ever discussed with Jefferson. It came in the penultimate paragraph of his final letter to him. The next paragraph included the famous statement of the younger man, the junior member of America's most important political partnership, that "you cannot look back to the long period of our private friendship & political harmony, with more affecting recollections than I do. If they are a source of pleasure to you, what ought they not to be to me?" Knowing Jefferson was about to die, Madison assured him that posterity would recall him fondly—as it in fact already did. How fitting that Jefferson's grandest political partnership, his political career, should have closed on this emblematic note: with Madison relaying to Jefferson the way he had dulled the edges of Jefferson's final pronouncement on behalf of Jefferson's leading principle, which their allies in Congress continued to hold most dear. Just as in 1776.

Chapter 2

Freedom of Conscience

Thomas Jefferson considered liberty of conscience to be the basis of all other freedom.[1] He held to this position fervently from his earliest surviving comments on the subject to the very end of his days. His role in establishing Virginia's devotion to it stood for him among his most significant achievements.[2] He ranked it with writing the Declaration of Independence and establishing the University of Virginia, including it with them on his gravestone.

Besides drafting the most significant statute in American history, Jefferson also encouraged religious freedom at other junctures. The most well-known instance of this is in the Declaration of Independence, where he asserted that men were "endowed by their creator with certain inalienable rights," thus anchoring the entire American republican project in a theological assertion—one that has retained its purchase on Americans' hearts and minds even as their more conventional theological commitments have waned. He also famously provided the most memorable summary of the Religion Clauses when he wrote as president that the First

Amendment had "buil[t] a wall of separation between church and state," a metaphor whose place in American culture would come to be extremely significant, though in drastically un-Jeffersonian fashion, beginning a century later. A decade after that, he planned for the new University of Virginia to accept students of all religious persuasions, to own a full library of texts about Christian history and other religions, and to offer no courses on religion. Inquiry, yes, but inculcation, no.

That Jefferson should have taken this approach to what we now call matters of church and state is somewhat surprising in light of his background. As the old saying says, dukes don't emigrate. Yet, when it came to matters of religion, that is what Thomas Jefferson—son of a Church of England vestryman and one himself—did.

Jefferson was born into a colonial society in which the Church of England theoretically commanded the adherence and support of all. In his father's lifetime, the large landowners who dominated Virginia politics and society had engaged in a frenzy of church-building whose monuments can be seen in virtually all of the Tidewater counties even now. Not only did the fine new buildings of the early eighteenth century signal that the Old Dominion was a Christian country, but they also served as monuments of the gentry's dominance of an overwhelmingly rural society.[3]

Historian Holly Brewer calculates that at the time of the revolution, about eighty-five families owned about two-thirds of the land in present-day Virginia. This land ownership entailed dominance of the county courts, the county militias, the counties' seats in the House of Burgesses (the only representative body in colonial Virginia), and the county vestries. Because no Church of England bishop was ever sent to govern the nominally Episcopalian church in the several colonies (New York, Maryland, Virginia, North Carolina, South Carolina, and Georgia) in which it was officially established, the vestries held sway there. They selected priests, more or less. They decided where chapels would be located. They financed parishes' other activities, including provision of relief to the halt and the lame, the blind and the deaf.

In short, power in the Virginia elite ultimately depended on ownership of land and slaves, which led to places on courts, on vestries, as
militia officers, and in the House of Burgesses. How odd, then, that Jefferson should set out to undermine the Virginia elite's social position by
eliminating the religious establishment, thereby putting religion entirely
on a voluntary basis.

Here he seems to have been under the influence of the most radical
English thinkers, including John Locke, John Milton, and Anthony
Ashley Cooper, the third earl of Shaftesbury.[4] We have no evidence
to substantiate the idea that Jefferson was ever a Trinitarian—that is, a
Christian. Jefferson was seventeen when he went to the College of
William & Mary, and though he had a pretty low opinion of the faculty,
he did greatly admire and appreciate the sole layman of the group: Professor William Small. Jefferson credited Small with extensive "rational"
conversation and with exposing him to "the system of things in which we
are placed"—which is Jefferson-speak for Enlightenment teachings concerning, among other things, religion.[5]

We have extensive notes, apparently compiled when he was in his early
thirties, from Jefferson's reading of Locke and Shaftesbury on matters of
government and religion.[6] Those notes tend to support the ideas that government involvement in religion is intellectually inconsistent, that it is
contrary to Christ's example, and that it is a usurpation of the duty of
every man. In his notes on Locke and his separate "Notes on Episcopacy,"
Jefferson also advocates the *sola scriptura*-based claim of the radical
Protestants, in England and abroad, that "Christ . . . does not make it
essential that a bishop or presbyter [elder] govern them."

The notes on Locke's "A Letter Concerning Toleration" (1689), in particular, foreshadow Jefferson's later writings on the subject. "Our savior,"
he says, "chose not to propagate his religion by temporal pun[ish]m[en]ts
or civil incapacitation, if he had it was in his almighty power, but he
chose to extend it by it's influence on reason, thereby showing to others
how they should proceed." Civil officials, he goes on to say, have only the

power the people have given them, and they have never given them authority over religion. As to individuals, "No man has *power* to let another prescribe his faith with[ou]t believing." In fact, "I cannot give up my guidance to the magistrate; because he knows no more of the way to heaven than I do & is less concerned to direct me right that I am to go right." Members of the polity in general have "no right to prejudice another in his civil enjoyments because he is of another church." Besides, "[tr]uth will do well enough if left to shift for herself . . . she has no need of force to procure entrance into the minds of men." Although he accepts Locke's teaching in these respects, Jefferson notes of Locke's statement that atheists should not be tolerated that "where he stopped short, we may go on."

Jefferson's notes on Shaftesbury's "A Letter Concerning Enthusiasm" (1708) are equally liberal in spirit, and their implications are equally as radical as those on Locke. So, for example, Jefferson wrote that "in the middle ages of [Christianity], opposition to the state op[inio]ns was hushed. the consequence was, [Christianity] became loaded with all the Romish follies. Nothing but free argument, raillery, & even ridicule will preserve the purity of religion." Here we see that Jefferson accepted the standard Protestant/Enlightenment criticisms of Catholic dogmas and traditions such as transubstantiation, monasticism, veneration of relics, and so on. As far as he was concerned, these elements of Western Christian tradition were pure nonsense which had been saved from widespread disrepute only by governments' energetic devotion to stamping out any questioning of them.

Earlier in his notes on Shaftesbury, Jefferson had noted the great Englishman's summary of "the antients'" experience with religious toleration. "As the Pythagoreans & latter Platonicks joined with the superstition of the times," he summarized, "the Epicureans & Academicks were allowed all the use of wit & raillery against it. Thus matters were balanced; reason had [full] play & science flourished." Not only that, he mused, but "superstition & enthusiasm thus let alone never raged to bloodshed persecution &c."

One cannot draw a straight line from a young man's reading and re-marking upon the arguments of particular writers to his later taking a lead in making their favored policies law in his commonwealth. One cannot do so where, as in Jefferson's case, he appended to his draft of the law in question a preamble rehearsing their arguments. A careful scholar cannot even go so far where the man, as in Jefferson's case, refers to one of the authors as a member of his personal "trinity" and displays an oil painting of him (in this case, of Locke) on his wall.[7] Still, we can be confident that Jefferson's Lockean position on church-state relations owed greatly to Locke's influence upon him.

His first effort in this regard came in 1776, when independence opened up an opportunity for thoroughgoing reform of Virginia's religious establishment. In those days, a quorum of Virginia's congressional delegation had to be on the floor to cast Virginia's vote, and thus Jefferson could not simply resign and head home to help draft a new constitution. Jefferson's repeated requests to be replaced by Virginia's legislature fell on deaf ears, so he could not leave. Stuck in Congress, then, Jefferson put pen to paper and produced a document contemplating a thorough reform of Virginia society. Among other things, it said, "All persons shall have full & free liberty of religious opinion," and none would have to attend or give financial support to any services.[8]

Here we see the priority that Jefferson always gave to liberty of religious opinion—to the freedom of the mind. First came the right to think as one would, and only thereafter the right to act as one would.

In any event, Jefferson's proposal on religion did not become part of the Old Dominion's first written constitution. However, the Declaration of Rights did include a final section committing Virginia to the notion that Virginians were entitled to the "free exercise" of religion. That section was the handiwork of Jefferson's future friend James Madison.[9] Frustrated in his desire to achieve fundamental reforms of Virginia society through provisions of the Virginia Constitution, Jefferson decided to push his reform program as a legislator instead.

In his old age, Jefferson drafted an autobiographical sketch.[10] A hodge-podge of his life from his birth in 1743 to his assumption of the office of secretary of state in 1790, his account includes lengthy descriptions of events he adjudged important and omits much that we might like to know. Fortunately, among the events he includes is the 1776 debate in the House of Delegates over the future of the new republican state's Episcopalian religious establishment. Jefferson's goal, as he put it elsewhere, was "the demolition of the church establishment."[11]

As Jefferson summarized his effort, "it could only be done by degrees" in a struggle spanning the period from 1776 to 1785, with considerable help from James Madison.[12] In fact, contrary to Jefferson's implication, the matter had been on the General Assembly's radar since 1769, largely as a result of the growing prominence of the dissenting movements—notably, in Jefferson's Albemarle County, the Baptists—in that period.[13] Instructions were given to the House of Burgesses' Committee on Religion in 1774 to report a bill providing toleration for all Protestants, but nothing came of it.

The substitution of Madison's "free exercise" formula for the "toleration" contemplated by George Mason's draft of the Declaration of Rights' section on religion (section 16) seems to have emboldened the dissenters and liberals such as Jefferson. Numerous petitions poured into the newly renamed House of Delegates in the latter months of 1776. In response, Jefferson and eighteen others were named to a Committee on Religion, with conservative Carter Braxton as chairman. As Jefferson put it in his "Autobiography," the legislature had been "crowded with petitions to abolish . . . spiritual tyranny," and, "These brought on the severest contests in which I have ever been engaged."[14]

Jefferson explained the severity of the struggle by claiming that "although the majority of our citizens were dissenters, . . . a majority of the legislature were churchmen [that is, Episcopalians]." Led by Edmund Pendleton and Robert Carter Nicholas (the last colonial treasurer, thus the highest-ranking colonial to side with the revolution in Virginia), these men put on a rearguard action whose effect was to delay the success of the reformers' efforts to disestablish the church for a few years. It was to them that Jefferson gave most of the credit for the fact that in 1776, 1777, and 1778, the legislature merely put the colonial tithe in abeyance instead of abolishing it altogether.

Jefferson drafted resolutions for the Delegates in 1776, and that house considered very similar ones saying, among other things, that, "all and every act or statute, either of the parliament of *England* or of *Great Britain*, by whatever title known or distinguished, which renders criminal the maintaining any opinions in matters of religion, forbearing to repair to church, or the exercising any mode of worship whatsoever, or which pre-scribes punishments for the same, ought to be declared henceforth of no validity or force within this Commonwealth" and that the petitioners' re-quest to be excused from compliance with the tithes was reasonable. An act more or less to this effect passed the House of Delegates on Novem-ber 30, after Jefferson had left for home. This was chiefly George Mason's doing, though he and Jefferson shared similar sentiments in this area.

Almost as soon as the new constitution had been adopted, Jefferson had begun agitating for a revisal of the laws. This revisal would be a thorough combing of Virginia's law to ensure that it was consistent with republi-can government. As Jefferson put it, the project would result in "a system by which every fibre would be eradicated of ancient or future aristocracy; and a foundation [would be] laid for a government truly republican."[15] Perhaps he was inspired to take this approach by the example of his idol, Sir Francis Bacon, who had proposed a similar project for England.

Although five members of the newly rechristened House of Delegates accepted appointment to the committee charged with preparing a revisal, ultimately only three—Jefferson, Edmund Pendleton, and George Wythe—did the work. As Jefferson explained in his "Autobiography," "the first question was whether we should propose to abolish the whole existing system of laws, and prepare a new and complete Institute, or preserve the general system, and only modify it to the present state of things."[16] Although Pendleton and another member favored the more radical approach, Jefferson's side won out: reforms would be piecemeal.

What Pendleton advocated, in brief, was overthrowing Virginia's English common-law system and replacing it with civil law—law based on a code. As Jefferson put it, the legislature "had been in the practice of revising from time to time the laws of the colony, omitting the expired, the repealed and the obsolete, amending only those retained." He hazarded that this was what the legislature wanted the committee to do. Composing a new code, he said, would be an enormous task, and even if successfully performed, would leave the meaning of each section uncertain until there had been numerous court decisions determining it. In addition, "in order to be systematical," a code "must be the work of one hand," and none of the committee members stood ready to perform the work. Virginia would remain a common-law polity. There would be no Virginian Justinian.

Scattered reforms would be the committee's aim. The package they concocted came to 128 bills, of which 126 ultimately were presented to the House of Delegates.[17] Those 126 included several bills touching on the general issue of the relationship between the Old Dominion's government and religion. Although some of the revisal's most significant proposals never won adoption, the most important of the proposals on religion ultimately did secure passage. The committee divided its work among its three members, but Jefferson drafted all of the religion-related ones.

First among these was Bill No. 80, which provided for a complete reorganization of Virginia's sole institute of higher learning, the College of William & Mary.[18] The only college in colonial America south of New Jersey, William & Mary also stood as the sole seminary for the Church of England in those provinces. Jefferson recalled in his "Autobiography" that William & Mary had been "an establishment purely of the Church of England," whose visitors, like people in similar stations in England, legally (we might add "logically") "were required to be all of that Church."

Besides that, professors had "to subscribe its 39 Articles" (which were the basic points of the Anglican Church's teaching), students had to learn its teaching, and training men to the ministry was one of its prime purposes.

The college had been established with six professorships: two in a "school of sacred theology" (one to teach Hebrew and exegetics and the other "for explaining the common places of divinity, and the controversies with heretics"); two in a "school for philosophy" (one to teach "rhetoric, logic, and ethics" and the other "physics, metaphysics, and mathematics"); one to teach Latin and Greek; and one "for teaching Indian boys reading, writing, vulgar arithmetic, the catechism and the principles of the Christian religion."

Jefferson found all of this unappealing. He would have replaced the College of William & Mary as it had been with a secular institution of higher learning. Instead of having its college inculcate English Christianity, Jefferson would have had it teach various more "practical" subjects. Under the plan Jefferson floated, all would change. The six professorships would now be eight, with Enlightenment assignments including "one of moral philosophy, the laws of nature and of nations, and of the fine arts," a professor "of law and police," a professor of "history, civil and ecclesiastical," one "of mathematics," another "of astronomy and medicine," a professor "of natural philosophy and natural history," "one of the ancient languages, oriental and northern," and "one of modern languages." The college for instruction of young Indians would be abandoned in favor of a periodic mission among the Indians, whose chief function would be "to investigate their laws, customs, religions, traditions, and more particularly their languages, constructing grammars thereof, as well as may be, and copious vocabularies." As opposed to fellow creatures in need of Christian conversion, the Indians were to become objects of study. To cap it all off, Jefferson provided that the college should engage the eminent American astronomer David Rittenhouse to construct a copy of his famous "model of the solar system" for William & Mary.

The bill said that his changes would "aid and improve the seminary [that is, the college], in which those who are to be the future guardians of the rights and liberties of their country may be endowed with science and virtue, to watch and preserve the sacred deposit." From their previous disappointment in their college, Virginians would come to see it as "more useful" if the changes here proposed were made—if William & Mary were transformed from a theological seminary into a training ground for republican politicians.

As Jefferson envisioned it, the college would no longer be under the thumb of the General Assembly, but instead would be a kind of self-perpetuating guild—in the fashion of a modern American university. This change, he did not need to add, would eliminate the Episcopalian Tidewater counties' domination of the college—thus making it more likely that the college would remain permanently insulated from Anglican tradition.

In the end, Bill No. 80 never became law. Jefferson said in his "Autobiography" that this was due to "the religious jealousies . . . of all the dissenters," whose antennae were finely attuned to any sign of favoritism for this Church of England institution. However, when he was governor, he did manage to eliminate the professorships of divinity and of Oriental languages (the latter of which concerned Hebrew, Chaldee, and Syriac—all three important to Protestant theological and historical study). For these, he said, the government "substitute[d] a professorship of Law and Police, one of Anatomy, Medicine, and Chemistry, and one of Modern languages; and the charter confining us to six professorships, we added the Law of Nature and Nations, and the Fine Arts to the duties of the Moral professor, and Natural history to those of the professor of Mathematics and Natural philosophy." Nevermore would William & Mary train young men to the priesthood. Jefferson thought this necessary to proper respect for religious freedom.

Far and away the most famous of the revisors' proposals was Bill No. 82, "A Bill for Establishing Religious Freedom."[19] Jefferson classed his authorship of this bill as one of his three greatest accomplishments. James Madison eventually secured its passage into law, and it now forms part of the Virginia state constitution. Madison summarized his legislative triumph in a letter to Jefferson by saying, "I flatter myself have in this Country extinguished for ever the ambitious hope of making laws for the human mind [*sic*]."[20]

Jefferson's bill had three sections. The first, which in Jefferson's published papers comes to fifty-six of the bill's total seventy-three lines, laid out the legislation's philosophical necessity. It began by saying that men do not choose what to believe, "but follow involuntarily the evidence proposed to their minds." The Senate deleted this statement, so that the bill as passed began by saying, "Whereas almighty God hath created the mind free . . ."

The balance of the paragraph develops this argument perfectly. Most powerfully, it notes that legal coercion cannot actually change men's opinions, but must "tend only to beget habits of hypocrisy and meanness." It is also, he continued, "a departure from the plan of the holy author of our religion, who being lord both of body and mind, yet chose not to propagate it by coercions on either, as was in his Almighty power." According to Jefferson's "Autobiography," an attempt was made to insert "Jesus Christ" after "the holy author of our religion" into this passage, but a huge majority voted down the proposal.[21] Thus Jefferson had fulfilled the ambitious goal he set for himself in his notes on Locke: he had led Virginia in extending religious liberty to "the Jew and the Gentile, the Christian and Mahometan, the Hindoo, and infidel of every denomination"— including even the atheist.

Virginia in adopting the bill also went on record against a general assessment in support of the Christian religion, or indeed, in support of any religion at all. "To compel a man to furnish contributions of money for the propagation of opinions which he disbelieves," the passed version said, "is sinful and tyrannical; . . . even the forcing him to support this or that teacher of his own religious persuasion, is depriving him of the comfortable liberty of giving his contributions to the particular pastor whose morals he would make his pattern, and whose powers he feels most persuasive to righteousness."

Besides blasting justifications for taxing people to support religion and for forcing them to participate in it, Jefferson also took aim at the long-standing English practice of conditioning rights and privileges upon religious opinion. In England during that time, a man could not attend Oxford University or Cambridge University, nor could he sit in the House of Commons, unless he was a member in good standing of the Church of England. Jefferson saw this as both unacceptable and absurd: "our civil rights," the final form of the bill said, "have no dependance on our religious opinions, any more than our opinions in physics or geometry." To deny a man these opportunities, then, was to deprive him of "a natural right."

Jefferson's statement of principle in the bill's first section ended in a characteristic fit of Enlightenment naiveté. "Truth," he thundered, "is great and will prevail if left to herself . . . She is the proper and sufficient antagonist to error, and has nothing to fear from the conflict unless by human interposition disarmed of her natural weapons, free argument and debate; errors ceasing to be dangerous when it is permitted freely to contradict them." Lurking behind this expression of Enlightenment faith is the smiling visage of Anthony Ashley Cooper, the third earl of Shaftesbury, whose opinion to the same effect had been carefully noted by Jefferson many years before he wrote this bill.

With all of that as prelude came the operative section, which stated simply that neither compulsion to religious practice nor punishment for "religious opinions or belief" would be known in Virginia. Rather, the bill said, "all men shall be free to profess, and by argument to maintain, their opinions in matters of religion, and . . . the same shall in no wise diminish, enlarge, or affect their civil capacities."

In England, the matter might have ended there. If ultimately the law had come to have enough purchase on the sentiments of Englishmen, it could have come to be seen as part of England's unwritten constitution, as a monument in the history of British liberty.

Jefferson and his Virginian contemporaries had started off down a markedly different path. Their constitution, just months old at the time of this bill's drafting, was a written document, not a set of customs and habits. However much Virginians might appreciate it, the bill was not part of the written Constitution of 1776. Thus, it could be repealed by simple legislative enactment.

The final section of the bill addressed this problem. "We all know," it said, "that this Assembly, elected by the people for the ordinary purposes of legislation only, have no power to restrain the acts of succeeding Assemblies, and that therefore to declare this act irrevocable would be of no effect in law." Yet, the General Assembly continued, "the rights hereby asserted are of the natural rights of mankind, and . . . if any act shall be hereafter passed to repeal the present or to narrow its operations, such act will be an infringement of natural rights." Its place in subsequent Virginia constitutions seems to indicate that succeeding generations in the Old Dominion have agreed.

To say that the Commonwealth's government would respect liberty of conscience—and that is what the Virginia Statute for Religious Freedom means—did not completely answer the question of what was to be the fate of Virginia's colonial religious establishment. Besides taxes, forced attendance, oaths, and heresy trials, the establishment had had other elements. Among those was the Church of England's possession of extensive property—church buildings, parsonages, and other property—in Virginia. Would that now revert to the Commonwealth and, perhaps, its other donors? The revisors proposed answers to this question.

Part of their response took the form of Bill No. 83, "A Bill for Saving the Property of the Church Heretofore by Law Established."[22] It said that "the English church till then established by law" would retain all of its property, including its right to outstanding payments, despite its disestablishment. The vestries were also to be given power to impose taxes to meet parish debts accrued prior to January 1, 1777. Where a vestry had in hand more money than it needed to meet outstanding obligations, it was to be allowed to spend that money on poor relief—a function otherwise already transferred from the Episcopal Church, which had it before the revolution, to the civil government.

One type of property a parish would be allowed to retain by Jefferson's bill was its glebe, or parsonage. If a parish had funds on hand, it could spend that money on acquiring a glebe before applying any of it to poor relief.

Having thus accounted for the chief elements of the Episcopal establishment by abolishing them, whether immediately or prospectively, Jefferson's package of legislation next turned to elements that were to be retained. First on the list we find Bill No. 84, "A Bill for Punishing Disturbers of Religious Worship and Sabbath Breakers."[23] This bill had three sections, each on a different subject.

The first section made it a crime for anyone to arrest a "minister of the gospel" while he was leading a religious service. Although they do not say when, the editors of Jefferson's papers note that the bill's reference to "the gospel"—a Christian term—was changed to the general word "religion" prior to its ultimate passage. The bill's second section provided criminal penalties for anyone who disturbed a religious service in progress. Penalties included imprisonment.

While these provisions seem consistent with the Bill for Establishing Religious Freedom, the same cannot be said for the next and final section. It continued prohibition for breaking the Sabbath, an ancient Christian prohibition traceable to Emperor Constantine I, bugbear of Western Christian antiestablishmentarians since the earliest days of the Reformation. "If any person on Sunday shall himself be found laboring at his own or any other trade or calling," it said, "or shall employ his apprentices, servants or slaves in labour, or other business, except it be in the ordinary household offices of daily necessity, or other work of necessity or charity, he shall forfeit the sum of ten shillings for every such offense, deeming every apprentice, servant, or slave so employed, and every day he shall be so employed as constituting a distinct offense." Not only must an individual observe the Sabbath by not working himself, but he would be punished for putting his servants to work as well. Eventually, through Madison's effort (!), this bill was enacted.

If this was not sufficiently contrary to the prevailing impression of Jefferson, Bill No. 85 ran directly counter to it.[24] Entitled "A Bill for Appointing Days of Public Fasting and Thanksgiving," it provided precisely what the title indicated: that the governor and the council could name public days of prayer and thanksgiving, just as in colonial times. Ministers would be required to hold services on those appointed days, as well as to preach on the assigned subject, on pain of a hefty fine of fifty pounds. Again surprisingly, Madison endeavored to secure the bill's passage, but his effort failed.

Bill No. 86 continued on the religious theme. Entitled "A Bill Annulling Marriages Prohibited by the Levitical Law, and Appointing the Mode of Solemnizing Lawful Marriage," it represented a revolution in the polity: elimination of the clerical monopoly upon the power to perform marriages. Rather than requiring three public announcements of intention to marry prior to the ceremony and reserving the power to perform it to the Episcopal priests, this bill contemplated simply obtaining a license and proclaiming the intention to be married with witnesses in attendance. Once they had met these requirements, a couple would "without further ceremony, be deemed man and wife, as effectually as if the contract had been solemnized, and the espousals celebrated, in the manner prescribed by the ritual of any church." The bill also included provisions prohibiting marriage between whites and others, which we will consider hereafter. This bill never passed, but it demonstrates precisely what Jefferson meant by his revolution: that the church would no longer have a monopoly of any kind of civil authority, although it could continue to provide services of the kind it always had for people who wanted them.

The final two religion bills in this portion of the revisal, Nos. 87 and 88, concerned usury and gambling.[25] Lending money at higher than a prescribed rate of interest and gambling had been criminal activities in England, and thus in Virginia, from time immemorial. Given his way, Jefferson would have kept them so. The usury bill, which became law, arbitrarily limited legal interest to 5 percent while establishing a penalty of forfeiture of the interest provided in the agreement plus a fine of the same amount. The gambling bill provided that gambling debts would be unenforceable. Instead, both the loser and the winner of any large amount (Jefferson left the amounts blank in his bill) would face stiff fines in proportion. People who bet in public would be barred from public office, and tavern keepers hosting such activity would lose their licenses. Finally, the bill made it a crime to run a lottery for one's own benefit—which is somewhat ironic in light of the fact that the Commonwealth ran one for Jefferson's benefit in his last years of life.

That these bills came at the end of the religion section of the revisal shows that Jefferson recognized them as springing from Christian teaching. He doubtless would have denied that his opposition to the behavior they banned reflected the grip of Christian thought on his mind.

There remain two more religious policies in Jefferson's bills to consider. First, Bill No. 98, "A Bill Prescribing the Oath of Fidelity, and the Oaths of Certain Public Officers," prescribed one of four different oaths to each of four classes of oath-takers.[26] Perhaps most significantly, the Jeffersonian oaths substituted an oath to the Commonwealth for the former oath to the monarch. Jefferson envisioned an oath for each of his groups ending "so help me God." Apparently he had not considered that invoking the deity, or taking an oath at all, involved subscribing to underlying religious assumptions; the key point was the replacement of the king with the Old Dominion as the object of the oath-taker's loyalty.

This bill ultimately was adopted in tandem with a companion bill, No. 119, "A Bill Permitting Those Who Will Not Take Oaths to Be Otherwise Qualified."[27] Attractively, the history of the American Revolution finds all of the states, as well as the United States, carving out exceptions to oath-taking requirements for dissenting groups such as Quakers, whose religion barred oath-taking. Jefferson's bill allowed such people to substitute the formula used by "their church, or religious society" "on similar occasions" for the oath prescribed by Virginia statute—but only if the testator's objection to the usual oath arose out of "religious scruples" and no other cause. If in court, the bill said, the scrupulous would be permitted to substitute "in solemn form" or "charged" for the usual "upon their oath" or "sworn." As in prescribing oaths, so in allowing them to be avoided, Jefferson ignored the futility of having the impious make such statements. His mind likely was on the imperative, described in the preamble of Bill No. 82, to avoid forcing dissenters into hypocrisy via an oath requirement.

Jefferson's first term as governor began just after he presented these last two bills to the House of Delegates, and his career as a legislator effectively came to an end at this point.[28] It seems somewhat poetic that it should have culminated in a proposal to exempt those with religious scruples against oath-taking from taking oaths, for respect for religious scruples as a component of the freedom of the mind was near the top of Jefferson's hierarchy of political principles. The proposed exemption seems to follow naturally from the claim, stated in the first section of the Virginia Statute for Religious Freedom, that "to compel a man to furnish contributions of money for the propagation of opinions which he disbelieves," as the passed version said, "is sinful and tyrannical; . . . even the forcing him to support this or that teacher of his own religious persuasion, is depriving him of the comfortable liberty of giving his contributions to the particular pastor whose morals he would make his pattern, and whose powers he feels most persuasive to righteousness." If making him contribute money was "sinful and tyrannical," surely making him actually do something that violated his religious scruples was worse.

As governor, Jefferson received a set of queries about "the state of Virginia" from a French diplomat resident in America at the time, François

Barbé-Marbois.[29] Rearranged by Jefferson, they became the foundation of his sole book, *Notes on the State of Virginia*. The title was a pun, and the reference to the book's major divisions as "queries" rather than "chapters" owed to its origin as a set of answers to a prominent Frenchman's questions.

Query XVII concerned "The different religions received into that state?"[30] Here Jefferson provided both a short history of the development of confessional diversity in the Old Dominion and a summary of the history of his reform efforts in this area. One may think him a bit harsh on the score of the colonial establishment, as his statement that "if no capital execution took place here, as did in New-England, it was not owing to the moderation of the church, or spirit of the legislature, as may be inferred from the law itself; but to historical circumstances which have not been handed down to us" bore little relationship to the actual Anglicanism of his friends such as John Page, George Wythe, and George Mason. Still, in the days immediately preceding the revolution, Baptists in his own and neighboring Piedmont counties did suffer persecution.[31]

He next described the state of Virginia's religious law circa 1781, when some of the establishment lay in abeyance or had been repealed, but other matters—such as passage of his Bill No. 82—were still in the future. Jefferson makes the point that although the taxes and so forth are not being enforced, the common law's religious provisions still technically can be, which means that people can be banned from holding office, even foreclosed from filing suit, deprived of custody of children, or jailed up to three years for denying the truth of the Christian religion or any of its chief components. "This," he concluded this part of the essay, "is a summary view of the religious slavery, under which a people have been willing to remain, who have lavished their lives and fortunes for the establishment of their civil freedom."

With his French intended audience in mind, Jefferson preached that "our rulers can have authority over such natural rights only as we have submitted to them. The rights of conscience we never submitted, we could not submit. We are answerable for them to our God." In other words, the obligation to God is antecedent to the social compact, and so government has no rightful say in this area, according to Jefferson's understanding. His conception of the social compact, like much of his thinking about the establishment of a state religion, came from John Locke, author of the famous *Second Treatise: On Civil Government.* Man had certain natural rights in a pre-civil setting, and he entered into a social compact with his fellows to secure their protection. Government has only the powers it received via its institution, and there was no need, according to Jefferson, for it to be given power over men's thoughts. "The legitimate powers of government," he continued, "extend to such acts only as are injurious to others. But it does me no injury for my neighbour to say there are twenty gods, or no god. It neither picks my pocket nor breaks my leg."

Jefferson left the door open for society to take certain steps in response to the religions of its members. If one believed the impious untrustworthy witnesses, he could reject their testimony at law. "Constraint," on the other hand, "may make him worse by making him a hypocrite, but it will never make him a truer man." Not coercion, but freedom of inquiry had enabled Christianity to make progress in Rome, and the Reformation would not have made its progress if not for that. Government has no particular insight in the area of religion, and so granting it power to mandate religion would make no sense.

Jefferson avers that Pennsylvania and New York have freedom of religion, and that it works well for them. Perhaps the Virginia establishment is a dead letter, but so long as it remains on the books, it may be resuscitated, and that would be a disaster. Best to eliminate it while the opportunity offers.

We have no direct evidence on the point, but even a cursory reading of this short chapter of Jefferson's book next to his friend Madison's "Memorial and Remonstrance: Against Religious Assessments" seems to indicate that the two of them had arrived at a common understanding of these issues, likely through conversation on the subject. Their sympathy in this area would be the ground of the ultimate solution to the problem in Virginia.

Jefferson's governorship ended abysmally. First an invading British force—commanded by General Benedict Arnold, no less—chased the governor and legislature from the new capital, Richmond, in January 1781, and then a cavalry detachment pursued them from Charlottesville and Monticello, to which they had retreated. Rather than accompany them to their transmontane temporary capital, Jefferson let the legislators await the arrival of his successor. Rumors swirled that Governor Jefferson had inadequately prepared for the invasion, and some said he had cravenly fled the cavalrymen sent to apprehend him on his mountaintop. A delegate from his own county—his own representative—filed a motion of impeachment. (As we saw in relation to the grand jurors who handed up a presentment against Congressman Cabell in 1797, the Virginia Constitution of 1776 allowed impeachment after one had left office.)

When the time came, Jefferson presented an impassioned defense of his performance as governor. The legislature gave him a unanimous endorsement, and then he retired from public life. Feeling put upon, he vowed not to accept public office again. Soon enough, in 1782, Jefferson's young wife, whom he kept pregnant despite her evident physical weakness, died of a postpartum malady. Jefferson despaired, his daughter later describing him in a way that impresses one with the likelihood that he was clinically depressed.

In 1784, concerned with his friend's emotional state and determined to draw him back into public life, Madison succeeded in coaxing Congress into naming Jefferson America's minister (now it would be ambassador) to France. Jefferson spent five years in Europe's cultural center, where he witnessed, and even participated in, the earliest days of the reform movement that ultimately became the cataclysmic French Revolution. He also drank deep of the bounteous French high culture. His envy of various elements of it—notably the musical—was paired with a heightened appreciation of some of his homeland's virtues.

He did not keep his observations to himself, but instead dove into a campaign to vindicate America's reputation. Yes, his country was backward, but it had much to recommend it. Madison, meanwhile, left Congress in 1783 and returned to Virginia. He was in the House of Delegates when the Old Dominion's leading politician, Patrick Henry, proposed a general assessment in 1785.[32] Arguing that popular morality had declined since the religious reforms of 1776, Henry proposed a solution: a bill providing for support of "teachers of the Christian religion." Not a revivification of the colonial taxes to support the Anglican (now Episcopal) Church, Henry's measure would have required that every Virginian pay a levy to the Christian pastor of his choice.

Madison sat aghast as Henry's bill passed its first reading, then its second reading, by large House of Delegates votes. By the terms of the 1776 Virginia Constitution, one more vote in favor would pass the bill, and then, despite Section 16 of the Declaration of Rights, Virginians would be back under a requirement to contribute to Christianity. Patrick Henry nearly always got his way in the House of Delegates, and there seemed little chance of beating him on the bill's final reading. What to do?

Madison had a brilliant idea: get Henry out of the House of Delegates. The Constitution of 1776 empowered the General Assembly to elect the governor, and so Madison proposed that Henry, who had been Virginia's first republican governor, be elevated to the chief magistracy once again. The House of Delegates agreed. Once Henry had been ceremoniously installed in his new position, Madison seized the occasion. Because the electorate had not considered the question, he said, the house should postpone a decision on Henry's measure until members had the opportunity to determine their constituents' preference. Only then could they make so momentous a decision confident that they had the people's blessing.

There followed the first statewide political campaign in Virginia history. Each member was given numerous copies of Henry's bill to circulate in his home district. Petitions circulated on both the pro and the con side of the question. Prompted by Mason and George Nicholas, Madison aided the pro cause by penning a very pithy summary of the freedom-of-religion argument, "Memorial and Remonstrance: Against Religious Assessments." In this pamphlet, Madison made several of the same arguments as Jefferson had made concerning church-state relations in *Notes on the State of Virginia*: that man's duty to his creator was antecedent to government, that government had no appropriate role in religion, that government had never really helped religion and religion was not necessary to government, and so forth. While we cannot prove that Madison relied on Jefferson's arguments, and while Madison certainly knew the radical arguments of Locke and others just as well as Jefferson did, we can be pardoned for deducing that Jefferson likely influenced the shape of Madison's argument—particularly in light of what followed the publication of "Memorial and Remonstrance."

The overall campaign was a debacle for the general assessment's supporters. Nine times as many people signed the petitions against the bill as signified their support. With that, Madison told the reconvened House of Delegates it should lay the bill aside. No third vote was ever taken. Next, he offered an alternative: the Bill for Establishing Religious Freedom. Soon enough, he won the day, and he wrote exultantly to Jefferson. Jefferson spread the news among the leading lights of France. He wanted them to think highly of the United States, and particularly of the Old Dominion. *Notes on the State of Virginia* had contributed to his effort, and the Virginia Statute for Religious Freedom (as it was now called) won praise from many mighty European minds—as he exulted to his friend the legislator:

The Virginia act for religious freedom has been received with infinite approbation in Europe & propagated with enthusiasm. I do not mean by the governments, but by the individuals which compose them. It has been translated into French & Italian, has been sent to most of the courts of Europe, & has been the best evidence of the falsehood of those reports which stated us to be in anarchy. It is inserted in the new Encyclopedie, & is appearing in most of the publications respecting America. In fact it is comfortable to see the standard of reason at length erected, after so many ages during which the human mind has been held in vassalage by kings, priests & nobles: and it is honorable for us to have produced the first legislature who had the courage to declare that the reason of man may be trusted with the formation of his own opinions.[33]

The "ages" Jefferson had in mind spanned essentially all of recorded history, for the age of established churches had followed hard upon the period when most governments were like the Romans' in making religious observance (though not, as among the Christians, religious belief) a matter of state responsibility. Virginia's abrupt divergence from this path stands out even at this distance as epochal.

Besides recognizing its authentic import, Jefferson clearly found great satisfaction in the reputation that came to him as author of the new statute. Its translation into French and Italian meant that it could be read by the informed and the powerful essentially anywhere in those days when French served the role of international language filled by English today. Inclusion in the *Encyclopédie* promised a kind of immortality to both the measure and the man. Jefferson hoped and expected that in time the enthusiasm of the literary class would yield European measures embodying this liberal American principle.

Jefferson retained essentially the same opinions on government and religion through the rest of his life. One historian summarized the remainder of his career on these questions as "commentary upon the Bill for Establishing Religious Freedom."[34] As Jefferson put it in a characteristically pithy formulation in 1800, he had "sworn on the altar of god eternal hostility against every form of tyranny over the mind of man."[35]

Jefferson's outstanding opportunities to implement these principles after the Virginia statute's adoption came during his presidency, 1801–1809. In that office, he made a point of breaking with his two august predecessors' custom of calling days of prayer, fasting, and thanksgiving.[36] He drew attention to this decision in his Second Inaugural Address:

> In matters of religion, I have considered that its free exercise is placed by the constitution independent of the powers of the general government. I have therefore undertaken, on no occasion, to prescribe the religious exercises suited to it; but have left them, as the constitution found them, under the direction or discipline of State or Church authorities acknowledged by the several religious societies.

His policy as the third president and his public explanation of that policy raise the interesting question of how one is to understand Bill No. 85 of the revisal, in which Jefferson had provided for continued proclamations of days of prayer and fasting by Virginia authorities, even going so far as to establish significant penalties for noncompliant ministers. If, as he said in the quotation above, such proclamations violated the Tenth Amendment, what of their relationship to Section 16 of the Virginia Declaration of Rights and the Virginia Statute?[37] We have no surviving commentary from him directly on this point.

A president of course is not solely an official, but is also a symbol. Jefferson recognized this in several ways, including by refusing to don court garb in meeting with the British minister, in refusing to adopt diplomatic seating at White House dinners, and in discontinuing what he considered the monarchical habit, established by Washington and continued by Adams, of presenting State of the Union Addresses orally. He also recognized it in attending religious services in the US Capitol throughout his presidency.[38]

It is in this light that we must interpret the most famous presidential utterance on church and state, Jefferson's 1802 Letter to the Danbury Baptist Association.[39] Jefferson wrote to that beleaguered organization with the ideas both of bucking up a persecuted religious minority friendly to his Republican Party and of disseminating his own views, what he hoped would become American views, about the proper relationship between government and religion.[40]

Danbury, Connecticut, the town in which my university is located, lay in a state founded by some of the first families of Massachusetts. Connecticut's reason for being, like that of the Bay Colony, was to be a Puritan community. Although by 1802 six of the nine states that had had colonial religious establishments had abolished them, not only did Connecticut retain its establishment, but that establishment remained socially and politically powerful. The wealthy, the high officials, and Yale College all remained Congregationalist.

New England churchmen had lambasted Jefferson soundly both in 1796 and in 1800. Yale's president, Congregationalist minister Timothy Dwight IV, captured the general hysteria in saying that in case Jefferson were elected in 1800, "we may see the Bible cast into a bonfire, the vessels of the sacramental supper borne by an ass in public procession, and our children . . . chanting mockeries against God . . . [to] the ruin of their religion, and the loss of their souls."[41]

The Baptists of Connecticut represented what everywhere was a bedraggled minority. Generally from lower rungs on the social ladder, they had to pay taxes to support the state church. Congregationalists cordially shunned them. In 1802, Congregationalist Connecticut was two-thirds of the way to its historic feat of being one of only two states whose electoral college votes were cast against Jefferson for president all three times he was a candidate—in 1796, 1800, and 1804. Jefferson's victory in the second of those elections came to Connecticut Baptists as such a wonderful development, so pregnant with positive implications concerning the future of American church-state relations, that they wrote a letter soon after Jefferson's March 1801 inauguration telling him how happy they were.

Unbeknownst to them, their letter would evoke from Jefferson an immortal statement of his civil faith. No doubt he reveled in its implications concerning the privileged status of New England's Congregationalist ministers.

The meat of Jefferson's Letter to the Danbury Baptists[42] said:

Believing with you that religion is a matter which lies solely between Man & his God, that he owes account to none other for his faith or his worship, that the legitimate powers of government reach actions only, & not opinions, I contemplate with sovereign reverence that act of the whole American people which declared that their legislature should "make no law respecting an establishment of religion, or prohibiting the free exercise thereof," thus building a wall of separation between Church & State. Adhering to this expression of the supreme will of the nation in behalf of the rights of conscience, I shall see with sincere satisfaction the progress of those sentiments which tend to restore to man all his natural rights, convinced he has no natural right in opposition to his social duties.

I reciprocate your kind prayers for the protection & blessing of the common father and creator of man, and tender you for yourselves & your religious association, assurances of my high respect & esteem.

All three of America's remaining establishments (in Massachusetts and New Hampshire, besides the Nutmeg State) traced their descent from Puritanism. The Puritans were the people who had expelled Anne Hutchinson for heresy and Roger Williams for dissenting from the New England Way, drawn the wrath of Charles II down upon their own heads by persecuting Quakers (first expelling, then hanging them), and given American history its most shameful example of fanatical extremism by hanging numerous people for witchcraft in the still-notorious Salem witch trials. Their Congregationalist heirs also had thundered from their pulpits the warning that electing Jefferson threatened the future of Christianity in the United States. For Jefferson, their behavior was an archetype of closed-minded intolerance. As he put it soon after drafting the Letter to the Danbury Baptists, "I know it will give great offence to the New England clergy; but the advocate of religious freedom is to expect neither peace nor forgiveness from them."[43] Jefferson ran the draft letter by Postmaster General Gideon Granger before promulgating it, and that Connecticut native echoed Jefferson's view of the establishment, replying that the letter would "undoubtedly give great Offence to the established Clergy of New England while it will delight the Dissenters as they are called."[44]

Note that Jefferson took the opportunity to explain that his vision of proper church-state relations rested on his understanding of the limitations of government power. Where, as in New England in his day, a "man" did not enjoy freedom of religion, he was being deprived of "his natural rights." The limitations to which Jefferson referred followed from the political theory underlying the Declaration of Independence and other Jeffersonian statements concerning the proper basis of government before and during the revolution, which by 1802 had come to be publicly associated with Jefferson. Jefferson famously had claimed in the Declaration of Independence that "their Creator" had given people "certain unalienable Rights," and government must respect, even protect, those rights. In fact, it was "to secure [those] rights that Governments [were] instituted among Men." How appropriate that Jefferson should make his most famous claims concerning the rights of conscience in a missive to an oppressed religious community in the state least committed to respecting them. Jefferson underscored his and the Baptists' common position by closing with his prayer and an invocation of the theistic (they may have inferred Christian) faith he shared with them.

By the end of Jefferson's life on July 4, 1826, he'd had the pleasure of seeing his Republican confreres triumph even in the Federalist heartlands of Massachusetts and Connecticut. Although the Bay State retained its taxpayer support for religion, even New Hampshire and Connecticut had done away with it. (Massachusetts would in 1833.)

Although he retired from politics effective March 4, 1809, Jefferson would have one last opportunity to make an important statement concerning church-state relations: his work in establishing the University of Virginia. Central to his vision was that the institution should be secular—open to religious inquiry without pushing religious orthodoxy.

Chapter 3

Colonization

Though long fascinated by their work in remaking British North America into thirteen "free and independent states," I have always taken the Jeffersonian position that the revolutionaries should not be considered secular saints. Yes, they did many notable things, but they also erred.[1]

Still, historical personages must be considered historically. That Ben Franklin had no interest in companionate marriage tells us more about his time than about him. John Jay's notable anti-Catholic, anti-French animus reflected his family's recent experience of being expelled from France for being Protestant, as well as his firm commitment to Protestantism. Thomas Jefferson's life as a slave owner . . . Well, many—even some prominent scholars—think that is a bit different.

As I finished writing this book in 2015, state Democratic Party leadership in four states decided to drop Thomas Jefferson's name from their annual fundraising dinners. A Jefferson-Jackson Dinner, they decided, did not reflect the priorities and commitments of the contemporary

Democratic Party, at least in Georgia, Missouri, Iowa, or Connecticut. Connecticut's state party chairman Nick Balletto said he hoped the Nutmeg State Democrats' act would prompt other states' parties to do the same thing.[2] Connecticut NAACP leader Scot X. Esdaile called it a "symbolic first step" toward correcting "the wrongs of the past." Ironically, Missouri Democrats renamed their fundraiser for native son Harry S. Truman, who famously had strongly negative things to say about the ideas of a desegregated US military and interracial marriage (which he said the Bible banned).[3]

Democrats' decision to take this step puts them on the same side of the question as historian Paul Finkelman. Finkelman takes a frankly critical approach to Jefferson, saying that the appropriate "test" is "whether he was able to transcend his economic interests and his sectional background in order to implement the ideals he articulated."[4] Pointing to contemporaries such as George Washington and John Randolph of Roanoke (who freed their slaves in their wills), as well as Robert Carter (who freed more than four hundred slaves in his lifetime), Finkelman long has called Jefferson's omission to do any such thing "treason against the hopes of the world." This judgment, Finkelman insists, is not presentist, but rather reflects the standards of the best of Jefferson's own generation— which is the company among which we would hope and expect to find republican Virginia's second governor and the United States' third president. Both Finkelman's somewhat unhistorical attitude toward Jefferson and his assessment of the evidence put him in the minority when he first expressed his opinion.

Critical scholarship on the revolutionaries' slavery-related record led William W. Freehling to publish a widely cited journal article demanding two cheers for the Master of Monticello in 1972. A couple of decades later, Freehling revised the piece substantially for its appearance in a collection of his articles. He had been too easy on Jefferson the first time, he contended. Jefferson's "conditional antislavery" depended on conditions that never came to be.[5]

Later in the 1990s, historians Joseph Ellis and Andrew Burstein remained skeptical. In his prizewinning *American Sphinx*, Ellis came down on the negative side on the question of a Jefferson–Sally Hemings sexual relationship.[6] Burstein, who privately said, "I love Jefferson," seemed every bit the infatuated teenager in Ken Burns's documentary *Thomas Jefferson*, as well as in his popular book *The Inner Jefferson: Portrait of a Grieving Optimist*.[7] Law professor Annette Gordon-Reed, the first African-American scholar with a significant role in this saga, swayed a considerable segment of expert opinion with her 1997 book *Thomas Jefferson and Sally Hemings: An American Controversy*, but many remained unconvinced.[8] As Scot French and Edward L. Ayers had shown, skepticism of the idea of a Jefferson-Hemings relationship went back to the very first significant Jefferson biographers, who gave substantial deference to accounts of life at Monticello provided by Jefferson's white descendants.[9] From that point in the early nineteenth century until 1968, essentially no historian gave tales of miscegenation at Monticello any credence. Not until 1997 were most scholars persuaded.

When DNA testing demonstrated in 1998 that at least some of Sally Hemings's descendants were also descended from a male in the Jefferson line, thus almost conclusively vindicating Finkelman, Gordon-Reed, and Sally Hemings, Burstein wrote a new Jefferson book consistent with this information.[10] Ellis coupled recantation of his position on l'affaire Hemings with the argument that since Thomas Jefferson had fathered children by a slave, and since President Bill Clinton's perjury and obstruction of justice had occurred in sworn testimony in a sexual harassment case, Clinton should be acquitted of high crimes and misdemeanors in his Senate impeachment trial.

Critics commonly accuse Thomas Jefferson and his peers of hypocrisy. They purported to believe that "all men are created equal," the charge goes, and yet they owned slaves and did nothing to give effect to their stated belief in human rights. Equality was just for white, propertied men, the indictment holds.

Insofar as Jefferson is concerned, this charge is inaccurate. Jefferson did not do nothing about the plight of enslaved blacks in America.[11] He did not passively accept that slaves would remain slaves in Virginia forever, or even that there would be slavery in America. Instead, he conceived of a solution to the race problem consistent with his own fears and, it seems, dislike of blacks. If Jefferson had had his way, all blacks would have been sent out of Virginia—indeed, out of America. This program was called "colonization."

In 1821, near the end of his life, Jefferson wrote an "Autobiography." Amounting to ninety pages in a 1984 edition, this quirky account of his life ended with his agreement to become George Washington's first secretary of state in 1790. Virtually free of personal information, the sketch is more or less an account of Jefferson's political career through his forty-seventh year.

Jefferson's version of his earliest days in the Virginia House of Burgesses, colonial Virginia's sole elected legislative body, features an extensive description of what he claimed was an attempt by him to bring Virginia slavery to an end. Among the numerous Jefferson cousins in senior leadership in the House was Richard "Spectacle Dick" Bland, whom Jefferson judged the foremost expert on matters constitutional he ever knew.[12] (Recall that Jefferson's best friend and ally was James Madison.) As it was customary in the House of Burgesses for junior members to be seen and not heard, Jefferson persuaded Bland to present a bill providing for the eventual disappearance of slavery from the Old Dominion. The bill provided that beginning on a date certain, anyone born into slavery in Virginia would be free upon reaching the age of majority.

John Adams remarked decades later that although the two of them sat in Congress together for years, he never heard Jefferson give a significant speech. Perhaps Bland's experience that day accounts for Jefferson's reticence. As he remembered fifty-odd years later, Bland was subjected to everything but assault by the critics of the Bland-Jefferson proposal.

Ordinarily among the House's leaders, Bland on that day was called an enemy to his country. As Jefferson told it, something even more important happened that day too.

Jefferson wanted his readers to understand that Bland's travails determined Jefferson's attitude toward Virginia slavery reform for the rest of his life. Watching and listening silently, he is supposed to have decided that Virginians not only lacked any interest in eliminating slavery but passionately rejected the idea. If serious change was to come through the master class's voluntary action, it would come later.

In this same period, 1767–1774, Jefferson practiced law. The leading historian of his law practice says, "In several cases he acted gratis for persons alleging that they were being wrongfully held in slavery."[13] In one case, attorney Jefferson argued on behalf of a mulatto (that is, mixed-race person) that "under the law of nature, all men are born free, and every one comes into the world with a right to his own person, which includes the liberty of moving and using it at his own will." The court dismissed the suit on the ground that Jefferson had not proven the mulatto grandmother to have been free, and thus had not shown that freedom descended to her grandson. Jefferson also accepted court appointment as counsel to a mulatto suing for his freedom in 1772. However, his client died while the suit was pending. Never again did Jefferson argue for freedom of a slave without also pushing colonization.[14] His law practice came to an end at the climax of the imperial crisis. At that point, Jefferson gave serious attention to the slavery issue in his three great revolutionary works: "A Summary View of the Rights of British America," his draft Virginia constitutions, and his draft Declaration of Independence. Written over a period of two years, they made numerous statements about slavery.

In "A Summary View," Jefferson concludes his section decrying the act of Parliament dissolving the New York assembly by saying that if four million people in America, "every individual of whom is equal to every individual of them in virtue, in understanding, and in bodily strength," are to have 160,000 in Britain "give law to" them, then the four million "should be suddenly found the slaves" of the British voters.[15] This terminology was widely employed by patriots before and after 1776, but in our day, the idea of Jefferson and his slaveholding ilk calling their political situation "slavery" can seem rather jarring. (Jefferson used the slavery metaphor again later in the pamphlet, when he criticized George III for preventing colonists to the west from having representation in Virginia's legislature.)

Far from ignoring actual slavery, however, Jefferson came to it later in "A Summary View." Complaining of George III's use of his power to suspend laws adopted by colonial legislatures in North America, Jefferson asserted that the king, "for the most trifling reasons, and sometimes for no conceivable reason at all," had "rejected laws of the most salutary tendency." Slavery-related laws were Exhibits A through C.

What kind of slavery-related laws? Why, laws aimed at preparing the ground for "the infranchisement of the slaves we have." Before that could be done, Jefferson wrote, cutting off further slave imports would be necessary. "Yet our repeated attempts to effect this by prohibitions, and by imposing duties which might amount to a prohibition, have been hitherto defeated by his majesty's negative: thus preferring the immediate advantages of a few British corsairs to the lasting interests of the American states, and to the rights of nature deeply wounded by this infamous practice." Not only should George III be blamed for omission to put slavery on a path to ultimate elimination, in other words, but he should be seen as having done this for the pecuniary interests of a few.

In mid-1775, Jefferson helped write the Continental Congress's "Declaration of the Causes and Necessity of Taking Up Arms."[16] His draft of this congressional justification of the decision to organize the Continental Army noted in its final paragraph that in respect of their conduct toward their British cousins, the Americans "did not invade their island carrying death or slavery to its inhabitants."[17] Jefferson's draft Declaration of Independence mined the same vein.

Virginia's ruling Revolutionary Convention moved on May 15, 1776, that Congress should declare independence.[18] On June 7, Richard Henry Lee made the motion in Congress.[19] Jefferson represented Virginia on the five-man congressional committee to draft a declaration appointed that day.[20] As he recorded events in his contemporaneous notes, "the committee for drawing the declaration of Independence desired me to do it." When finally Congress turned to the committee draft, Jefferson noted, "the clause . . . reprobating the enslaving the inhabitants of Africa, was struck out in complaisance to South Carolina & Georgia, who had never attempted to restrain the importation of slaves, and who on the contrary still wished to continue it. Our Northern brethren also I believe felt a little tender under those censures; for tho' their people have very few slaves themselves yet they had been pretty considerable carriers of them to others."

The passage whose omission Jefferson lamented blamed George III personally for having "waged cruel war against human nature itself, violating it's most sacred rights of life and liberty in the persons of a distant people who never offended him, captivating & carrying them into slavery in another hemisphere or to incur miserable death in their transportation thither. This piratical warfare, the opprobrium of *infidel* powers, is the warfare of the *Christian* king of Great Britain. Determined to keep open a market where *Men* should be bought & sold, he has prostituted his negative for suppressing every legislative attempt to prohibit or to restrain this execrable commerce. And that this assemblage of horrors might want no fact of distinguished die, he is now exciting those very people to rise in arms among us, and to purchase that liberty of which he has deprived them, by murdering the people on whom he also obtruded them: thus paying off former crimes committed against the *Liberties* of one people, with crimes which he urges them to commit against the *lives* of another."

This stood as the twentieth of twenty paragraphs in which Jefferson/ Congress leveled charges against King George of violating their rights and thus his duty to protect his subjects in those rights' exercise. Quite a climax it was. If Jefferson intended the Declaration to be read aloud, as the best scholarship shows, not the philosophical preamble but the long series of "He has . . ." allegations formed its rhetorical, constitutional, and emotional center.[21] Jefferson intended his slavery paragraph to be the centerpiece of the entire document. Far from endorsing it, Congress excised it.

Jefferson's explanation that the Deep South and the North acted out of interest in voting to remove it should not be ignored. Seldom do politicians' acts deviate far from their constituents' material interests. Yet, one cannot help but suspect that at least some of the Virginian's congressional colleagues found these charges against George III more than a little ridiculous. Had George III personally made war on poor Africans? Had he personally subjected them to the horrors of the Middle Passage? Would it be useful in a document intended to make the American cause seem justifiable, even attractive, to outside observers for Congress to paint slavery—in which many of its members, including Jefferson, not to mention General George Washington, would remain invested—in such lurid colors? Did not everyone know better?

Pauline Maier says that Congress improved the committee draft in editing it, notably in excising this central paragraph.[22] Jefferson certainly disagreed. Over the following months, he sent copies of the committee version and the final version to friends, noting that they were different and evidently hoping his correspondents would endorse his version as superior.[23] Some of them energetically complied.[24] It is hard for us to decide what exactly Jefferson hoped to accomplish in this paragraph. Did he think of slavery as something George III had "obtruded" upon him? If so, did he think he was stuck with it? Here is the single passage in all of Jefferson's enormous body of surviving writings most likely to persuade us that Paul Finkelman was right and that Jefferson's pose in regard to slavery bordered on the risible. It is lucky that Congress saved him from himself.

. . .

As Congress drafted its Declaration, Jefferson looked longingly upon the Virginia Convention's process of writing and implementing the first written constitution adopted by the people's representatives in the history of the world: the Virginia Constitution of 1776. He would much have preferred to aid in that effort rather than taking the lead in drafting the document that cemented his fame. He asked Virginia's political leadership to relieve him of his congressional post.[25] Drafting the state constitution, Jefferson pleaded, "is a work of the most interesting nature and such as every individual would wish to have his voice in." Not only was it important, but "in truth it is the whole object of the present controversy; for should a bad government be instituted for us in future it had been as well to have accepted at first the bad one offered to us from beyond the water without the risk and expence of contest." No relief came. Since the state could not vote in Congress without a quorum of its delegation present, Jefferson had to stay in Philadelphia.

He did, however, write out three drafts of a state constitution.[26] In those documents, he laid out much of the reform agenda he hoped to see Virginia implement. If he had his way, the state church would be disestablished, the death penalty would be restricted only to people convicted of the worst crimes, every Virginia citizen not already in possession of substantial land would be given a share of the public lands, and all free children would be educated in public schools. White Virginians, in particular, would be made legal equals by an extensive program of reform. However, unfortunately for Jefferson, his draft made its way into the hands of George Wythe too late to be used as the basis of the new constitution.[27] Wythe told him that some few of his draft's provisions had been used, and clearly the preamble was.

Jefferson's draft constitutions mentioned blacks and slavery here and there as well. The preamble to his first draft said that George III had tried to subject Virginians to "a detestable & insupportable tyranny . . . by prompting our negroes to rise in arms among us; those very negroes whom by an inhuman use of his negative he hath <*from time to time*> refused us permission to exclude by law." This statement was rearranged slightly in his third draft's preamble. Besides blaming George III for inciting slave rebellion and keeping Virginians from halting slave imports, the Jefferson draft would have put slavery on the path to elimination. Article IV of that third draft, entitled "Rights Private and Public," included a statement that "no person hereafter coming into this country shall be held within the same in slavery under any pretext whatever." By "this country," Jefferson meant Virginia.

One could see such a policy as antislavery. Jefferson and others cast it that way. Alternatively, one could see it the way the South Carolina delegates to the Philadelphia Convention of 1787 saw Virginian George Mason's call for an end to slave imports: as a means of propping up the value of Virginians' slave property, which would fall if additional slaves were taken into the market.

In October 1776, Jefferson accepted appointment to a House of Delegates committee charged with proposing revisions to Virginia law.[28] He and others believed that the break with George III left them with a legal regime in many ways more fitted to monarchical than to republican society, and they intended to correct the situation with a thoroughgoing reform.

The five men appointed to the committee soon became three, as two legal laymen resigned from the group. That left only Jefferson and Virginia's two most prominent attorneys, his friend Edmund Pendleton and his legal mentor and fellow signer of the Declaration of Independence George Wythe. Of the three bills in the revisors' 126-bill package related to slavery and racial classification, Nos. 51, 53, and 54, the first is known to have been drafted by Jefferson and either or both of the other two may have been.[29]

The first of them, Bill No. 51, bore the title "A Bill Concerning Slaves."[30] Its chief significance lay in its first two paragraphs, which said that from that point, no one not either currently a Virginia slave or descended from a current Virginia female slave would be a slave in Virginia, that any black or mulatto transported into Virginia thereafter would be free once he had been in Virginia for a total of one year, and that if a person freed by these provisions did not depart from Virginia within a year after becoming free, he would be beyond the protection of the law. The next two sections say that slaves entering Virginia on their own initiative shall be outside the protection of the laws and that any white woman having a child by a black or mulatto must depart from Virginia or be out of the protection of the laws. It seems obvious that the point of this section of the bill was to establish rules gradually reducing the number of slaves, and of blacks generally, in Virginia. These sections, beginning with the passage out-lawing newcomer blacks and mulattos freed by the law after passage of one year, were not included in the law as ultimately adopted by the General Assembly. That the General Assembly rejected these harshly antiblack Jeffersonian proposals may perhaps be attributable to their greater compassion, or perhaps to the fact that Jefferson, unlike them, contemplated a future state of society in which all of the blacks had been freed and departed. When adopted, the bill included amendments pro-viding exceptions to the various prohibitions of importation and provi-sions for expulsion allowing Virginians to bring their own slaves from outside the state, and so forth. Where Jefferson's first priority was to impede the growth of Virginia's black population, that of the General Assembly was to respect slave property.

Thereafter, the bill bans blacks from being witnesses in legal pro-ceedings against whites. Jefferson and his colleagues could not know the irony of this provision at the time, but in 1806, while Jefferson was pres-ident, Wythe's notorious murderer got away with his crime scot-free. The only witnesses were black, the villain was white, and so no testimony was available.[31] Other provisions of the bill banned slaves from traveling out-side their masters' domains without passes, banned them from keeping "arms" or bearing them without written permission from their masters, and provided whipping as the punishment of any "negro or mulatto," not just of slaves, for various public infractions against the caste system: "riots, routs, unlawful assemblies, trespasses and seditious speeches." "He who will" was empowered by this section to carry offenders before the nearest justice of the peace.

Bill No. 53 provided a system for capturing and returning runaways, and No. 54 established one black grandparent as the test of mulatto status.[32] Historians have noted that it may well be that Jefferson's own offspring with Sally Hemings did not meet that threshold—and so were legally white. Since this bill was adopted on December 5, 1785, it was law in Virginia by the time Jefferson and Hemings returned from France to the United States in 1790. Oral tradition says that she had had one child by him by then.

Jefferson next took up the question of slavery in his one book, *Notes on the State of Virginia*.[33] The idea for his book came from a French diplomat, François Barbé-Marbois. The Frenchman, stationed in a more or less unknown USA, in 1780 sent out a set of queries to prominent men in each of the thirteen states.[34] He asked specifically about Virginia's rivers, mines, mountains, constitution, laws, manners, flora and fauna, and human inhabitants, among other things. Interestingly, one prominent scholar suggests that not the French diplomat, but instead his countryman the comte de Buffon, that day's most prominent biologist, drafted the questionnaire.[35] This possibility's fascination arises from the fact that Jefferson took the inquiry as an opportunity to write a book including, among other things, detailed attacks on some of the French naturalist's most important theories.

Besides that, Jefferson's fascinating book also includes his most detailed and extensive writings on the subjects of blacks' relationship to whites, their native abilities, and their place in American—or at least Virginian—society. They appear in two contexts: his chapter on "Laws" (Query XIV) and his essay on "Manners" (Query XVIII). It has been common for Jefferson's critics in our day to say that Jefferson cared only about slavery's negative effects on whites, which were the subject of the "Manners" chapter.[36] Yet, the "Manners" chapter's subject was peculiar Virginian manners, and Jefferson reasonably posited that whichever of their manners arose out of their practice of slaveholding would seem odd to a Frenchman, because there was no slavery in France. In "Laws," he did deal with the issue of blacks' rights, and he called slavery a serious offense to God.

As Paul Finkelman insists, *Notes on the State of Virginia* also finds Jefferson offering justifications of slavery "based on history, science, political theory, practical necessity, and, most of all, race."[37] Jefferson's arguments may have been the most influential pro-slavery arguments of the nineteenth century, which is when many prominent Americans came finally to propagating full-fledged defenses of the at-last-peculiar institution.

Because "Manners" is easily the shorter essay, we consider it first.[38] "There must," Jefferson begins, "doubtless be an unhappy influence on the manners of our people produced by the existence of slavery among us." Slavery, as he described (experienced?) it, constantly perverted masters' perceptions of themselves and of others: "The whole commerce between master and slave is a perpetual exercise of the most boisterous passions, the most unremitting despotism on one part, and degrading submissions on the other." For Jefferson, lover of nautical metaphors, "boisterous passions" came in gigantic waves, overwhelming a master.[39]

Jefferson paints a grim picture of the master's young child seeing the master vent those overwhelming passions in his dealings with his slaves. This alone ought to be enough, he says, to cause the slave owner to restrain himself. "But generally it is not sufficient." Rather, "the parent storms, the child looks on, catches the lineaments of wrath, puts on the same airs in the circle of smaller slaves, gives a loose to his worst of passions, and thus nursed, educated, and daily exercised in tyranny, cannot but be stamped by it with odious peculiarities." Summing up,

Jefferson avers that "the man must be a prodigy who can retain his manners and morals undepraved by such circumstances." This observation rings particularly ironic in light of our understanding of Jefferson's subsequent relationship with one of his slaves, Sally Hemings.

From these teachings about slavery's corrupting effect on slaveholders, Jefferson proceeds directly to a stern judgment upon the statesmen of slaveholding societies: "with what execration should the statesman be loaded," he says, "who permitting one half the citizens thus to trample on the rights of the other, transforms those into despots, and these into enemies, destroys the morals of one part, and the amor patriæ of the other." Note that although Section 1 of the Virginia Declaration of Rights of 1776 had been altered in the Convention that drafted it to imply that slaves were not citizens, Jefferson here assumes that they are citizens. Some scholars have treated every instance in which Jefferson's account of slavery in the *Notes* differs from his later views as evidence that he intended to deceive his European audience into thinking he was more liberal than he actually was. Perhaps deception is at work in this part of the "Manners" chapter. On the other hand, it is possible that Jefferson—who had not participated in drafting the Declaration of Rights—simply had not yet reached his mature understanding of this question.

Jefferson next lamented that "with the morals of the people, their industry also is destroyed." The reason was that in a hot place where slavery existed, no man would do physical work who could make a slave do it. "This is so true," he noted, "that of the proprietors of slaves a very small proportion indeed are ever seen to labour." Here was a true curse on a slaveholding people, in Jefferson's mind, as we will see hereafter.

The climax of Jefferson's little antislavery essay came, surprisingly, in a theological evaluation of the situation. One could search in vain for any other such passage in all of the tremendous body of Jefferson's surviving writings. "And can the liberties of a nation be thought secure," he asked rhetorically, "when we have removed their only firm basis, a conviction in the minds of the people that these liberties are the gift of God? That they are not to be violated but with his wrath?" As if the answer had been in doubt, he hurried to the awesome conclusion: "Indeed I tremble for my country [Virginia] when I reflect that God is just: this his justice cannot sleep for ever: that considering numbers, nature and natural means only, a revolution of the wheel of fortune, an exchange of situations, is among possible events: that it may be probable by supernatural interference!"

Not only was slaveholding unjust, but God might intervene to put down the whites and install the black race in the dominant position the whites had assumed. The direct intervention of the deity Jefferson invoked here is unique in all of his writings.[40] Generally, he mocked the idea of a god who intervened in the world. Here he used the idea of such a god to illustrate how truly irreconcilable with the good and true he held slavery to be. So what would he do about it?

"It is impossible," he wrote, "to be temperate and to pursue this subject through the various considerations of policy, of morals, of history natural and civil. We must be contented to hope they will force their way into every one's mind." Not some grand personal gesture, not some heroic example, but . . . hoping people changed their minds. He went on to say that he had seen evidence of progress in this direction since the revolution, then ongoing, had begun. "The spirit of the master is abating, that of the slave rising from the dust." What evidence he had for this claim, Jefferson left to inference. In time, he would admit that he had not actually seen any such evidence by 1780, or even prior to 1814.

Here is the best evidence that the slavery passages in *Notes on the State of Virginia* were intended to give a false impression. If there was to be "a total emancipation . . . with the consent of the masters, rather than by their extirpation," Jefferson had no more reason to think the day was near than he had had when Richard Bland had suffered the slings and arrows of outraged colleagues in the House of Burgesses over a decade earlier.

Thus, Query XVIII: "Manners." Far more extensive commentary on blacks, black-white relations, and the future of Virginia is to be found in

Query XIV: "Laws."[41] The chapter begins with a description of Virginia's legal system—its courts, etc.—before proceeding to a description of the laws. Six pages into the twenty-page chapter, Jefferson notes that "many of the laws which were in force during the monarchy being relative merely to that form of government, or inculcating principles inconsistent with republicanism, the first assembly which met after the establishment of the commonwealth appointed a committee to revise the whole code." In this context, he mentions in passing the proposal "to make slaves [who had been treated as real estate in colonial Virginia, thus under the doctrine of primogeniture all falling to the oldest son] distributable among the next of kin, as other moveables." After a couple of other proposals, he lists the one "to emancipate all slaves born after passing the act."

The more southerly northern states—New Jersey, New York, Pennsylvania, Connecticut, and Rhode Island—ultimately abolished slavery through this slow means. As Jefferson explained, the bill would have freed male slaves at age twenty-one and females at eighteen. We may note that since the policy would not have affected the status of people already held in slavery in the Old Dominion, slavery would have been slow to disappear even if the bill had become law. Which it did not. It was not even proposed.

As Jefferson explains it, "The bill reported by the revisors does not itself contain this proposition; but an amendment containing it was prepared, to be offered to the legislature whenever the bill should be taken up." Jefferson says the plan was for slaves to be taken from their parents at a certain age, then educated at the public expense. Once they had reached maturity, "they should be colonized to such place as the circumstances of the time would render most proper."

Jefferson's description assumes that white Virginians owed prospective freedmen a debt. As he explains, the contemplated amendment essentially required that the soon-to-be freedmen receive the same kind of provisions upon reaching maturity as indentured servants received upon completing their indentures: "arms, implements of household and of the handicraft arts, seeds, pairs of the useful domestic animals,

&c." They would be able to stand on their own two feet as agricultural laborers or even as yeoman farmers. Beyond that, Virginia ought "to declare them a free and independant people, and extend to them our alliance and protection, till they shall have acquired strength." As Peter S. Onuf explains, Jefferson "did know, with as much certainty as his own experience and observation could authorize, that African-American slaves constituted a *distinct nation*."[42]

This deportation of the formerly enslaved would cause substantial difficulties for the white people who remained behind, as Jefferson understood it. Therefore, additional white laborers must be recruited to take the blacks' former place. He contemplated "proper encouragements," but exactly what could have persuaded free men to accept slaves' place willingly is not explained. Of more pressing interest is the issue Jefferson actually does take up at this point: why the freedmen ought to be deported in the first place.

After all, if, as Jefferson hoped, Virginia was to remain an agricultural society, would it not be best to keep the current laborers to perform future labors? Why send them abroad and immediately try to replace them with someone else? Jefferson's answer is the most famous statement about race relations in the founding period: "Deep rooted prejudices entertained by the whites; ten thousand recollections, by the blacks, of the injuries they have sustained; new provocations; the real distinctions which nature has made; and many other circumstances, will divide us into parties, and produce convulsions which will probably never end but in the extermination of the one or the other race."

To unpack this sentence is a difficult task. We begin by noting that Jefferson generalizes to "the whites" a set of "prejudices" that, as we will see, he shared. He imputes to "the blacks," meaning the slaves, grievances impossible to overcome. He thinks "nature" "has made" "real distinctions" impossible for each race . . . well, no, impossible solely for the whites to ignore. He forecasts that in case an attempt is made to construct a multiracial society, cataclysmic race war must be the result.

The idea of whites' prejudices seizes our attention. In the book, as we have seen, "Laws" precedes "Manners." We have considered "Manners" first for the light it casts upon "Laws." Jefferson stated in "Manners" that all who were raised in slave-owning were similarly affected by it. That effect, he lamented, was strongly negative. Essentially, it made masters unfit for republican citizenship by habituating them to command. While Jefferson thought this experience universal, one of his closest political collaborators would argue powerfully that Jefferson erred. According to John Taylor of Caroline, the leading Jeffersonian publicist of the 1790s, the sponsor in the House of Delegates of the Virginia Resolutions of 1798, a three-time senator, and a prolific critic of Chief Justice John Marshall thereafter, owning slaves affected his passions barely at all. As Taylor told it, since they were so far below their masters, slaves' misbehavior provoked the master no more than the misbehavior of livestock.[43] In fact, Taylor thought that the relationship between master-class children and slaves could be a tender one, and he insisted that whites' observation of slaves' misdeeds could help to instill virtue in little masters.[44]

Taylor's view, not Jefferson's, became the basis of much southern thought on these questions in the two generations after the two died in the 1820s. If Taylor's understanding of the slave system appealed to many literate Virginians, how do we account for Jefferson's description of slaveholding's effects? One hazards the guess that Jefferson generalized from his own experience, assuming as many do that others' minds responded to specific situations as his, or those of masters he had known, had.

Interestingly, Taylor concluded his consideration of Jefferson's *Notes* by endorsing colonization. "If England and America would erect and foster a settlement of free negroes in some fertile part of Africa," he opined, "it would soon subsist by its own energies. Slavery might then be gradually re-exported, and philanthropy gratified by a slow reanimation of the virtue, religion and liberty of the negroes."[45] Taylor did not want his reader to think "that I approve of slavery because I do not aggravate its evils."[46]

Jefferson also foretold that in case of a general emancipation and elevation of the former slaves to some kind of equality with the former masters, a race war would result. Jefferson did not know that within two decades, the French colony of Saint Domingue—now Haiti—would be convulsed by slave rebellion. He thus did not know that over time, his assertions in "Laws" about the feasibility of a biracial society would come to seem more persuasive to his fellow southerners, particularly in Virginia. None of them knew what we know in the early twenty-first century: that blacks in America would answer their subjugation with remarkable support for American ideals and a notable forbearance. Despite the white misdeeds to which Jefferson referred, the race war never came.

Jefferson next considered various differences between white and black people. He started by noting that "the first difference which strikes us is that of colour." Whether this distinction's explanation lay in the structure of the skin or in some "secretion" unique to blacks, "is this difference of no importance?" The rhetorical effect of making this statement in the form of a question was to avoid taking responsibility for it. Jefferson followed with two more such questions, the first floating the idea that the difference in color was "the foundation of a greater or less share of beauty in the two races," the second elaborating by pointing to what he considered "that eternal monotony . . . that immoveable veil of black which covers all the emotions of" black people.

How important was this to Jefferson? He expanded: "Add to these, flowing hair, a more elegant symmetry of form, their own judgment in favour of the whites, declared by their preference of them, as uniformly as is the preference of the Oran-ootan for the black women over those of his own species." By the time Jefferson wrote this, the hypothesis that as each animal on the Great Chain of Being longed for the next one above itself, orangutans preferred black females and black males preferred white females, had been exploded.[47] Yet here he was peddling it. Having broached this baseline of racialist thinking, Jefferson went further in a sexual vein, saying, "The circumstance of superior beauty, is thought worthy attention in the propagation of our horses, dogs, and other domestic animals; why not in that of man?"

Warming to his subject, Jefferson elaborated on the physical differences between whites and blacks. Each difference, to his mind, favored the whites. "They [he meant blacks] have less hair on the face and body. They secrete less by the kidnies, and more by the glands of the skin, which gives them a very strong and disagreeable odor. This greater degree of transpiration renders them more tolerant of heat, and less so of cold, than the whites." Besides that, "they seem to require less sleep. A black, after hard labour through the day, will be induced by the slightest amusements to sit up till midnight, or later, though knowing he must be out with the first dawn of the morning."

Jefferson's letters are virtually never introspective. He seems to have observed only what was around him, never himself. This evaluation of blacks' smell and their sleeping habits, if produced by a master, could only have come from a master with essentially no self-awareness. (The passage is almost enough to force us to the realization that "Manners" was not autobiographical after all.) Completely absent from the entire passage are the ideas that perhaps slaves' body odor, if notable, had some relationship to the hard labor to which Jefferson and his white relatives, friends, and acquaintances customarily and consistently put them. So too blacks' supposed habit of working hard "through the day," then fraternizing well into the night despite knowing they would soon be rising early again. The only obvious alternative to that habit would have been just to drudge away for Jefferson all day, sleep regularly, and drudge away for Jefferson all the next day—one day after another, world without end, amen. Yes, there were slack times in a plantation's year, but black community is what made slaves' lives worth living—not, say, building and rebuilding Monticello, building the University of Virginia, constructing Montpelier's doorway, starting Jefferson's fire, or tending his crops. Jefferson's self-centeredness at this point is apt to leave the modern reader slack-jawed.

Jean-Antoine Houdon, the age's greatest sculptor, here captures Jefferson's personality more powerfully than any other portraitist ever would. Houdon also made plasters of numerous other prominent Americans for Jefferson. Jean-Antoine Houdon, *Thomas Jefferson*. 1789. Stone; Marble. © 2017 Museum of Fine Arts, Boston.

John Trumbull, son of a Connecticut governor, painted depictions of four notable scenes from the American Revolution. Jefferson dominates this, Trumbull's most famous painting. John Trumbull, *The Declaration of Independence, July 4, 1776*. Oil on Canvas. Courtesy Yale University Art Gallery.

Jefferson hoped that Virginian, and eventually American, public buildings would be based on ancient models. He designed the Virginia Capitol while away in France. **Virginia Capitol (photograph). Courtesy Library of Virginia.**

Here we see Vice President Jefferson as leader of the "Republican interest," as he called it. **Rembrandt Peale,** *Thomas Jefferson*. **1800. Oil on Canvas. © 2017 White House Collection/White House Historical Association.**

While Jefferson symbolized the
Republican Party, John Taylor
was its chief theoretician in the
1790s. He also sponsored the
Virginia Resolutions of 1798
in the House of Delegates and
wrote several anti–Marshall
Court books in later years—to
Jefferson's delight. **John Taylor
of Caroline. Oil on Canvas.
Courtesy Library of Virginia.**

Here we see Jefferson as he looked in
retirement, when he devoted much of
his energy to complaining about neo-
federalism and founding the University
of Virginia. **Giuseppe Valaperta,**
Thomas Jefferson **(1743–1826). 1816.
Bas Relief. Courtesy Collection of New
York Historical Society.**

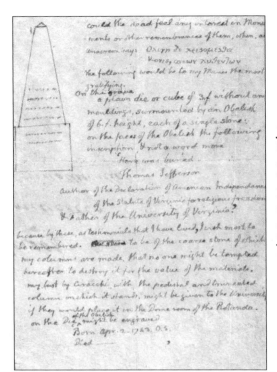

Jefferson took great care to shape his historical image, including sketching his own gravestone. The three achievements for which he wished to be remembered all reflected his desire to be seen as an Enlightenment leader. **Thomas Jefferson. Epitaph. c. March 1826. Courtesy Library of Congress.**

Edward Coles responded to Jefferson's suggestion that he give fellow young Virginians an example of a good slave owner by instead emigrating to Illinois. This depiction of the moment he freed his slaves adorns a wall of the Illinois State Capitol. **1819. Courtesy Illinois State Capitol.**

This heroic image of the leaders of the Voyage of Discovery stands in a prominent place in Charlottesville, Virginia—Jefferson's and Lewis's hometown. **Lewis and Clark and Sacagawea statue, Charlottesville, Virginia, erected in 1919. Courtesy Marika K. Gutzman.**

As they progressed westward, Lewis and Clark were to smooth American relations with Indian tribes by bestowing medallions depicting President Jefferson upon Indian leaders. This is one of those medals. **Jefferson peace medallion, obverse and reverse. Courtesy the National Park Service.**

At the center of his "academickal village" was to be Jefferson's Rotunda. Patterned on the Pantheon in Rome, it is if anything substantially more beautiful. **Courtesy University of Virginia.**

A prominent planter and military figure, John Hartwell Cocke was also a leading Virginia reformer. Besides joining Jefferson on the original University of Virginia Board of Visitors, Cocke privately lamented the influence of Jefferson's having had a relationship with a slave woman. **William James Hubard, *John Hartwell Cocke*. 1836. Oil on Canvas. Courtesy Collection of the Fralin Museum of Art at the University of Virginia.**

Joseph Carrington Cabell served in the Virginia Senate as the University of Virginia's chief legislative patron. Besides that, he joined Jefferson on the university's original Board of Visitors. **Louis Mathieu Didier Guillaume, *Joseph Carrington Cabell*. 1856. Oil on Canvas. Courtesy Collection of the Fralin Museum of Art at the University of Virginia.**

This is the old Jefferson whom the University of Virginia's first students would have known. Thomas Sully, *Portrait of Thomas Jefferson*, 1821–1830. Oil on Canvas. Courtesy Collection of the American Philosophical Society.

Jefferson next gives black men a backhanded compliment. "They are at least as brave" as whites, he concedes, but he guesses that "this may perhaps proceed from a want of foresight, which prevents their seeing a danger till it be present." They were brave, in other words, but the explanation lay in their lack of intelligence. As if that were not bad enough, "they are more ardent after their female: but love seems with them to be more an eager desire, than a tender delicate mixture of sentiment and sensation." He did not think to adduce any particular evidence in support of this harsh judgment.

"Their griefs," Jefferson adjudged coldly, "are transient. Those numberless afflictions, which render it doubtful whether heaven has given life to us in mercy or in wrath, are less felt, and sooner forgotten with them. In general, their existence appears to participate more of sensation than reflection." Here we must note that Jefferson lived at the cusp of the modern period in the history of human sentimentality.[48] His slaves, and other slaves he knew, did not. What we take to be common emotional attachment seems to have been markedly different for premodern people. Besides that, however, Jefferson and the members of his class denied some of the common attachments, such as of parents to children and of one spouse to another, to their slaves. Enslaved children could be sold away from their parents, and one spouse might be moved away from another. If slaves learned to harden their hearts, a description of them based on this fact makes a weak basis for an evaluation of their character.

Jefferson thought that blacks were more prone to sleep when not entertained or employed than were whites. This was predictable, he said, because "an animal whose body is at rest, and who does not reflect, must be disposed to sleep of course." If blacks seemed not to exercise their mental faculties to any great extent, the reason lay in the supposed facts that while their memory was on a par with whites', they were "in reason much inferior, as I think one could scarcely be found capable of tracing and comprehending the investigations of Euclid." (No one drew his attention to the fact that a person who was legally required to be kept illiterate was unlikely to read Euclid—or anything else. What effect this passage had on Jefferson's initial, European audience is difficult to say. Since Jefferson allowed elsewhere in the book that Virginia had no public schools, at least someone must have realized that surely enslaved blacks could not read. Historians' best estimate is that the literacy rate among white men in Virginia was about 50 percent.)

Jefferson, ever liberal in his allowances to his African-descended subjects, says, "It be unfair to follow them to Africa for this investigation. We will consider them here, on the same stage with the whites, and where the facts are not apocryphal on which a judgment is to be formed." Seemingly oblivious to the fact that he had not heretofore made such allowances, he adds that "it will be right to make great allowances for the difference of condition, of education, of conversation, of the sphere in which they move." Yes, of the millions who had made the Middle Passage, most had "been confined to tillage," but many could have taken advantage of the presence of their cultured masters. "All have lived in countries where the arts and sciences are cultivated to a considerable degree, and have had before their eyes samples of the best works from abroad." Indians, lacking these wonderful advantages, could carve, draw, and orate with great skill, "but never yet could I find that a black had uttered a thought above the level of plain narration; never seen even an elementary trait of painting or sculpture." Notice Jefferson's non sequitur: free Indians had achieved some artistic successes, yet enslaved blacks had not. Here he at once praised the indigenous Americans and slandered the blacks.

On and on Jefferson goes in the same fashion, granting that blacks are reputed for musical sense but noting that "whether they will be equal to the composition of a more extended run of melody, or of complicated harmony, is yet to be proved"; asserting that misery prompts people to poetry, and then noting that their abundant misery seems not to have moved blacks to poetry; asserting that blacks' love "is ardent, but it kindles the senses only, not the imagination." Turning to a famous black contemporary, Jefferson offers the back of his hand: "Religion indeed has produced a Phyllis Whatley [*sic*]," he says, "but it could not produce a poet. The compositions published under her name are beneath the dignity of criticism." In their day, Phillis Wheatley's poems were widely admired. Why Jefferson scorned them is unclear. In the next passage, Jefferson levels withering criticism at the work of another contemporary black writer, Ignatius Sancho, before expressing doubt that "the letters published under his name" were really products of his pen.

"The improvement of the blacks in body and mind, in the first instance of their mixture with the whites, has been observed by every one, and proves that their inferiority is not the effect merely of their condition of life," Jefferson claims. The conditions under which slaves among the Romans lived were far worse. Besides that, Roman slaves were segregated by sex. On the other hand, American slaves "multiply as fast as the free inhabitants." Cato the Elder, he says, taught that one must sell his old, exhausted slaves, and this did not happen in America. Too, Romans commonly exposed slaves they thought terminally ill by putting them on "the island of Æsculapius, in the Tyber," and again, American slaves did not have to fear such a fate. Roman law required that testimony be extracted from slaves by torture, while American law simply excluded slave testimony. These and other cases in which American slavery supposedly weighed more lightly on the slaves than its ancient Mediterranean antecedent serve Jefferson as buildup to a list of several Roman slaves he classed among the "rarest artists. They excelled too in science, insomuch as to be usually employed as tutors to their master's children. Epictetus, Diogenes, Phaedon, Terence, and Phædrus, were slaves." One might have expected, he implies, that their intellectual attainments would be as tightly circumscribed as those of black slaves at Monticello circa 1781. "But they were of the race of whites. It is not their condition then, but nature, which has produced the distinction."

Seemingly Jefferson here has at last leveled a categorical judgment. He proceeds to say, however, that the question "whether further observation will or will not verify the conjecture, that nature has been less bountiful to them in the endowments of the head" remains an open question. He defends them in the matter of their seeming disposition to criminality: "That disposition to theft with which they have been branded, must be ascribed to their situation, and not to any depravity of the moral sense." After all, Jefferson reasoned, where the law did not respect a man's right to property, he could be expected to develop disrespect for others'. He quotes Homer saying "whatever day Makes man a slave, takes half his worth away," but then notes that several Homeric slaves demonstrated "the most rigid integrity" and other excellent moral qualities. His explanation: "the slaves of which Homer speaks were whites."

Jefferson now comes to his conclusion. Like the rest of this extended consideration of blacks' abilities—a long digression in a chapter on "Laws"—it is at once diffident and negative. General conclusions about physical reality require many observations, he says, "even where the subject may be submitted to the Anatomical knife, to Optical glasses, to analysis by fire, or by solvents." When the issue is a faculty of the human mind—indeed, a quality of an entire race—and when "our conclusion would degrade a whole race of men from the rank in the scale of beings which their Creator may perhaps have given them," circumspection is of the essence. "I advance it therefore as a suspicion only," he concluded, "that the blacks, whether originally a distinct race, or made distinct by time and circumstances, are inferior to the whites in the endowments both of body and mind." Nature having made the races different, according to Jefferson, the devotee of natural history must maintain them that way. Thus, Americans faced a more daunting task than the Romans had. The Romans had but to free a slave, who then "might mix with, without staining the blood of his master." In North America, the slave, "when freed, . . . is to be removed beyond the reach of mixture." To Jefferson's mind, "science" required colonization. Otherwise, free whites and freed blacks might make mixed-race babies, and that was just too much to contemplate.

Jefferson came back to the general issue of race over and over in the forty-four years that remained to him, yet his position remained remarkably close to the one he elaborated in *Notes on the State of Virginia*. Slaves, and blacks in general, were probably mentally inferior to whites. He would have liked to be persuaded that they were equal to whites; seeming evidence that they were capable of intellectual feats on a par with whites', however, always left him unpersuaded. Instead, he repeatedly said that he doubted such evidence as was presented to him actually had been produced by unassisted blacks.

He never grew inured to slaveholding, either. Time after time, he conceded the injustice of his owning other men. In his youth and early middle age, he held out hope that a positive turn in his fortunes would make possible the ultimate disentanglement of his fate from slavery's. As he put it in 1786, "I am miserable till I shall owe not a shilling: the moment that shall be the case I shall feel myself at liberty to do something for the comfort of my slaves."[49] By the time he left federal politics in 1809, however, this possibility seemed unlikely. The decline in his personal fortunes resulting from his self-indulgent spending habits, the collapse of the market for tobacco, and the bankruptcy of a political ally for whom he had cosigned a large loan finally made this impossible.

In 1786, Jefferson's close ally James Madison worked to have the Virginia General Assembly adopt the reform program Jefferson and the other revisors had advocated in 1779. The omission of the provision for slavery's elimination drew French commentary, and Jefferson intervened to absolve the legislature of blame.[50] Although he and Wythe had both been absent from the House of Delegates at the time—he in France, Wythe in the judicial branch—there had been members perfectly desirous and capable of raising the issue. "But they saw," he said, "that the moment of doing it with success was not yet arrived, and that an unsuccesful effort, as too often happens, would only rivet still closer the chains of bondage, and retard the moment of delivery to this oppressed description of men." The time would come, but it had not yet. Pushing off responsibility for slavery onto his unconverted countrymen, Jefferson added, "What a stupendous, what an incomprehensible machine is man! Who can endure toil, famine, stripes, imprisonment or death itself in vindication of his own liberty, and the next moment be deaf to all those motives whose power supported him thro' his trial, and inflict on his fellow men a bondage, one hour of which is fraught with more misery than ages of that which he rose in rebellion to oppose." Lest one think he might soon manumit his own bondmen, he continued by saying, "But we must await with patience the workings of an overruling providence, and hope that that is preparing the deliverance of these our suffering brethren. When the measure of their tears shall be full, when their groans shall have involved heaven itself in darkness, doubtless a god of justice will awaken to their distress, and by diffusing light and liberality among their oppressors, or at length by his exterminating thunder, manifest his attention to the things of this world, and that they are not left to the guidance of a blind fatality." God would soften the hearts of other white Virginians, and until then, waiting was all one could do.

If God was going to soften white Virginians' hearts, perhaps one way for Him to accomplish this task would be to provide examples of blacks performing notable intellectual feats. As in *Notes on the State of Virginia*, Jefferson hoped to see such evidence. Benjamin Banneker, whom Jefferson had made the first black civilian employee of the federal government by hiring him for the commission to survey the District of Columbia, contacted Jefferson about his intellectual achievements.[51]

Banneker told Jefferson that he had caught wind of Jefferson's reputation as an *ami des noirs*. He confided in Jefferson that his father had been born in Africa and had been enslaved, but that the younger Banneker had avoided that fate. White Americans, Banneker noted, had pledged their faith in the doctrine that "all men are created equal," and yet they continued to hold blacks in slavery. Ingeniously, Banneker used the word "you" in leveling this allegation, playing on the obscurity of the word—

whether it was singular or plural—so that one reading the letter the first time cannot tell whether he is saying that Jefferson himself had stated that principle but continued to hold slaves or is saying that Americans generally make the claim and do the deed, but finally he falls into the plural usage.

His reason for writing this epistle, Banneker says, is to send Jefferson a gift. Banneker made an almanac, carefully calculating the lunar cycles, the solstices, and so forth. Perhaps guessing that Jefferson would be skeptical about the identity of this work's actual author, Banneker says that although he could have waited to send Jefferson a published copy of the almanac, he has sent a handwritten manuscript to remove any doubt that it is his work.

As was his custom, Jefferson responded in an indulgent mood.[52] After conveying the requisite thanks, Jefferson hurried to add that "no body wishes more than I do to see such proofs as you exhibit, that nature has given to our black brethren, talents equal to those of the other colours of men, and that the appearance of a want of them is owing merely to the degraded condition of their existence both in Africa and America." He also claimed the first rank among those who hoped to see adopted a system for ameliorating blacks' condition. Besides that, he told Banneker he had sent the almanac to the marquis de Condorcet, "Secretary of the Academy of sciences at Paris, and member of the Philanthropic society," so that the reputation of "your whole colour" might have the benefit of this accomplishment.

Jefferson wrote to Condorcet, a prominent Enlightenment figure and French revolutionary politician, that very day.[53] His enthusiasm was notable. "I am happy to be able to inform you," he began, "that we have now in the United States a *negro*, the son of a black man born in Africa, and of a black woman born in the United States, who is a very respectable Mathematician. I procured him to be employed under one of our chief directors in laying out the new federal city on the Patowmac, and in the intervals of his leisure, while on that work, he made an Almanac for the next year, which he sent me in his own handwriting, and which I inclose to you." Besides this, Jefferson gushed, "I have seen very elegant solutions of Geometrical problems by him. Add to this that he is a very worthy and respectable member of society. He is a free man. I shall be delighted to see these instances of moral eminence so multiplied as to prove that the want of talents observed in them is merely the effect of their degraded condition, and not proceeding from any difference in the structure of the parts on which intellect depends."

Historian Winthrop Jordan notes the confusion Banneker's impressive achievements wrought in Jefferson's mind.[54] "Moral eminence" had nothing to do with intellect in the Jeffersonian understanding. Jefferson's reference to the moral faculty, with which he believed that all men were equally endowed, shows him perhaps unconsciously resisting the conclusion that this son of an African native had mental faculties on a par with those of whites.

Jefferson proved similarly resistant to evidence of black intellectual attainment when presented by whites. So, in response to receiving from the Abbé Grégoire a copy of his *De la littérature des nègres, ou Recherches sur leurs facultés intellectuelles, leurs qualités morales et leur littérature* [*On Blacks' Literature, or Researches on Their Intellectual Faculties, Their Moral Qualities, and Their Literature*] (1808), President Jefferson wrote to the author somewhat enthusiastically.[55] Jefferson began by saying, as he had to Banneker, that "no person living wishes more sincerely than I do, to see a complete refutation of the doubts I have myself entertained and expressed on the grade of understanding allotted to them by nature, and to find that in this respect they are on a par with ourselves." His skepticism on that score, he said, had been based on "personal observation on the limited sphere of my own State," and in Virginia, slavery meant that "the opportunities for the developement of their genius was not favorable, and those of exercising it still less so."

Jefferson insisted that he had adjudged blacks inferior in mind "with great hesitation." As a political matter, he hastened to add, native intellect should have no bearing: "whatever be their degree of talent it is no measure of their rights. Because Sr. I. Newton was superior to others in understanding he was not therefore Lord of the person or property of others." Yet, blacks' reputation for intelligence was "gaining daily in the Opinions of nations, & hopeful advances are making towards their reestablishment on an equal footing with the other colours of the human family." Grégoire had done Jefferson a service through "the many instances you have enabled me to observe of respectable intelligence in the race of men, which cannot fail to have effect in hastening the day of their relief."

While polite to this prominent Enlightenment figure who, considering Jefferson to be a fellow citizen of the Republic of Letters, had shared his findings with the American, Jefferson criticized him angrily in a letter to the Connecticut poet Joel Barlow.[56] "He wrote to me . . . ," Jefferson said of the Abbé, "on the doubts I had expressed five or six & twenty years ago, in the Notes on Virginia, as to the grade of understanding of the negroes, & he sent me his book on the literature of the negroes." While Jefferson confided that he had given the Frenchman "a very soft answer," his appraisal of Grégoire's book to Barlow dripped contempt. "His credulity," Jefferson wrote, "has made him gather up every story he could find of men of colour (without distinguishing whether black, or of what degree of mixture) however slight the mention, or light the authority on which they are quoted." Not only was the authorship of some works in Grégoire's collection dubious, Jefferson meant, but the editor had not even bothered to distinguish among authors purely black and those with various degrees of white ancestry. What Jefferson meant here was that racial "science" of the kind to which Jefferson subscribed held that blacks' intelligence was apt to be greater as the proportion of white "blood" rose, so that one would expect to find more literary merit in works by people of mostly white ancestry than in those of purely black people.

These ruminations predictably brought the 100 percent black Banneker to mind. Jefferson sank to the challenge: "the whole do not amount in point of evidence, to what we know ourselves of Banneker. We know he had spherical trigonometry enough to make almanacs [by this point, Banneker had followed up the 1791 almanac he had sent Jefferson with at least five more years' worth[57]], but not without the suspicion of aid from Ellicot, who was his neighbor & friend, & never missed an opportunity of puffing him." The only known ground of this "suspicion" is that Banneker was black, and so the burden of proof in any dispute about his intelligence lay upon him and his advocates.

Jefferson added that he had "a long letter from Banneker which shews him to have had a mind of very common stature indeed." Unlike Barlow, we need not take Jefferson's word on this. We have ready access to Jefferson's correspondence. Although Banneker's sole letter to Jefferson is too lengthy to reproduce here, the curious reader with access to the Internet can judge for himself.[58] It certainly seems the product of a more cultivated mind than Jefferson admitted.

Despite again slighting evidence of black intellectual achievement, Jefferson continued to cling to a nuanced position. "as to Bishop Gregoire," he said, "I wrote him, as you have done, a very soft answer. It was impossible for doubt to have been more tenderly or hesitatingly expressed than that was in the Notes of Virginia, and nothing was or is farther from my intentions than to enlist myself as the champion of a fixed opinion, where I have only expressed a doubt." Besides, there was a virtual laboratory experiment under way: "S. Domingo will, in time, throw light on the question."

The fears of interracial war Jefferson expressed in *Notes on the State of Virginia* reflected a pervasive attitude among American slave owners, and not only in Virginia.[59] Even today, stately homes in Charleston, South Carolina's historic district commonly have spiked barriers atop the walls erected to serve the purpose performed by fences in today's America. Periodically, rumors of slave plots racked each of the chief American slave societies, from the Chesapeake to the Lowcountry, across the Deep South to Natchez, New Orleans, and beyond. Not only the master class, but hostile outsiders considered cataclysmic slave rebellion a possibility. It remained to John Brown to try to spark it from the white side of the color line in 1859. How important Brown's effort was to driving southerners out of the Union in 1860–1861 is impossible to say, but it certainly played a role.[60]

Long before Brown, however, in the heyday of Jefferson's political career and influence, Jefferson's theory received validation: slaves in the French colony of Saint Domingue launched the only successful slave uprising in the history of the Western Hemisphere. Just think of the coincidence: slavery had existed from time immemorial, all over the world, and yet the sole successful slave uprising began while Thomas Jefferson was George Washington's secretary of state, less than a decade after he wrote his *Notes* and a mere handful of years after he published them.

As the Haitian Revolution of 1791–1804 progressed, many whites fled the island colony for the North American mainland. Some brought their slaves with them. They told tales of the most extreme barbarity, thus seemingly stoking fears of the likelihood of similar events in America's slave states.[61] The Haitian Revolution concluded with extermination of the remaining white residents, giving flesh to Jefferson's greatest fears.[62]

As America's foreign minister, then ultimately as its chief executive, Jefferson was at the forefront of policy-making concerning Haiti. Responsibility for refusing Haitian leaders' proffer of an alliance between the Western Hemisphere's only two republics rests ultimately with him. Instead of befriending the blacks, the Washington administration—with Jefferson as secretary of state—sent French planters $700,000 (a princely sum in a day when the federal government's annual budget was in the low millions) to try to put down the revolt. As president, Jefferson first scuttled the good relations with the slave rebels established by his Massachusetts predecessor John Adams, then in 1806 got Congress to suspend trade with the black republic.[63] Although he had realpolitik motives as well, Jefferson's prime motive, to borrow a phrase from a Frenchman he admired, was "pour encourager les autres"—to give an example to slaves in the United States.[64] Jefferson held that it simply would not do for American slaves to see a successful black republic established through slave rebellion very near the American coast. The 1806 law was succeeded by the famous Embargo of 1807, which continued the policy to the end of Jefferson's presidency. Haiti remained unrecognized by America for decades thereafter.[65]

Jefferson retired temporarily from public office in 1793, yet he continued an extensive correspondence. One interesting exchange involved a Virginia Quaker named Robert Pleasants. As was typical of Quakers, Pleasants was embarked on the project of educating blacks. Enclosing his own plan, he asked Jefferson for the former governor's thoughts on the matter.[66]

Jefferson replied that he had drafted a Bill for the More General Diffusion of Knowledge, and that it might easily be amended to satisfy Pleasants's desires.[67] "Very small alterations," Jefferson confided, "would make it embrace the object of your paper, it's effect would be general, and the means for carrying it on would be certain and permanent. Permit me therefore to suggest to you the substitution of that as a more general and certain means of providing for the instruction of the slaves, and more desireable as they would in the course of it be mixed with those of free condition." Pleasants had contemplated educating some black slaves separately, but Jefferson held that they ought to be educated alongside free ones. "Whether, for their happiness, it should extend beyond those destined to be free, is questionable. Ignorance and despotism seem made for each other." Perhaps only those destined to be free ought to be educated; enlightenment could only leave slaves more unhappy.

Jefferson won election to the presidency in the House of Representatives early in 1801. The House resolved the tied election of 1800, in which the pre–Twelfth Amendment Constitution's provisions for election of the president and vice president had left Jefferson and his running mate Aaron

Burr tied in the electoral college.[68] Not only did the election lead to serious divisions within the Republican Party, but the venomous public disputation associated with it coaxed Virginia slaves to rebellion.

Thinking this was at last their chance to throw off their shackles, because numerous white men (so the partisan Virginia newspapers told them) sympathized with slaves, an indeterminate number of bondmen joined in a plot spearheaded by Gabriel "Prosser" to overthrow the system.[69] Only the coincidence of the heaviest rainstorm in a century with the planned insurrection thwarted the careful plan to seize the Richmond armory, hand out the weapons to fellow slaves, and establish black rule in Richmond.

The first slaves tried for participation in the plot received full due process, including legal representation by some of the foremost members of Virginia's bar. Convicts, including ultimately Gabriel himself, were hanged. Yet, as the executions proliferated, Jefferson's ally Governor James Monroe sensed political danger. Surely it did not look good heading into the 1800 election for the capital city of the main Republican state to be hanging numbers of slaves. Although Monroe had moved the hangings outside the city, he still thought there might be negative political repercussions. Jefferson too believed there had been hangings enough. In the end, many common participants were transported outside Virginia as punishment.

Once President Jefferson had been safely sworn in, the Virginia General Assembly considered the question how to prevent such things from happening again. Monroe wrote President Jefferson on June 15, 1801, conveying a resolution of the General Assembly calling for acquisition of land outside the Commonwealth "to which persons obnoxious to the laws or dangerous to the peace of society" could be sent.[70] He explained that this seemed more humane than killing them, as current law arguably required.

Monroe noted that the resolutions had not specified whether the place should be within or outside the USA, and he added that although probably a place in the country's vacant western lands had been contemplated, in case "a friendly power" offered a place outside the country, the General Assembly might find it congenial. Monroe dared go further: one resolution referred to people whose presence might be dangerous to society as among those whom the Commonwealth might like to deport. The governor said that this did not by its terms seem limited only to convicts, but could also extend to blacks generally, whose presence already had caused the Old Dominion trouble and likely eventually would cause it substantially more.

Slavery, he said, was "an existing evil which commenced under our colonial system [that is, was started by the British], with which we [Virginians] are not properly chargeable, or if at all not in the present degree, and we acknowledge the extreme difficulty of remedying it." Before it could arrive at the best solution to the problem, the legislature needed the broadest choice of options. To that end, it needed a place to which slaves might be sent. He hoped Jefferson would undertake the task of finding such a place, "which in a peculiar degree involves the future peace, tranquility and happiness of the good people of this Commonwealth."

Jefferson answered him more than five months later.[71] He began by noting the ill repercussions likely to result from any public disclosure of his letter's contents. Having instructed Monroe to keep what Jefferson said to himself, Jefferson proceeded to lay bare his own thoughts and feelings on the issue.

"Conspiracy, insurgency, treason, rebellion" among the slaves could be handled using the same measures as had always been employed in such cases before. Yet, the likelihood that the General Assembly's resolutions contemplated some more wide-ranging response meant that he should consider all options.

He quickly ruled out relocating Virginia's slaves into the Old Northwest—formerly Virginia's trans–Ohio River territory. Much of that land had already been laid out for purchase and settlement, he noted, and would thus likely be expensive for the state to buy. Besides that, whether

Virginia would want a new state to join the union with that type of population seemed dubious.

The land to the USA's north, British territory, was populated either by whites or by Indians. Neither group seemed apt to be so well disposed toward America as to welcome this project. Jefferson also doubted that expatriate ex-slaves from America would fare well in Canada's forbidding climate. Spain owned the land to America's south and west, which different Indians possessed, and this combination seemed as little likely to welcome the idea of a colony of freedmen from the USA as did America's northern neighbors. Even more certain was that Spain would not "alienate the sovereignty." Besides, again, would America want such a community so nearby?

Jefferson answered that it would not. "However our present interests may restrain us within our own limits," he rhapsodized, "it is impossible not to look forward to distant times, when our rapid multiplication will expand itself beyond those limits, & cover the whole Northern, if not the Southern continent with a people speaking the same language, governed in similar forms, & by similar laws: nor can we contemplate, with satisfaction, either blot or mixture on that surface."

By "blot or mixture," he referred to dark-hued residents and mixed-race children. Jefferson wanted an all-white continent, or perhaps two, and he assumed that where white and black people remained in close proximity, there was bound to be interracial procreation. Certainly there was abundant such activity in Jeffersonian Virginia. Not only did the evidence of one's eyes show it, but many prominent Virginians other than Jefferson participated in it. One close acquaintance of his, fellow University of Virginia founding father (original Board of Visitors member) John Hartwell Cocke commented on it:

> It is too well proved, they [interracial children] are not few, nor far between. I can enumerate a score of such cases in our beloved Ant. Dominion that have come in my way thro' life, without seeking for them. Were

they enumerated with the statistics of the State they would be found in the hundreds. Nor is it to be wondered at, when Mr. Jeffersons notorious example is considered.[72]

Cocke would have known, as he sat on one of the highest rungs of the same social hierarchy as did Jefferson, whose home he had often visited.[73]

Spain, France, and Portugal owned much of South America, and Jefferson told Monroe that if Virginia's legislature wanted him to, he would inquire of them concerning a place to which freed slaves might be sent. However, what seemed more sensible to him was to colonize blacks from Virginia, from America, in the Caribbean. "The West Indies," he warmed to his subject, "offer a more probable & practicable retreat for them. Inhabited already by a people of their own race & colour; climates congenial with their natural constitution; insulated from the other descriptions of men; Nature seems to have formed these islands to become the receptacle of the blacks transported into this hemisphere." Jefferson's observations reflected several ideas: that each race of men was destined for particular climes; that "race & colour" were immutable characteristics establishing real divisions among different varieties of *Homo sapiens*; that separation from whites and Indians would be optimal for blacks; and that nature meant particular places for particular groups of people. All of these ideas clearly pointed toward the desirability of colonization.[74]

Jefferson confided that as in regard to unsettled or thinly settled portions of North America, obtaining West Indian territory from European powers for this purpose might be difficult. He thought the odds rather better, however, because the West Indies were already generally populated by blacks. "The island of St. Domingo," in particular, struck Jefferson as "the most promising portion of them" in this regard, because blacks already controlled the place "under regular laws & government."

Remarkably, Jefferson offered Monroe the commonsense but still striking observation that blacks whom Virginia's government might hope to expatriate "for acts deemed criminal by us" might be attractive immigrants for acts deemed "meritorious perhaps by" the ruler of Haiti. The president did not think much of potential danger from Virginia slaves sent to Saint Domingue, because America likely would remain much more powerful than the new black republic indefinitely. Even were such difficulty more likely than he thought, Jefferson concluded, this consideration "is over-weighed by the humanity of the measures proposed, & the advantages of disembarrassing ourselves of such dangerous characters." As in *Notes on the State of Virginia*, he considered slavery deleterious to blacks and to whites, and he thought ridding the Old Dominion of potential rebels a highly desirable goal.

Possibly the two Virginia titans' efforts would fail.[75] In that case, Jefferson noted, there was always Africa. It offered "a last & undoubted resort, if all others more desireable should fail us." He awaited only the General Assembly's final judgment on these matters, he said, before he turned his full authority as president to the pursuit of this goal.

Perhaps the most brilliant commentator on Jefferson and blacks, Winthrop Jordan, says that Jefferson's notion of "the real distinctions which nature has made" between whites and blacks and his visceral revulsion at any "blot or mixture" on the North American landscape reflect the general binary tendency in his thought.[76] Everywhere he saw zeros and ones, either-or choices, wolves and sheep, freedom and "priestcraft," free people and a tyrannical king, republicans and monocrats, virtuous farmers and corrupt city dwellers, black and white. If such distinctions' significance could be negated at the polls, as in 1800, fine. If not, a war for independence, a French Revolution, or colonization of blacks abroad might be the answer.

Soon after the exchange with Governor Monroe, Jefferson wrote to America's representative in London, Rufus King, on the subject.[77] Would the British allow America to colonize its slaves in Sierra Leone, their new West African colony? British abolitionists had established this experimental colony to be a receptacle for freedmen, so it seemed just right for Jefferson's, and Virginia's, purpose.[78]

Jefferson told King that the example of Saint Domingue had encouraged American slaves to similar endeavors. Gabriel's Rebellion had been easily suppressed, he said, but that experience had led Virginia's legislature to have its governor relay its hopes to President Jefferson. As Jefferson told it, the best hope was for transportation of blacks "guilty of insurgency" from Virginia abroad.

Jefferson floated the idea of a commercial enterprise cooperatively established by the Americans and African natives to help defray the costs of the Virginia project by its profits. Sending these people to Sierra Leone made sense, he intimated, because it was intended to receive "civilized blacks" such as those found in Virginia. Amazingly, the president described these "undesirable" residents of Virginia this way:

> It is material to observe that they are not felons, or common malefactors, but persons guilty of what the safety of society, under actual circumstances, obliges us to treat as a crime, but which their feelings may represent in a far different shape. They are such as will be a valuable acquisition to the settlement already existing there, and well calculated to cooperate in the plan of civilisation.

Jefferson suggested that to cover the cost of their transportation, the settlers be sold as indentured servants, as he said poor German immigrants commonly were at the time in America, and that ships' captains be allowed to trade with the coastal Africans. This would defray the project's considerable costs. Jefferson added that not only rebels but any other black freemen should be allowed to migrate to Sierra Leone, if King could arrange it. "The consequences of permitting emancipations to become extensive," he noted, "unless a condition of emigration be annexed to them, furnish also matter of solicitude to the legislature of Virginia." We know what he meant, and King, who had been a passionate foe of slavery in the Philadelphia Convention and would be again as a senator during the Missouri Crisis of 1819–1821, must have known too. Jefferson hastened to add, however, that most emancipations were either of a master's entire workforce or of particularly deserving individuals, not of the recalcitrant or criminal.

Yet, President Jefferson failed. He left office without having made any significant progress toward colonizing blacks out of the country, let alone ending slavery. This is not to say, however, that his presidency marked no progress toward the goal of eliminating slavery from the country. By his 1806 call upon Congress to adopt legislation banning further slave imports at the earliest constitutionally permitted date, which his allies on Capitol Hill heeded, Jefferson acted on his stated conviction that reducing the share of slaves in the population made it more likely that the institution would be abolished.[79] Even Finkelman concedes that this law saved hundreds of thousands of Africans from being brought to the USA in chains.[80] However, Finkelman rightly notes that Jefferson as president did not do some of the things—proposing gradual emancipation in the District of Columbia, recognizing Haiti—that he might have done to further the antislavery cause. Finkelman explains Jefferson's omissions by reference to racism. Other possibilities are that Jefferson thought these measures would make colonization less likely and—this never occurs to Finkelman— that he had other priorities.

On Christmas Day 1810, John Lynch—founder of Lynchburg, Virginia, freer of his own slaves, and one of the state's most prominent citizens— wrote Jefferson an impassioned letter.[81] The Philadelphia Quaker abolition campaigner Anne Mifflin had visited Virginia and, disappointed in her expectation of encountering the Sage of Monticello, asked Lynch to relay a message to him. Mifflin wanted Jefferson to intervene with French and American authorities on behalf of a freedmen's colony in western Africa. This colony, she said, would contribute to the "Civilization of the Affricans," and Lynch noted it would also do Virginia the service of providing an outlet for American free black population.

Jefferson responded that "I have no hesitation in saying that I have ever thought it the most desirable measure which could be adopted for gradually drawing off this part of our population most advantageously for themselves as well as for us. Going from a country possessing all the useful arts, they might be the means of transplanting them among the inhabitants of Africa, and would thus carry back to the country of their origin the seeds of civilisation, which might render their sojournment and sufferings here a blessing in the end to that country."[82]

As Jefferson recalled, he had received a communication from Governor James Monroe in 1801 asking that he attempt to find someplace to which Virginia blacks could be relocated. Some of those people having been sent to Sierra Leone, the British authorities soon found them undesirable settlers—much less desirable than blacks from Britain's own West Indies possessions. That outlet for Virginia's black population thus had become unavailable. Portugal had replied to President Jefferson's inquiries with expressions of lack of interest too.

Ex-president Jefferson said that he could not communicate with foreign governments, but the federal government—James Madison's administration—would be quite willing to do so. (Lynch must surely have been able to read between the lines: if Jefferson said Madison would do something, he may well have had inside information to that effect.) He wished America would establish its own West African settlement of this kind. If this enterprise should be successful, he gushed, all might benefit, economically as well as politically. Yet, he doubted Americans would be thrilled at the prospect. Probably few blacks would willingly participate, he guessed.

That would not be the last time Jefferson heard about this subject. On July 31, 1814, Edward Coles sent Jefferson a momentous letter.[83] Son of Jefferson's friend and peer (and Dolley Madison's cousin) John Coles II, Edward was and for the rest of his life would remain a Jefferson admirer and supporter. Though a scion of the Virginia aristocracy, Coles had imbibed Jeffersonian principles in so pure a form as to be unable to reconcile his beliefs with his slaveholding inheritance. Therefore he asked Jefferson to advocate the old cause. Although "I never took up my pen with more hesitation," he began, and although he feared "appearing presumptuous" in suggesting political action to the revered ex-president, Coles begged him to pick up the standard of Republican leadership once again. Hinting at having read Jefferson's famous evaluation of the matter in *Notes on the State of Virginia* and throwing a bit of flattery in the direction of a prey strongly attracted to that bait, Coles said, "I will not enter on the *right* which man has to enslave his Brother man, nor upon the moral and political effects of Slavery on individuals or on Society; because these things are better understood by you than by me. My object is to entreat and beseech you to exert your knowledge and influence, in devising, and getting into operation, some plan for the gradual emancipation of Slavery."[84]

Foreseeing Jefferson's likely response, or at least recognizing that the august retiree might resist reentering the lists, Coles noted that this "difficult task" could only be "successfully performed by the revered Fathers of all our political & societal blessings." Moreover, Coles did not want Jefferson to think that the task could be championed chiefly by one of the other "Fathers"—not by President James Madison, say, and certainly not by Chief Justice John Marshall or former governor John Tyler Sr. Rather, "it is a duty . . . that devolves particularly on you" as the chief American apostle of "the rights of man, & the liberty & independence of your country." Coles noted that Jefferson had been "honored with the most important trusts by [his] fellow-citizens, whose confidence and love [he had] carried with [him] into the shades of old age and retirement." Still playing on the Sage of Monticello's outsize ego, Coles pressed the point: "In the calm of this retirement you might, most beneficially to society, and with much addition to your own fame, avail yourself of that love and confidence to put into complete practice those hallowed principles contained in that renowned Declaration, of which you were the immortal author, and on which we bottomed our right to resist oppression, and establish our freedom and independence."

Next, Coles brandished his thorough subscription to Jefferson's argument in his draft Declaration of Independence, referring to slavery as "this most degrading feature of British Coloniel policy, which is still permitted to exist, notwithstanding its repugnance as well to the principles of our revolution as to our free Institutions." Only inertia, not American initiative, accounted for the existence of so un-American a system as that of chattel slavery in the otherwise lovely, republican Old Dominion which Jefferson had taken the lead in creating. Even if Jefferson made the effort and failed, Coles added, he would leave the marker for future generations of his "disciples." Coles closed, shockingly, by revealing that he had determined to abandon Virginia forever rather than continue to hold slaves.

Jefferson's response strikes one even now as a thundering disappointment.[85] Coles's letter, he began, "was read with peculiar pleasure. The sentiments breathed thro' the whole do honor to both the head and heart of the writer." Yet, Jefferson's own ideas "on the subject of the slavery of negroes have long since been in possession of the public, and time has only served to give them stronger root." While "the love of justice and the love of country" pressed the thinking toward a resolution of the issue, nothing had been done on that score.

As was his custom, Jefferson referred to slavery as a problem both for "them" (the slaves) and for "us" (white Virginians). Both groups needed relief from slavery. The prerevolutionary generation had accepted slavery as normal, and Jefferson's sponsorship of a House of Burgesses measure advocated on the House floor by his senior cousin Richard Bland—"one of the oldest, ablest, and most respected members"—proved a debacle. The younger man "was more spared," but Bland "was denounced as an enemy to his country, & was treated with the grossest indecorum."

In Jefferson's account, the revolution drew him away from high Virginia politics into federal service. We know, however, that in 1779–1781, he served not only in Virginia politics but also as the Old Dominion's governor. If no attempt was made to alleviate slaves' bondage, a two-term governor must share the blame. In his missive to Coles, he says his postings in Europe and in the federal capital left him "little opportunity of knowing the progress of public sentiment here on this subject." One wonders what Coles, surely aware that Jefferson often returned to Monticello as secretary of state in 1790–1795, lived in Virginia full-time in 1795–1797, and as vice president in 1797–1801 regularly returned, made of this assertion of ignorance. We have no way of knowing what Coles knew of Jefferson's behind-the-scenes role in Virginia politics in 1797 and 1798, but we at least are aware that he did not maintain a hands-off posture. More on that anon.

We also do not know whether Jefferson's next passage struck Coles as patronizing. If touchy of his honor—as Virginia gentlemen generally were—he must have found it so. Jefferson insisted that he had long hoped that young Virginians' having been raised in a republican environment would make them more sensitive to the wrong being done the slaves than their fathers had been. Lo! Coles's letter was the first tangible sign that his hopes were being fulfilled. "The hour of emancipation is advancing in the march of time," he piously pontificated. "It will come."

Jefferson next told Coles that the best method of achieving this aim seemed to him to be a gradual emancipation law. Adopted in numerous states, including New York, Connecticut, New Jersey, and Pennsylvania, such laws set future dates after which anyone born into slavery would become free, and Virginia's might say they would be expatriated—that is, sent abroad—upon attaining adulthood. This would leave time for educating them, and it would "give time for a gradual extinction of that species of labor and substitution of another." Freeing them all at once was out of the question, Jefferson averred, because slaves' lifelong subjugation left them "as incapable as children of taking care of themselves." To free them all at once would be cruelly to sentence them to die off due to the lack of parenting skills among them, and "in the mean time they are pests in society by their idleness, and the depredations to which this leads them." Lest Coles think that blacks might intermarry with whites, Jefferson hurried to add that "their amalgamation with the other colour produces a degradation to which no lover of his country, no lover of excellence in the human character can innocently consent."

To Coles's point that Jefferson's unique stature made him the one American who above all others must take the lead in wrapping up the history of American slavery, Jefferson answered that his time, and his contemporaries' time, for political leadership had passed. Now it was for the young—for people such as Coles—to take up that burden. Abandoning Virginia seemed to Jefferson precisely the wrong thing to do. He urged Coles to make persuasion of other Virginians his life's calling. While treating his own slaves well, as Jefferson thought he had done, Coles should propagandize other sons of the Old Dominion until the time arrived when emancipation commanded the sympathies of most Virginians. "It is an encoraging observation," the old man wrote, "that no good measure was ever proposed which, if duly pursued, failed to prevail in the end. We have proof of this in the history of the endeavors in the British parliament to suppress that very trade which brought this evil on us."

In sum: not my job; not my fault; good luck to you. Jefferson's response must have come to Coles as a mighty blow, for it set him on a life course he cannot have foreseen.[86] Virginia law required that any slave who was freed leave the Commonwealth within a year. Therefore, Coles decided to take all of his slaves to Illinois and free them. He did in 1819, giving them parcels of land into the bargain, and his wonderful deed is immortalized in the dome of the Illinois Capitol.[87] Eventually, Coles played the lead role in the successful opposition to attempts to revoke the ban on slavery in Illinois, of which he was governor at the time. While Jefferson's grandson became Confederate secretary of war, Coles supported Abraham Lincoln for president in 1860 and sided with the Union against the Confederacy—and his native Virginia.

. . .

Jefferson's close political ally James Madison generally agreed with Jefferson on these questions. In 1816, he agreed to become the first president of the new American Colonization Society (ACS). This group, whose membership at various times included not only Madison but future president John Tyler, Henry Clay, John Randolph of Roanoke, John Taylor of Caroline, and various other prominent politicians among its tens of thousands of members, had as its goal raising private and government funds for the purpose of relocating free blacks from America to Africa.[88]

Ultimately, with the sponsorship of Jefferson's friend and onetime mentee President James Monroe, the ACS took the lead in establishing Liberia on Africa's west coast. With a capital, Monrovia, named for Monroe, Liberia had as its first settlers thousands of black Americans.

Despite his very close relationships with ACS President Madison and US President Monroe, Jefferson never joined the ACS. He never said why. We can speculate that here as in rejecting requests that he advocate reform of the state constitution and as in brushing aside Edward Coles's request that he take the lead in advocating a Virginia gradual emancipation act, Jefferson decided that his education program would be harmed if he associated his name with the ACS. He may also have feared the constitutional implications of the ACS's program.[89]

In 1817, Jefferson became executor of the will of his friend, the Polish veteran of the American Revolution Tadeusz Kościuszko.[90] This Polish republican had directed that approximately $17,000 be devoted to the task of purchasing, manumitting, and providing real property to American blacks. Following nearly a century of litigation, ultimately the money was put to completely different purposes.

As we have seen, the Missouri Crisis of 1819–1821 elicited vociferous defenses of slavery from Thomas Jefferson. He compared news of the crisis to "a fire bell in the night," which Virginians associated with slave rebellion.[91] For Jefferson, slavery in Missouri meant diffusion of the slave population across the North American landscape, and thus diminution of the share of slaves in Virginia's overall population. If slavery were confined to lands in which it currently existed, on the other hand, slaves' share of their populations would grow, state-level emancipation would become less likely, and interracial children would proliferate. Ex-Federalists such as Rufus King, in trying to cabin black population within the eastern slave states, threatened the ultimate success of Jefferson's revolution itself. As Patrick Henry's son-in-law, court of appeals chief judge Spencer Roane, put it, Virginians were "averse to be dammed up in a land of Slaves, by the Eastern [meaning northeastern] people." Sometime governor William Branch Giles, for his part, envisioned the Louisiana Territory's lands as "an almost boundless reservoir for the reception of slaves."[92] The Virginian could not "contemplate, with satisfaction, either blot or mixture on th[e] surface" of republican North America, but the North's Missouri Crisis position threatened to make it inevitable. Other Virginians, agreeing, considered dividing the union a reasonable alternative to insistence that Missouri could come into the union only with an antislavery constitution.[93]

Jefferson's friend James Madison presided over the American Colonization Society in his post-presidential retirement.[94] Jefferson joined with the ACS after 1821 in favoring federal government sponsorship of colonization. Private, even state, resources simply did not measure up to the magnitude of this project's expense, and so a more desperate approach was justified, he held.

Jefferson advocated removal of blacks from Virginia, and from all America, to the end of his life. At age eighty, he offered a detailed plan for colonization of blacks abroad to prominent Unitarian and *North American Review* editor Jared Sparks.[95] Jefferson lauded an article Sparks had recently run in that periodical on the subject of colonization. Such an effort, the ex-president averred, "may introduce among the aborigines the arts of cultivated life, and the blessings of civilization and science. By doing this, we may make to them some retribution for the long course of injuries we have been committing on their population."

That was not Jefferson's chief interest, as he hurried to make clear: "The 2d object, and the most interesting to us, as coming home to our physical and moral characters, to our happiness and safety, is to provide an Asylum to which we can, by degrees, send the whole of that population from among us, and establish them under our patronage and protection, as a separate, free and independant people, in some country and climate friendly to human life and happiness." By that population, he meant "the people of color." Jefferson's hope was to see them all expatriated.

Jefferson then explained to Sparks that although purchasing and transporting all blacks from America was "impracticable," he did not believe "that getting rid of them is forever impossible. For that is neither my opinion nor my hope." The goal could be accomplished, he said, "by emancipating the after-born, leaving them, on due compensation, with their mothers, until their services are worth their maintenance, and then putting them to industrious occupations, until a proper age for deportation." He had said the same thing, he noted, in *Notes on the State of Virginia* "five and forty years ago." What he had calculated as a $600 million expense of attacking deportation frontally would be reduced to "thirty-seven millions and a half" via this scheme, because each newborn "would probably be yielded by the owner gratis." Here we find a characteristic touch of Jeffersonian fantasy. That the master class would simply give away all infant slaves could hardly have impressed a more hardheaded man as likely.

Jefferson found the money required by his plan ready to hand. Where was it to be acquired? "Why not from that of the lands which have been ceded by the very States now needing this relief? And ceded on no consideration, for the most part, but that of the general good of the whole." In case Sparks objected that those lands had already been settled, Jefferson drew his attention to "the territories since acquired . . . or so much, at least, as may be sufficient." Besides claiming that the common lands formerly Virginian, etc., should rightly be used to finance the removal of blacks from America and their transportation to Africa, Jefferson added that northerners as recently as 1821—three years earlier—had claimed deep interest in ameliorating the condition of American blacks, particularly slaves. "The object," he continued, "although more important to the slave States, is highly so to the others also, *if they were serious in their arguments on the Missouri question* [emphasis added]." Jefferson did not believe they had been, but here was a chance to hoist them on what he took to be their own petard. If the North was to make great sacrifices, well, the "slaves States . . . would also contribute more by their gratuitous liberation, thus taking on themselves alone the first and heaviest item of expense." Maybe you, dear Sparks, will be giving up part of the national land, but we will be freeing our young slaves, so the burden will be fairly distributed.

As we have seen, Jefferson advocated colonization partly to vindicate blacks' right to self-government—that is, their claim on his dogma that all men are created equal. One other ground on which he relied was his aversion to racial mixture. Thus, when his acquaintance William Short proposed early in 1826 to convert American slaves into serfs, and thus to eliminate the slave trade, Jefferson gave a positive response.[96] "On the subject of emancipation," Jefferson began, "I have ceased to think because not to be a work of my day. The plan of converting the blacks into Serfs would certainly be better than keeping them in their present condition." Still, there was a better idea, he said: colonization. Blacks from America could be sent "to the governments of the W.I. [West Indies] of their own colour." Not only was this "entirely practicable," but it was "greatly preferable to the mixture of colour here." Enserfment—tying agricultural laborers to particular land, as in Russia at that time—would eliminate the practice of moving people around by sale and purchase, but it would not end miscegenation, to which Jefferson expressed his "great aversion."

Why was Jefferson at such pains to dissociate himself from interracial procreation, all the way to the end of his life? Former generations of historians pointed to the combination of attacks on him as a miscegenator and the presence at Monticello of his late father-in-law's half-black off-spring as enough to drive anyone into that posture.[97] Now virtually all Jefferson scholars agree that Jefferson fathered at least some of his slave Sally Hemings's children.[98] This casts his statements about miscegenation, its inevitability and its repugnance, in an entirely different light. Jefferson left no recorded statements on this matter, however.

Chapter 4

Assimilation

All of Jefferson's writings concerning Native American Indians must be put into a specific context.[1] Jefferson did not simply study Indians for study's sake. Rather, he was a participant in the transatlantic Republic of Letters.[2] His chief interlocutors in this field were the day's leading biologist, Georges-Louis Leclerc, the comte de Buffon, and his circle. To great acclaim, Buffon long argued that the Western Hemisphere was the site of degeneration of animals generally, including humans. Calling Buffon "the best informed naturalist who has ever written," Jefferson set himself the patriotic task of refuting Buffon's argument.

Good student of Aristotle that he was, Buffon first described what men had in common, then turned to classifications and distinctions. In light of the "fact" that animal life in general degenerated in the Western Hemisphere, he said, Europe's quadrupeds were of greater size and variety than their puny American cousins. Apparently under the prodding of correspondence and samples from Jefferson and Benjamin Franklin, Buffon eventually abandoned the notion that his general theory applied to European-descended people in America.[3] Perhaps Buffon had heard of the Abbé Raynal's experience at a dinner also attended by Franklin. The French disciple of Buffon asserted that men degenerated in the Western Hemisphere, and so Franklin demanded that first his American, then his French guests stand up. As Jefferson told it, the half-dozen Americans possessed the "finest stature and form; while those on the other side were remarkably diminutive, and the Abbé himself, was a mere shrimp."[4]

Indians, however, Buffon continued to insist were notably inferior to European humans. As Jefferson has Buffon tell it, animals "shrink and diminish under a niggardly sky and an unprolific land," and "all the animals that have transported from Europe to America . . . have become smaller . . . and those which were not transported [and] which are common to both Continents . . . are also considerably less than those of Europe."[5] While eventually deciding that Europeans did not degenerate in America, and indeed all might improve, Buffon clung to his insistence that Indians were backward.[6]

Various American men of letters responded to Buffon's argument.[7] Ben Franklin, characteristically, mocked the Frenchman's assertions on numerous occasions. John Adams repeatedly confuted the "shameless falsehoods" of Buffon and his circle. Thomas Jefferson, however, went further than any other: he made answering Buffon a major project, one on which he worked for many years.

Jefferson offered his most extensive counterstroke in his sole book, *Notes on the State of Virginia*. Besides discussing Indians in Query XI, which answered a question his correspondent François Barbé-Marbois had not asked—"A description of the Indians established in that state?"—Jefferson in Query VI, "Productions Mineral, Vegetable and Animal," included copious information about Virginia's animals, including people.[8] Jefferson began by describing Buffon's general position:

The opinion advanced by the Count de Buffon, is 1. That the animals common both to the old and new world, are smaller in the latter. 2. That those peculiar to the new, are on a smaller scale. 3. That those which have been domesticated in both, have degenerated in America: and 4. That on the whole it exhibits fewer species.

Jefferson considered Buffon's explanation of this supposed phenomenon—that America is cooler and moister than the Old World, and that both of these conditions impede the growth of large animals. He called every element of this argument into question, notably by offering examples of American types that were larger than the comparable European animals. Although he wrote *Notes* in the 1780s, he would still be collecting specimens in support of his case during the last decade of his life, the 1820s.

After ten pages of text and charts, Jefferson at last turned to Buffon's assertions concerning European man and the American Indian.[9] He quoted Buffon as saying, "Although the savage of the new world is about the same height as man in our world, this does not suffice for him to constitute an exception to the general fact that all living nature has become smaller on that continent." Buffon hastens to add details in support of this assertion, saying, "The savage is feeble, and has small organs of generation; he has neither hair nor beard, and no ardor whatever for his female."

In Buffon's telling, Indians' supposed lack of sexual ardor has wide-ranging consequences. "There is no need," he says, "for seeking further the cause of the isolated mode of life of these savages and their repugnance for society: the most precious spark of the fire of nature has been refused to them; they lack ardor for their females, and consequently have no love for their fellow men." Sexual longing, in Buffon's schema, accounted for sociability generally. Its absence from Indians meant that he could say "their other feelings are cold and languid; they love their parents and children but little; the most intimate of all ties, the family connection, binds them but loosely together; between family and family there is no tie at all; hence they have no communion, no commonwealth, no state of society."

Ethnohistorians today reject completely Buffon's sketch of wandering, atomistic Indians rendered unsociable by the weakness of their sex drives. Buffon spun out a tale of Indians with only the most limited, brutish, intermittent sexual interest, which he blamed for Indian men's treatment of their wives "as beasts of burden, which they load without consideration with the burden of their hunting, and which they compel without mercy, without gratitude, to perform tasks which are often beyond their strength." Buffon's American Indian made his woman into a mindless drudge instead of a love object. "Nature," Buffon insists, "by refusing him the power of love, has treated [the Indian] worse and lowered him deeper than any animal."

Jefferson rejects this caricature altogether. "An afflicting picture indeed," he calls it, "which, for the honor of human nature, I am glad to believe has no original." Jefferson says that any distinction between North American Indians and Europeans in this regard is owing entirely to "diet and exercise." Too, the Indian is "affectionate to his children, careful of them, and indulgent in the extreme . . . His affections," Jefferson says, "comprehend his other connections, weakening, as with us, from circle to circle, as they recede from the center." Even the most severe warriors among the Indians, their Virginian defender notes, cry "most bitterly on the loss of their children."

Even where he finds superior attributes in the Indian, Buffon manages to make the whole picture unattractive. This is particularly true when it comes to martial attributes, which were if anything held in even higher esteem in the eighteenth century than today. "Although swifter than the European because he is better accustomed to running," Buffon avers, "he is, on the other hand, less strong in body." More to the point, "He is also less sensitive, and yet more timid and cowardly; he has no vivacity, no activity of mind; the activity of his body is less an exercise, a voluntary motion, than a necessary action caused by want."

Again Jefferson comes to the Indian's defense: "he is brave," the American counters, "when an enterprise depends on bravery; education with him making the point of honor consist in the destruction of an enemy by stratagem, and in the preservation of his own person free from injury; or perhaps this is nature; while it is education which teaches us to honor force more than finesse." Beyond this stab at European pretension to superiority, Jefferson adds "that he will defend himself against an host of enemies, always chusing to be killed, rather than to surrender." Besides that, Jefferson notes the Indian's superiority in another regard: his supreme capacity for enduring torture, which he bears "with a firmness unknown almost to religious enthusiasm with us."

Jefferson goes on to describe the experience of white men who have married Indian women, which he says is that Indian women have proved as fertile as their white counterparts. "Instances are known," he says, "of their rearing a dozen children." Jefferson explains the fertility disparity by the difference between living conditions among the whites and among the Indians. In addition, he insists that Buffon's concession concerning the size of Indians—that they are "about the same size as the man" of the Eastern Hemisphere—explodes his overall contention about the Western Hemisphere's effect on animals. Jefferson makes great sport of the idea that while Indians are of the same stature as Europeans, more or less, their mental faculties have been negatively affected by New World conditions.

It is here that Jefferson adduces the most famous of his arguments concerning Indians' genius: the famous speech of the Mingo chief Logan. As Jefferson tells the story, Logan had come to be the last of his line through whites' killing off his wife and children. Logan, long a friend of the whites, took his vengeance in the ensuing war, but then surrendered at the war's climax. Rather than attend the surrender, Logan submitted the following speech:

I appeal to any white man to say, if ever he entered Logan's cabin hungry, and he gave him not meat; if ever he came cold and naked, and he clothed him not. During the course of the last long and bloody war, Logan remained idle in his cabin, an advocate for peace. Such was my love for the whites, that my countrymen pointed as they passed, and said, "Logan is the friend of the white men." I have even thought to have lived with you, but for the injuries of one man. Col. Cresap, the last spring, in cold blood, and unprovoked, murdered all the relations of Logan, not sparing even my women and children. There runs not a drop of my blood in the veins of any living creature. This called on me for revenge. I have sought it: I have killed many: I have fully glutted my vengeance. For my country, I rejoice at the beams of peace. But do not harbour a thought that mine is the joy of fear. Logan never felt fear. He will not turn on his heel to save his life. Who is there to mourn for Logan?—Not one.

In case any denied his assertion that Logan's eloquence matched that of any oration ever uttered by Demosthenes or Cicero (symbols respectively of Greek and of Roman oratorical achievement), Jefferson pointed out that the Indians did not have writing, and so his cultural inheritance must be taken into account in weighing the merits of Logan's production.

Note that Jefferson's account of Logan's speech mirrored Jefferson's own view of the American Indian.[10] He was, in this account, essentially good. His finest exemplar had been drawn into a fruitless war by unrepresentative, violent whites, and in the end he had been overpowered. Having demonstrated his valor in war, he would leave no progeny. Jefferson seemingly hoped for more for the Indians at this point, but by the end of his career, one can see the outline of the United States' ultimate Indian policy faintly outlined in Jefferson's own behavior.

In his dispute with Buffon, on the other hand, Jefferson would have none of the idea that the New World's men were inferior to those of the Old. If differences could be observed, they owed only to the cultural, not to the biological, situation of the Indians. Europeans such as Buffon who argued to the contrary had employed "more eloquence than sound reasoning . . . in support of this theory." Buffon remained for Jefferson the preeminent zoologist, but here he erred.

Why did Jefferson devote so much attention to this quarrel in what was, after all, primarily a work of description and not of disputation? One possible answer is that Jefferson and Franklin, among other Americans who took up this case, had their eyes on potential immigrants to and investors in North America. To accept that all was decay in the United States would have meant seeing potential migrants to America stay away, the argument goes, and that way lay the failure of the revolutionary dream of America.[11]

Jefferson's attention to Indians did not begin with *Notes on the State of Virginia*, nor did it end there. Early in his life, Jefferson conducted a pioneering excavation of an Indian burial mound near Shadwell, the plantation of his birth, just miles from his adult home of Monticello in Piedmont Virginia's Albemarle County. He recalled having repeatedly been in the presence of a prominent Indian leader in his boyhood. This was due to Peter Jefferson's—Thomas's father's—position as the leading man of Thomas's home county.

While Indians lived throughout Tidewater Virginia at the time of Jamestown's 1607 settlement, they were by the time of Jefferson's birth in 1743 nearly unknown in the Old Dominion's coastal region. In fact, Jefferson only occasionally saw a few in Albemarle, which was essentially the westernmost point of Virginia settlement in mid-century. White migration westward, with European agriculture's exclusive domination of the land, meant that the Indians had been pushed farther west. Jefferson's father had been party to extending the boundary of Virginia far to the west, and as the most prominent man in their part of the colony, he had been on personal terms with leading Indians in the area. Young Thomas recalled having met them in his boyhood. The days of extensive Anglo-Indian interaction in the Piedmont, however, had long passed.

Yet, Indians had left numerous monuments, and one of them sparked

Jefferson's interest. In the *Notes*, he describes having excavated an Indian burial mound.[12] Of such mounds, he says "many are to be found all over this country [meaning Virginia]." Jefferson's work as an archeologist has long drawn significant respect from experts in the field, so that Jefferson scholar William Peden could summarize one scientist's account as saying that Jefferson "anticipated by a century the aims and methods of modern archeological science."[13]

Jefferson explains his decision to excavate by reference to his curiosity about the mounds' organization. Of the three conjectures in circulation, he would find which was correct. His characteristic ingenuity and perceptiveness strike one in every sentence of his description of the excavation, as does his powerful curiosity.

Immediately upon completing his three-page description, Jefferson provides further observations demonstrating his painfully disrespectful attitude toward Indian culture. Jefferson notes that some mounds were earthen and some were stone, but "that they were repositories of the dead, has been obvious to all." About thirty years prior to his writing the book, he says, a large group of Indians went to the seemingly abandoned barrow near his home and, "without any instructions or enquiry, and having staid about it some time, with expressions which were construed to be those of sorrow, they returned to the high road, which they had left about half a dozen miles to pay this visit, and pursued their journey." Beginning about twelve years prior to his writing, he concludes, the barrow he had excavated and another in its neighborhood had been "put under cultivation," so that they were "much reduced in their height, and spread in width, by the plough, and [would] probably disappear in time." In other words, he had dissected a burial mound at which people still commemorated their ancestors who were interred in it, and other Virginians had reduced its size by farming. Rather than excuse Jefferson's behavior as typical of archeological practice generally, we might instead bewail archeologists' practice. His neighbors' deeds, on the other hand, speak for themselves, unfortunately.

Also of interest to Jefferson in writing the "Aborigines" chapter of his book were the Indians' languages.[14] He lays out his theory of Native American origins in tentative form for readers' consideration. One cannot but be impressed with Jefferson's learning in this area as he explains why he believes it likely that North American people had contact with Europeans beginning very long ago, and as he relates the then-recent voyages of Captain Cook to his theory that East Asians did as well. Physiognomy persuades him that Indians and East Asians share common stock, and he laments that numerous Indian peoples have been suffered to disappear without their languages' having been recorded for future study; a linguist armed with extensive American lexicons, he asserts, could prove dispositively how the peoples of the New World and the Old were related. "Were vocabularies formed of all the languages spoken in North and South America, preserving their appellations of the most common objects in nature, of those which must be present to every nation barbarous or civilized," Jefferson mused, ". . . and these deposited in all the public libraries, it would furnish opportunities to those skilled in the languages of the old world to compare them with these, now, or at a future time, and hence to construct the best evidence of the derivation of this part of the human race."

Jefferson considered the future of American ethnography in the fifteenth chapter of *Notes*, "Colleges, Buildings, and Roads."[15] After explaining that the College of William & Mary's Brafferton professorship had been endowed "for the instruction of the Indians, and their conversion to Christianity," he laid out his own plan. Rather than a special institute in Williamsburg, the Indians should be sent a professor to live among them, instruct them in Christianity, and "collect their traditions, laws, customs, languages, and other circumstances which might lead to a discovery of their relation with one another, or descent from other nations. When these objects are accomplished with one tribe, the missionary might pass to another."

Jefferson would find himself better positioned than anyone else in history to follow up on this insight. In 1801, the choice of the House of Representatives made him president of the United States, and the electoral college elected him to a second term in 1804. In the interval, he accepted the offer of Napoleonic France to sell America the Louisiana Territory, a gigantic inland empire whose extent was nearly as great as that of the republic Jefferson represented. Immediately, reasons of state and scientific curiosity coincided.

Jefferson by this point had made clear to all and sundry that he thought the Indians might eventually be incorporated into Anglo-American society. He had said in the *Notes* that their mental endowments matched those of the white man, after all. To do so, then, they would first have to overcome a cultural inheritance Jefferson had denominated "savage" in his draft Declaration of Independence.[16]

The term "savage" in the eighteenth century retained its original meaning, referring to people who were simply uncultured. Despite his interest in and sympathy for Indians, he had not the slightest doubt of American culture's superiority to theirs—and of the benefit to them in case they adopted American ways.

Jefferson laid out his understanding of an "American theory of savagism" in an 1824 letter.[17] As he put it, "Let a philosophic observer commence a journey from the savages of the Rocky Mountains, eastwardly towards our sea-coast. These he would observe in the earliest stage of association living under no law but that of nature, subsisting and covering themselves with the flesh and skins of wild beasts. He would next find those on our frontiers in the pastoral state, raising domestic animals to supply the defects of hunting. Then succeed our own semi-barbarous citizens, the pioneers of the advance of civilization, and so in his progress he would meet the gradual shades of improving man until he would reach his, as yet, most improved state in our seaport towns. This, in fact, is equivalent to a survey, in time, of the progress of man from the infancy of creation to the present day."

Note that Jefferson's account of the levels of societal organization be-tween the Atlantic and the Rockies assumed the equality of the Indians and the whites. Indians could move through time simply by adopting the white man's ways, just as white men on the frontier had in Jefferson's account moved from civilization to "semi-barbarous" life. For the Indians to do so would be the ultimate vindication of Jefferson's argument against Buffon—and a complete vindication of America as a whole. As Jefferson confided to another French correspondent, his (imaginary) observation of Indians led to the conclusion that "I am safe in affirming, that the proofs of genius given by the Indians of North America, place them on a level with whites in the same uncultivated state."[18] Not only that, he said, but people who had "lived among them . . . all agreed in bearing witness in favor of the genius of this people."

Jefferson went into detail. "As to their bodily strength," he allowed, "their manners rendering it disgraceful to labor, those muscles employed in labor will be weaker with them, than with the European laborer." How-ever, the comparison did not favor the European uniformly, for "those which are exerted in the chase [hunting], and those faculties which are employed in the tracing an enemy or a wild beast, in contriving ambus-cades for him, and in carrying them through their execution, are much stronger than with us, because they are more exercised." Unlike when weighing the capacities and merits of blacks, Jefferson made significant allowance for the state of civilization in which Indians found themselves. This led him to a conclusion diametrically opposite the one he had reached in *Notes* concerning the blacks: "I believe the Indian, then, to be, in body and mind, equal to the white man." Perhaps guessing that his correspondent would be familiar with his book, Jefferson closed this passage by admitting that "I have supposed the black man, in his present state, might not be so; but it would be hazardous to affirm, that, equally cultivated for a few generations, he would not become so."

Another way to demonstrate the falseness of Buffon's claims against the American environment would have been to demonstrate that the

Indians had made great civic achievements in the past.[19] Since the trans-Appalachian United States was in Jefferson's day spangled with various kinds of structures built by bygone Indian civilizations over the previous five thousand years, evidence was abundant. Despite having conducted an archeological excavation early in his life, Jefferson never returned to that science. He did, however, encourage various people in their attempts to record and analyze these monuments (invariably called "mounds," whatever their various forms). Yet, despite finally abandoning fanciful theories about the Carthaginian or other origins of the monuments, Jefferson was very slow to accept the magnitude of the evidence presented to him. His quarrel with Buffon did not require him to believe that North American Indian culture had once achieved a high level, and so he only grudgingly admitted it. By his life's end, however, he expressed pleasure at the fact that "it is truly pleasing to hope that, by [the American Antiquarian Society's] attention, the monuments of the character and condition of the people who preceded us in the occupation of this great country will be rescued from oblivion before they will have entirely disappeared."[20]

Jefferson hoped as secretary of state in 1790–1793 to pave the way for better relations with the Indians. However, doing so would have required maintenance of an adequate military force to ensure that white settlers did not involve America in conflict with its neighbors to the west. When the centralizing tendency of Hamilton's fiscal and constitutional positions became clear, Jefferson fell into consistent opposition to monarchical inclinations. This meant, as the leading scholar of the question put it, that, "his social ideals with respect to the rights of Indians and a humane civilization policy could never be realized." The politician who opposed Washington's suppression of the Whiskey Rebellion would also oppose using the army in the same part of the country to protect Indians. Surely he would not advocate Secretary of War Henry Knox's call for a standing army to be sent to protect the Indians, let alone that anti-Indian malefactors be tried by courts-martial.[21]

In 1803, Jefferson described his hopes concerning Indians' future in a letter to a federal Indian agent.[22] The ideal approach, he said, was "to let our settlements and theirs meet and blend together, to intermix, and become one people. Incorporating themselves with us as citizens of the United States, this is what the natural course of progress of things will, of course, bring on, and it will be better to promote than to retard it. Surely it will be better for them," he philanthropically mused, "to be identified with us, and preserved in the occupation of their lands." Four years later, Jefferson—still president—conceded that "both duty & interest" pressed Americans to make Indians into "useful members of the American family" by imparting the ways of "civilized life."

Jefferson had substantial opportunity to act on his interest in Indians' place in North America generally while president of the United States from 1801 to 1809. The law of nations essentially mandated that he do what he could to establish America's claim to the Louisiana Purchase and the Oregon Territory, and so he had to launch something like the Voyage of Discovery, aka the Lewis and Clark Expedition.

From the beginning of European exploration of the Western Hemisphere, European powers had agreed on two essential points of law.[23] First, the European power that discovered a particular portion of the New World had a claim on that land to the exclusion of other European powers—that is, sovereignty. That claim involved not just the immediate area it had discovered, but the immediately connected area as well. Second, this claim did not preclude continued traditional use of that territory by the Indian inhabitants; rather, those inhabitants could continue there, but in case they left or sold it to the discovering power, the discovering power obtained full title—fee simple—to the place.

Jefferson accepted this understanding throughout his public career. As we have seen, he certainly did believe in its underlying assumption that European civilizations were superior to those of the Indians. His reference to Captain Cook in the *Notes* demonstrates familiarity with that

English seaman's mission to "take possession . . . for His Majesty by setting up proper marks and inscriptions as first discoverers and possessors." The Spanish had responded to Cook's taking down some of their marks of possession by effacing his and restoring their own, and Jefferson was going to ensure that America maintained its valid claim. More significantly for our story, and indeed for contemporary purposes generally, Cook took care to establish British possession of British Columbia, on the northwest coast of North America, in 1776–1778.

As secretary of state in 1790, Jefferson had had occasion to lay out his understanding of these matters. In response to queries concerning the State of Georgia's title to land within its borders, right to grant that land even when still inhabited and used by Indians, and power to extinguish the Indians' title, Jefferson responded that:

> If the country, instead of being altogether vacant, is thinly occupied by another nation, the right of the native forms an exception to that of the new comers; that is to say, these will only have a right against all other nations except the natives. Consequently, they have the exclusive right of acquiring the native right by purchase or other just means. This is called the right of preemption, and has become a principle of the law of nations, fundamental with respect to America. There are but two means of acquiring the native title. First, war, for even war may, sometimes, give a just title. Second, contracts or treaty.

Also in 1790, Jefferson laid out his understanding of discovery doctrine in relation to Cherokee lands in North Carolina.[24] The Cherokee there, he averred, "were entitled to the sole occupation of the lands within the limits guaranteed to them," while the state under the law of nations "established for America by universal usage, had only a right of preemption of these lands against all other nations: It could convey, then, to its citizens only this right of pre-emption, and the right of occupation could not be united to it till obtained by the United States from the

Cherokees." Only the United States could extinguish the Indian title, not North Carolina. In 1793, Jefferson issued a similar opinion regarding Virginia.[25]

Although Jefferson as philosophe argued for Indians' equality with white men, and although in the abstract he hoped to see them subsumed into American society, as a high official of the federal government's executive branch, he faced other imperatives that took precedence over these preferences.[26] Most notable of these imperatives was that of beating other European countries to the punch when it came to claiming the lands of North America's West Coast, and thus establishing the United States as a transcontinental society.

This imperative explains Jefferson's decision, which at first he resisted, of accepting France's offer to sell the Louisiana Territory.[27] Jefferson's constitutional views prodded him to seek amendment of the Constitution prior to the purchase, but he ultimately relented—he thought unconstitutionally—in the name of raison d'état. He said he hoped the Americans would forgive him for taking this step, as so gigantic a bounty could not be sacrificed even to the Constitution. America had to extend from ocean to ocean.

How could that be accomplished? Jefferson's solution was the voyage of the Corps of Discovery, since known to one and all as the Lewis and Clark Expedition.[28] Often depicted as a gratuitous research mission, the expedition was more properly a diplomatic and military one. The word "Discovery" in its official name did not refer to "finding things," but to the law-of-nations doctrine. Jefferson intended, and Meriwether Lewis and William Clark set out, to stake an American claim to the Northwest with priority over those of the European countries.

This helps to explain much about the tasks the expedition performed. For example, one might consider conveying medals with Jefferson's image and pledges of friendship to local Indian leaders absurdly patronizing, a kind of parody of uninformed Americans interacting with supposedly ignorant Indians.[29] Lewis told the Indians that:

[Our great chief] has . . . commanded us to tell you that when you accept his flag and medal, you accept therewith his hand of friendship, which will never be withdrawn from your nation as long as you continue to follow the councils which he may command.[30]

Lewis gave similar speeches to dozens of Indian peoples, whom he also instructed to give Jefferson all the flags and medals they had previously received from their former overlords, the French and Spanish.

When put in the context of the types of rituals always understood as evidence of one European power's discovery of a particular portion of the New World—burying bottles containing written claims, say, or planting markers with a sovereign's name on them—this made perfect sense. For a local Indian leader to be bedecked with a symbol of his and his people's relationship with the US government would satisfy the long-standing legal requirement that the claiming power's discovery be notorious. This was true even where, as mocking ethnohistorians have sometimes noted, the Indians cannot be thought to have understood the relationship in the same way as the Americans did: it did not matter, so far as the law of discovery was concerned, what the Indians thought of it.

In conveying their medals, Lewis and Clark told the Indians with whom they interacted that they were subject to the sovereign United States and could benefit from trading with them. The Indians were also told that they could benefit from a military relationship with them. There should not be any further relations between the Indians and any foreign country—France, Britain, Spain, Russia—just as the doctrine of discovery required.

Here Jefferson's lifelong interest in the Indians dovetailed nicely with diplomatic imperatives. Jefferson and the two army captains were perfectly in sync in regard to the kinds of data the latter should collect on their journey. Jefferson wanted to know all about inland North America's flora and fauna, and that extended to the humans perforce. The Corps took with it a long list of English words Jefferson wanted translated into

Indian languages. Lewis wrote down extensive lists of local words—for day and night, sun and moon, grass and trees, bird and bear, mother and father, warm and cold, and so forth—to take back to Jefferson. A diplomat would need to know such things. The chief executive omnimath would revel in having them, even learning them.[31]

When Lewis and Clark sent shipments of the fruits of their labors back to Washington, DC, they included much material to please Jefferson's intellect: maps to stimulate the son of Peter Jefferson, Virginia's first great mapmaker; antlers and prairie specimens to arm Monsieur Jefferson, antagonist of the comte de Buffon; sketches to decorate the parlor of Thomas Jefferson, ingenious architect of Monticello; and list upon list of Indian words for the great Virginian anthropologist.

Upon finally reaching the West Coast, the Corps of Discovery built a "permanent" settlement, Fort Clatsop, on the Oregon coast. Why go to such effort in a place that the explorers would only inhabit for one winter? Because legal discovery required permanent occupation, and a fort was more arguably permanent than a campsite. Meanwhile, nearby Indians were to be sold the idea that they too were subject to the sovereignty of the United States and its Great Father, Thomas Jefferson.

To ensure that others would learn of the American "discovery" of the Oregon coast, Lewis and Clark posted a letter at the fort.[32] It laid out the history of the expedition to that point, the course the travelers had taken en route to the Pacific, and the dates of their arrival and departure. The goal of this posting cannot have been anything other than to reinforce America's claim to the land. Along the way, the two leaders armed nearby Indian groups with copies of their letter, which they asked them to deliver to passing Europeans. Here was a perfect symbol of the subordination of Jefferson's ethnohistorical and humanitarian goals to imperatives of state: Indians might be interesting biological subjects and promising potential members of American society, but beating Russia, Spain, and Britain to the west was absolutely essential.

Farther east, Jefferson adopted a variegated approach to the problem of extracting land from Indian peoples.[33] He would buy it if possible. He would bribe Indian leaders where the opportunity presented. He urged military officers to push Indians off the land they occupied. As he put it in a letter to Andrew Jackson, who had complained of an Indian agent's excessive sympathy with the Indians, the federal government's chief goals were two: "1. The preservation of peace; 2. The obtaining lands." He went on to say that the particular Indian agent was committed to those goals and the policy of civilization, in the context of explaining that he had pushed the Indian agent to purchase a particular plot.[34] This could be done in case of Indian attacks upon Americans, yes, but he recommended use of a particular stratagem in peacetime too. Indians, Jefferson confided, ought to be loaned as much money as they wanted to borrow by the federal government. Whenever an Indian proved unable to fulfill his debt obligations, he could then be required to provide title to his land in satisfaction. Over time, Jefferson envisioned Indians being converted from hunter-gatherers to American yeomen using this tactic. Whether they were was of secondary importance to him, however: the main thing was to obtain their land.[35]

As president, Jefferson saw acquisition of Indians' land as going hand in hand with civilizing the savages.[36] As he explained to his secretary of war (the cabinet member responsible for Indian relations), occupation of the land along the Mississippi and of the land along the Spanish frontier in the South would give America substantial borders with the great European powers. Civilization would lead Indians to sell their land for money to buy implements, which they could use in the farming that would denude the land of game—and thus drive further Indian population from the land. Government supply stores could encourage Indians to run up debt, which might be extinguished in exchange for further cessions. "Our proceedings," he concluded, "should tend systematically to that object, leaving the extinguishment of title in the interior country to fall in as occasion may arise. The Indians being once closed in between strong settled countries on the Mississippi & Atlantic, will, for want of game, be forced to agriculture, will find that small portions of land well improved, will be worth more to them than extensive forests unemployed, and will be continually parting with portions of them, for money to buy stock, utensils & necessities for their farms & families."[37] Soon thereafter, Jefferson spelled out to William Henry Harrison—his chief agent in the Midwest—the desirability of pushing uncooperative tribes beyond the Mississippi River.[38] Here was the germ of Indian Removal. Before that policy was adopted, however, Jefferson himself had been responsible for acquisition of "close to 200,000 square miles of Indian territory in nine states of the present Union, mostly in Indiana, Illinois, Tennessee, Georgia, Alabama, Mississippi, Arkansas, and Missouri." The purpose was geostrategic, not economic; white population was not yet available to populate this territory, which the Indians did not yet want to abandon.[39]

American Indians' control of most of the area east of the Mississippi came to an end chiefly as a result of purchase and sale, not of warfare. Where it did not end that way, it sometimes ended as a result of a cycle of white encroachment, Indian atrocity, and US government military intervention, at the conclusion of which "a cession was demanded by federal authorities as the price of peace."[40] Whatever the process, Jefferson considered the result inevitable. As he explained in his Second Inaugural Address, Indians had been content in their continent when "the stream of overflowing population from other regions directed itself on [American] shores." Indians were "overwhelmed by the current, or driven before it." By 1805, they no longer could subsist by hunting on their drastically reduced lands, so whites had to teach them "agriculture and the domestic arts; to encourage them to that industry which alone can enable them to maintain their place in existence." Therefore, his administration had "liberally furnished them with the implements of husbandry and household use; we have placed among them instructors in the arts of first necessity; and they are covered with the aegis of the law against aggressors from among ourselves."[41] These efforts had had to contend, Jefferson lamented, with some Indians' attempts to persuade the rest to remain faithful to their ancestors' ways. Jefferson characterized the choice Indians faced as one between "habit" and "the duty of improving our reason."

Ultimately, Congress in 1830 followed President Andrew Jackson's suggestion and adopted the Indian Removal Act, thus not only depriving the Indians of the protective "aegis of the law" but actively driving them from what remained of their ancestral lands. The resulting expulsion of Indians from Georgia and Alabama left only a few hundred of them in Tidewater Virginia and upstate New York.

Jefferson's critics have seen Jacksonian Democrats' policy as of a piece with Jefferson's. There is much truth in this. The Cherokee had become about as acculturated as they could have, with little white schoolhouses, European-style agriculture, American dress, and even Protestantism with a Bible translated into their own language—whose written form was invented specifically to facilitate their practice of Christianity. They had lived up to Jefferson's stated hopes for them.

In the end, it did them little good. A decade after Jefferson's death, Georgia Democrats wanted Indians' land, and their political leaders rushed to give it to them. Perhaps it is somewhat ironic that the Georgia governor most responsible for Indian dispossession, George Gilmer, was a son of Jefferson's dear friend Dr. George Gilmer and a brother of Francis Walker Gilmer, Jefferson's first choice to be the University of Virginia's first law professor. Or perhaps it is not ironic at all. After all, Jefferson's land-hungry Indian policy as president clashed with the one he sketched out in *Notes on the State of Virginia*, and even in his public statements as president. Just as American principles yielded to American practice in regard to the Indian, so did Thomas Jefferson's.

Chapter 5

Mr. Jefferson's University

The final line on Thomas Jefferson's gravestone refers to him as "Father of the University of Virginia."[1] Here Jefferson claims credit for what in his day was the sole portion of his wide-ranging education plan to come to fruition: the establishment of the University of Virginia (UVA), which one scholar has called the first of the modern universities.

Jefferson devoted much of his time in retirement to establishing Central College and having the General Assembly transform it into the state university. As he said in 1817, "I have only this singular anxiety in the world. It is a bantling of 40 years birth and nursing, and if I can once see it on its legs, I will sing with sincerity and pleasure my nunc dimittis."[2] He hoped that the University of Virginia would eventually serve as the keystone of a great edifice of public education designed to promote democratic self-government and the life of the mind in the Old Dominion. With the aid of important lieutenants such as state senator Joseph Carrington Cabell, Governor Wilson Cary Nicholas, former president James Madison, and President James Monroe, he managed to have the university made in accordance with his own vision for the place. In doing so, he capped off not only his forty-seven-year public education project, but also his fifty-seven-year career as the most influential and effective statesman in American history.

Jefferson's efforts on behalf of education for the nonaffluent majority of Virginia's population flowed naturally from his republican commitments. Republicanism meant government by the common people, and the common people needed to be educated if they were going to govern well. "Preach," he told one of his close political allies, his own law teacher George Wythe, "a crusade against ignorance; establish & improve the law for educating the common people."[3] So Jefferson intended to do.

We tend to think of the founding fathers—leaders of the revolution and early republic—as state builders first. Jefferson had other priorities. As he put it to his closest friend and collaborator James Madison, "Say, finally, whether peace is best preserved by giving energy to the government, or information to the people. This last is the most certain, and the most legitimate engine of government. Educate and inform the whole mass of the people. Enable them to see that it is their interest to preserve peace and order, and they will preserve them. And it requires no very high degree of education to convince them of this. They are the only sure reliance for the preservation of our liberty."[4]

Note, "of our liberty." In the aftermath of the revolution, not only common people, but members of the social elite would rely on the adequacy of popular education for their liberty. When Jefferson wrote this letter to Madison in 1787, he sat in Europe, surrounded by the passive many (the ignorant masses) and the oppressive few (the nobility and the monarchs). Division of America into two such classes must be avoided, and honing the people's intelligence was the path to avoiding it.

The story began in 1776, when Jefferson and his friend Edmund Pendleton started to discuss the idea of a revision of the laws.[5] Off in Philadelphia, Jefferson had had to watch from afar as the Virginia Convention adopted a first republican constitution rather unlike what Jefferson had

hoped to see it adopt. If he had had his way, that first republican constitution written by the people's representatives in the history of the world—
the Virginia Constitution of 1776—would have included substantial
legal reforms. Among them would have been provisions that capital punishment was only for the most severe crimes, that each free man who did
not possess as much be given fifty acres of the Commonwealth's land, and
that the Old Dominion's feudal land tenures were abolished. The law of
Virginia remained mired in the feudal past, and Jefferson had intended his draft constitution to remedy the situation.

It was not to be. Jefferson's proposals, other than his preamble and his
use of the title "Senate" for the legislature's upper house, were mostly rejected.

Pendleton thought the policy matters omitted from the Convention's
handiwork should be addressed by the newly reconstituted General Assembly. Perhaps inspired by his hero Sir Francis Bacon, who had suggested such a project for Parliament, Jefferson prodded the General
Assembly to launch the revisal of the laws. Five members were appointed
to a committee to draft a revisal for the House of Delegates' consideration.
Two of the five, George Mason and Francis Lightfoot Lee, begged off,
leaving three core members to perform the task. They were Edmund
Pendleton and George Wythe, the most prominent legal figures in revolutionary Virginia, and the substantially younger Thomas Jefferson. Jefferson seized control of the project, taking responsibility for the most
significant reform proposals.

Ultimately, the revisors submitted 126 bills for the Delegates' consideration. Among them were three—Nos. 79, 80, and 81—directly related
to education. Far the most important of the three was Bill No. 79, "A Bill
for the More General Diffusion of Knowledge."[6] Soon after drafting it,
Jefferson called it the most important bill of the 126 the revisors drafted.[7]
It envisioned establishing primary schools throughout Virginia to which
all free children would be sent. If their parents could not pay, the taxpayers would. The bill also would have established regional secondary

schools to which the best students would be sent, again at the public expense. Finally, it provided for sending the crème de la crème to the College of William & Mary on the taxpayers' tab. The wealthy would be allowed to send their offspring to the secondary schools and to William & Mary as well.

This proposal marked a radical innovation. Up to this time, and indeed until public pre-collegiate education was finally established in Virginia after the Civil War, the wealthy commonly educated their sons by hiring tutors to perform the task in their own households. Alternatively, such boys might instead be sent to regional schools for the social elite run by local ministers. After completing this cycle, a boy likely would proceed to William & Mary. Alternatively, he could be sent to Scotland to study medicine or to England's Inns of Court to prepare for a legal career. Most boys preparing to be lawyers in Virginia, as in other colonies, undertook apprenticeships in the offices of established practitioners instead.

The existing situation reflected and perpetuated the moneyed elite's position atop Virginia society. Jefferson objected to this nonsystem as arbitrarily denying the Commonwealth the benefit of its native talent, for he assumed that most of the ablest young men were from among the more populous lower levels of Virginia society.[8] Those poor fellows usually went through life without the benefit of any particular schooling at all. Not only did the Old Dominion suffer for lack of formal education for such people, but those people themselves would be better situated to exploit their natural right to "the pursuit of happiness" if their minds were cultivated. Thus, Jefferson entitled his proposal "A Bill for the More General Diffusion of Knowledge," not "A Bill for the More General Diffusion of Merit" or ". . . of Ability."

The preambles to Jefferson's draft bills generally explained the reasoning behind them in detail. Certainly his education bill's preamble did. It started by saying that while some types of government were more appropriate to "the free exercise of [individuals'] natural rights and . . .

better guarded against degeneracy," even such governments were prey to the general tendency of officials to transform them into tyrannical ones. The best way to prevent that from happening, it continued, was to educate the people, particularly in the history of "other ages and countries." Armed with that knowledge, they could thwart the schemes of wicked officials.

The second ground for the bill was that "the sacred deposit of the rights and liberties of their fellow citizens" should be guarded by those "whom nature hath endowed with genius and virtue," made fit to make and administer the laws "by liberal education." However, "the indigence of the greater number disabling them from so educating, at their own expence, those of their children whom nature hath fitly formed and disposed to become useful instruments for the public," the public should found and fund schools at the public expense. Otherwise, "the happiness of all [might] be confided to the weak or wicked."

For the purpose of organizing the elementary schools, Jefferson proposed that voters in each county choose "aldermen" each year. Those officials were to be tasked with dividing the county into "hundreds" (a colonial term for a small area; Jefferson eventually would call such districts "wards"). Each hundred should be "of such convenient size that all the children within each hundred [might] daily attend the school to be established therein." The boundaries of hundreds would remain unchanged unless population changes required redrawing them. The site of each school was to be selected by the local electorate.

The electorate would not control the curriculum, however. Rather, "at every of these schools shall be taught reading, writing, and common arithmetick, and the books which shall be used therein for instructing the children shall be such as will at the same time make them acquainted with Græcian, Roman, English, and American history." Each school's teacher would follow the "general plan of reading and instruction recommended by the visitors of William and Mary College." Jefferson thought that reading, writing, and math were essential to full participation in both the civil life and the political affairs of the newly republican state. Knowledge of history, as we have seen, would equip his fellow citizens to guard their liberties against potential usurpers. Therefore, "all the free children, male and female, resident within the respective hundred, shall be intitled to receive tuition gratis, for the term of three years," and they could stay longer if their families wanted to pay for it.

Jefferson's inclusion of female children in this provision is interesting. As he admitted many years later, he had not given "systematic contemplation" to the subject.[9] In his day, the education of girls in Virginia was even more slapdash than that of boys. As he explained, he had thought about it "only as the education of [his] own daughters occasionally required." He suggested that "the inordinate passion prevalent for novels" be avoided by women, as "when this poison infects the mind, it destroys its tone and revolts it against wholesome reading. Reason and fact, plain and unadorned, are rejected." Girls ought instead to be steered toward "interesting and useful vehicles of sound morality," of which he listed a few. Besides those, a few classic writers, including Shakespeare, Pope, and the classic French writers, "may be read with pleasure and improvement." French was necessary for both sexes as "the depository of all science" (meaning knowledge). Besides those, dance, drawing, and "household economy, in which the mothers of our country are generally skilled," were essential. "The order and economy of a house," he summed up, "are as honorable to the mistress as those of the farm to the master, and if either be neglected, ruin follows, and children destitute of the means of living." The constrained prospects of common Virginia women likely explain why Jefferson proposed sending girls only to the primary schools. (Jefferson made no express provision for education of free blacks, let alone slaves. However, he proved open to the former, and even the latter, in a 1796 exchange with Virginia Quaker Robert Pleasants. Pleasants wrote asking Jefferson's opinion of his plan for beginning to educate black children.[10] Jefferson answered that the Bill for the More General Diffusion of Knowledge could be amended for that purpose.[11] He did wonder, however, whether children not destined for freedom would actually benefit from having the veil of ignorance lifted.)

The teacher's pay and expenses, like the expenses of building and maintaining the schoolhouse, would be provided by the hundred's taxpayers. This provision, if Jefferson and other proponents of public education are to be believed, proved the most important in the plan.

Bill No. 79 also provided for "grammar schools"—intermediate schools—in each region. Jefferson specified which counties would be grouped into each region, including in the sparsely populated trans-Appalachian section of the state. The location would be chosen by each county's aldermen, and via eminent domain taken from its owner(s) and the school built thereon. "In these grammar schools," the bill said, "shall be taught the Latin and Greek languages, English grammar, geography, and the higher part of numerical arithmetick, to wit, vulgar and decimal fractions, and the extraction of the square and cube roots." Visitors from each county would join in electing a rector for each grammar school, who would oversee the school's operations "and see that any general plan of instruction recommended by the visiters of William and Mary College [should] be observed."

Jefferson said of the teachers of both the hundred schools and the grammar schools, as well as of the groundskeepers of the grammar schools, that they had to "give assurance of fidelity to the commonwealth" before entering upon their duties. In that day, republicanism could not be taken for granted. Jefferson would not have a monarchist or a foreigner cultivating young citizens.

Each September, the overseer of each hundred school was to select an outstanding student who had finished at least two years' schooling to continue to the regional grammar school at public expense. Two or more of the aldermen were to interrogate the child publicly, with help from other contenders' parents, friends, teachers, or guardians. If the aldermen vetoed the overseer's selection, the process would begin again until a selection was approved. At the grammar school, each September would see one-third of the rising second-year scholarship students discontinued on the basis of their laggard progress. Of those who were entering their third year at the school, only one would be continued, and he could stay for four years more and "thence forward be deemed a senior."

The regions in the northern and eastern parts of the state would each send one senior to William & Mary every even-numbered year, and those in the southern and western parts of the state in every odd-numbered year would each send one select senior to William & Mary. Those scholars would receive room, board, tuition, and clothing from the public while they continued at the college.

The editor of Jefferson's papers observes that while some other jurisdictions, notably in New England, had at least some public schooling even for those whose parents could not afford it, there was a novel element to Jefferson's plan.[12] Jefferson's scheme would identify "natural gradations and disparities among men; it saw nothing dangerous or inimical to the liberties of the people in accepting and making use of . . . a natural aristocracy of virtue and talent; and its unique and revolutionary feature, never yet put into practice by any people, was that, in order to permit such a natural aristocracy to flourish freely, it would remove all economic, social, or other barriers that would interfere with nature's distribution of genius or virtue."

Jefferson early received a prominent Virginian's warning that his plan likely would encounter substantial opposition. The Presbyterian reverend Samuel Stanhope Smith of Hampden-Sydney Academy (now Hampden-Sydney College), who eventually ascended to the presidency of the College of New Jersey (now Princeton University), warned that although he admired Jefferson's plan, it would elicit significant resistance from organized religious opponents.[13] Due to the role Jefferson envisioned for Episcopalian-dominated William & Mary, Smith said, "Be assured Sir, that while she continues under her present influence, the proposal will alarm the whole body of Presbyterians."

Jefferson cannot have been much surprised by this, because he intended to remove religious thought from its historic role in education.[14] Jefferson admired Henry Home, Lord Kames, who in *Essays on the Principles of Morality and Natural Religion* (1751) said that God gave humans a natural "common sense" of morality which fitted them to be social creatures. Jefferson intended to rely on this, not on the imposition of inculcated religious doctrine concerning morality, to guide his students. This intention would have both curricular and disciplinary implications for Virginia scholars in Jefferson's lifetime, and it would lead to political difficulties for Jefferson's proposals.

Also unfortunately for Jefferson's plan, another way in which it was novel in its Virginia context was its expense. Each taxpayer would have borne a significant burden in obtaining the land for his hundred school and his regional grammar school, in hiring a teacher for each and a groundskeeper for the grammar school, and in paying shares of indigent children's tuition at both, board at the grammar school, and expenses at William & Mary.

As Virginia's governor in 1779–1781, Jefferson received a series of queries about the Old Dominion from the French diplomat François Barbé-Marbois.[15] The marquis asked Jefferson about Virginia's geography, its natural resources, its constitution, and various other aspects of its natural and human resources. In the fourteenth chapter, entitled simply "Laws," Jefferson described the revisal project. He commented extensively on Bill No. 79.[16]

Jefferson's purely utilitarian explanation of the competitive element of his plan stands in marked contrast to his previous accounts of it. After beginning by saying that "another object of the revisal is, to diffuse knowledge more generally through the mass of the people," Jefferson describes the education to be provided in the hundred schools and the system for providing a scholarship to the best indigent student's use at the regional grammar school each year. "The best genius of the whole," Jefferson says, is to be "selected, and continued six years, and the residue dismissed. By this means twenty of the best geniuses [one for each of Virginia's proposed twenty regional grammar schools] will be raked from the rubbish annually."

After six years' instruction, Jefferson continues, "one half are to be discontinued (from among whom the grammar schools will probably be supplied with future masters)." While those students are to be put to work instructing the less advanced scholars, "the other half, . . . are to be chosen for the superiority of their parts and disposition, and to be sent and continued three years in the study of such sciences as they shall chuse, at William and Mary college," whose curriculum was also to be reformed. Thus, all would receive three years' basic education, ten per year would also graduate with decent knowledge of Greek, Latin, geography, and higher arithmetic, and ten more would have attained great heights in "such of the sciences as their genius [should] have led them to."

Only after thus describing the system he envisioned did Jefferson explain the plan's purposes. Besides the elitist one of culling the population for its few brightest members and giving everyone the rudiments of learning, Jefferson said that his three-tiered system would provide the wealthy with schools to which they could send their children as they desired and provide all "an education . . . directed to their freedom and happiness."

That happiness would be promoted by replacing the "Bible and Testament," traditional grist of the educational mill, with "the most useful facts from Grecian, Roman, European and American history." (No doubt this provision helped account for the opposition of many Protestant ministers to Jefferson's education proposals.[17]) Without skipping a beat, he added that "The first elements of morality too may be instilled into their minds." Instruction in languages in the grammar schools seemed to Jefferson ideal, as he judged children aged eight to fifteen or sixteen possessed of great ability to memorize, though not to exercise advanced judgment. It was at the conclusion of that stage that the best students would proceed from the grammar schools to the college. Thus, Jefferson said, "we hope to avail the state of those talents which nature has sown as liberally among the poor as the rich, but which perish without use, if not sought for and cultivated." The bright were as apt to be poor as anyone else, so society could only be sure of enjoying their gifts if provision were made for poor people's education at public expense.

Jefferson's description of the education bill concluded with a lengthy passage on the utility, even necessity, of public education in a republic. No aim of the bill was more important, he insisted, than that of equipping the people to guard their own liberty. This purpose accounted for the hundred schools' focus on historical reading. "History by apprising them of the past," he explained, "will enable them to judge of the future; it will avail them of the experience of other times and other nations; it will qualify them as judges of the actions and designs of men; it will enable them to know ambition under every disguise it may assume; and knowing it, to defeat its views."

All constitutions possessed "some germ of corruption and degeneracy," Jefferson ruminated. The "cunning" and "wicked" would cultivate that hint of trouble. This was why "every government degenerate[d] when trusted to the rulers of the people alone." The only way to prevent the overthrow of republicanism—government by the people—was to equip the people with the knowledge they would need to fend off the attempts at usurpation which officeholders were sure to launch. "The people themselves [were government's] only safe depositories. And to render even them safe their minds must be improved to a certain degree."

Corruption, for Jefferson, was best avoided by granting the suffrage to the entire citizenry. While England's extension of the suffrage to one-tenth of the adult males left them with power over nine-tenths, and thus with a powerful incentive to corruption, the American answer to this problem was to give each man a say. No private individual would be able to afford to corrupt the whole population. Properly educated, the people would sniff out attempts to deprive them of their freedom.

Jefferson's elevation to the governorship in 1779–1781, followed by his absence in France in 1784–1789, effectively removed him from the fray of political disputation concerning the Committee of Revisors' proposals. His close ally James Madison took the matter up in the House of Delegates in his absence. Madison finally gave Jefferson an account of the defeat of Bill No. 79 in an epistle dated December 4, 1786.[18] He said that while he had considered it imprudent to debate the bill at length the year before, he had pushed for a thorough debate this session. "In order to obviate the objection from the inability of the Country to bear the expence," he continued, "it was proposed that it should be passed into a law, but its operation suspended for three or four years. Even in this form however there would be hazard in pushing it to a final question, and I begin to think it will be best to let it lie over for the supplemental Revisors, who may perhaps be able to put it into some shape that will lessen the objection of expence."

Under the Virginia Constitution of 1776, each bill had to pass on three readings, and the narrowness of the second vote dissuaded Madison from going forward. Not until 1796 did the matter of public primary and secondary education come up again. At that point, the General Assembly passed a law giving each locality the option of implementing it. Virginians' famous aversion to taxes meant that, with the exception of schools in Norfolk, Jefferson's plan went nowhere.[19] Public primary and secondary education would not become a reality in Virginia until Reconstruction.

The second of Jefferson's three education bills, No. 80, bore the title "A Bill for Amending the Constitution of the College of William and Mary, and Substituting More Certain Revenues for Its Support."[20] This bill reflected Jefferson's intention to transform the college from an organ of the Church of England into a state university.[21] The college's organizers had stipulated that its organization must not be inconsistent with "the royal prerogative, the laws of England or Virginia, or the canons of the Church of England." By the time Jefferson wrote, the authorities had established four schools in the college. The first one, of "sacred theology," had two professors—one who taught Hebrew and scriptural exposition and another who taught "the common places of divinity and the controversies with heretics." The second school, of philosophy, also had two professors: one for "rhetoric, logic, and ethics," and the other for "physics, metaphysics, and mathematics." The third school was for Latin and Greek. The fourth and final school was given the task of instructing Indian boys in "reading, writing, vulgar arithmetic, the catechism and the principles of the Christian religion."

After providing a lengthy description of the numerous statutes, royal grants, and other sources of William & Mary's endowment and other money, besides laying out a description of its organization, Jefferson at last came to the bill's point. Nearly a century of experience had shown, he wrote, that the public's abundant provision for the college had not benefited Virginia as much as Virginia had a right to expect. Since responsibility for the college had always been in Virginia's government, in the wake of independence it was for the General Assembly to reorganize William & Mary. Especially in light of the republican turn in Virginia's political basis and the ongoing revolution, Virginians needed the legislature "to aid and improve that seminary, in which those who are to be the future guardians of the rights and liberties of their country may be endowed with science and virtue, to watch and preserve the sacred deposit."

Jefferson envisioned considerable reform of William & Mary. First, he called for reducing the eighteen visitors of the college to only five, and those five were to be appointed annually by the General Assembly (both houses voting jointly). Professors could be removed only by majority vote of the Commonwealth's three chancellors (equity judges), and then only for "breach or neglect of duty, immorality, severity, contumacy, or other good cause." Where formerly there had been a president and six professors, all selected by the visitors, now there would be eight professors, one of whom should serve as president. All would take an oath of "fidelity to the commonwealth" before assuming their positions. The professors would have "the ordinary government of the College, and administration of its revenues, taking the advice of the visiters on all matters of great concern."

What all of this amounted to was a substantial strengthening of the college's faculty. The school's president would now be one of the professors, and the professors were to have a status akin to what is now known as tenure: they would be removable only for cause. Day-to-day administrative matters, and even routine financial matters, were to be the faculty's responsibility, and the "visiters" were to have a role only in making significant policy decisions. Here, in concept, was something very much like the way contemporary American colleges theoretically function—though the most recent decades have seen inroads by professional administrators into areas of college decision-making long thought properly the province of the professors.

The eight William & Mary professors would, under Jefferson's scheme, be organized thus: "one of moral philosophy, the laws of nature and of nations, and of the fine arts; one of law and police; one of history, civil and ecclesiastical; one of mathematics; one of anatomy and medicine; one of natural philosophy and natural history; one of the ancient languages, oriental and northern; and one of modern languages." Even more radical than the transfer of authority to the faculty previously described would be this innovative curriculum. While since the time of Cato the Elder Western education had stressed instruction in the Greek and Latin languages, and while subsequent developments had given priority to Christian theology, Jefferson intended to drop the theology school and seriously downgrade the emphasis on the classical languages. In their places, he contemplated requiring students to master the latest developments in science, besides learning contemporary languages. He saw Christian theology as essentially worthless, referring to it consistently as "priestcraft" and with other negative epithets, and the subjects he wanted to stress struck him as eminently practical.

In place of the former Indian school, Jefferson proposed dispatching someone among the Indians occasionally "to investigate their laws, customs, religions, traditions, and more particularly their languages, constructing grammars thereof, as well as may be, and copious vocabularies." This person was to report his findings to the president and professors.

Often overlooked by scholars is the irreligious component of Jefferson's final curricular proposal. The College of William & Mary's organizers hoped North American Indians could become fellow Anglican Protestants, and so they called for their instruction in "reading, writing, vulgar arithmetic, the catechism and the principles of the Christian religion." Jefferson, on the other hand, proposed that the college treat Indians only as objects of curiosity, and so he proposed for them to be studied, observed, measured, and interrogated—but not in any sense helped. In light of Jefferson's lifelong interest in and sympathy for Indians, this may come as a bit of a shock. However, the reform was in this regard not as significant as it seems: very few Indians actually had been instructed at William & Mary—usually only a handful at a time. The Indian School's endowment, a dedicated portion of the rents from an English manor, had become unavailable with the coming of the revolution, and so suddenly any connection between the college and Indians would have to be conceived for the benefit primarily of Virginians.[22] With this in mind, Jefferson apparently thought the science of ethnography a desirable replacement for Indians' education.

Jefferson also proposed substituting a more dependable source of income to the college for the hodgepodge of sources outlined at the beginning of his bill. Finally, he provided that David Rittenhouse, "that greatest of astronomers" (and, coincidentally, an American), be paid by the Old Dominion to provide William & Mary a copy of his famous model of the solar system.

The historian of opposition to Jefferson's education proposals credits Episcopalians unhappy with Jefferson's Bill for Establishing Religious Freedom with ultimately blocking the plan to remake Virginia's old college—America's second-oldest college—from a Christian school into an Enlightenment one such as Jefferson envisioned.[23] They were right in opposing Jefferson's plan as anti-Episcopalian, for Jefferson said that he understood it that way. As he put it, William & Mary in 1780 was "an establishment purely of the Church of England; the Visitors were required to be all of that Church; the Professors to subscribe to its 39 Articles [Anglicanism's version of a creed]; its Students to learn its Catechism; and one of its fundamental objects was declared to be to raise up Ministers for that church."[24]

Although the General Assembly thwarted Jefferson's effort at first, he soon after accepted appointment as the Commonwealth's governor—and thus as one of William & Mary's governing visitors.[25] In that capacity, he later recalled, he "effected . . . a change in the organization of that institution, by abolishing the Grammar school, and the two professorships of Divinity and Oriental languages, and substituting a professorship of Law and Police, one of Anatomy, Medicine, and Chemistry, and one of Modern languages." Besides that, he continued, "we added the Law of Nature and Nations, and the Fine Arts to the duties of the Moral professor, and Natural history to those of the professor of Mathematics and Natural philosophy." The failure of Madison's efforts to have Bill No. 80 adopted in 1785–1786 marked only a partial frustration of Jefferson's efforts, then. William & Mary was not yet the secular modern university Jefferson wanted for Virginia, but it was no longer the medieval Christian school he had found it.

The final one of Jefferson's revisal bills concerning education was Bill No. 81, "A Bill for Establishing a Public Library."[26] This bill provided that every year the Virginia government would spend the substantial sum of "two thousand pounds" on "books and maps" to be added to the collection of a state library to be located in the capital, Richmond. The task of selecting items for purchase would be performed by three visitors chosen by the two houses of the General Assembly jointly. The books and maps were to be used on the library's premises.

The editor of Jefferson's papers notes that Jefferson intended the public library not as a circulating library after the fashion of Benjamin Franklin's famous Philadelphia library, but as a research center for the exceptionally gifted.[27] According to Jefferson's account in *Notes on the State of Virginia*, he meant for the library ultimately to form part of a joint complex with a public art gallery containing fine paintings and sculptures. Like the other two education proposals, it won little legislative sympathy in the revolutionary era.

As a congressman in 1784, Jefferson had opportunity to make his impress upon the educational history of the Old Northwest via the Land Ordinance of 1785. His proposal was that each township of thirty-six square miles should be divided into square-mile sections, which would be subdivided into acres. At each township's center would be a town school.[28]

While minister to France, Jefferson had repeated opportunities to hold forth to individuals who inquired of him concerning the proper form, content, and location of education for wealthy Americans. Not until 1794, however, did the former secretary of state and rising Republican Party leader have an opportunity to return to serious advocacy of a substantial departure in Virginia's state educational policy. A professor at the prestigious University of Geneva, François d'Ivernois, wrote him with a shocking question: would America be interested in having that school's entire faculty come to America for the purpose of starting a new school here?[29] For Jefferson, this meant Virginia could have a first-class European school—he ranked it one of Europe's two best—of its own, all at once.

An especially attractive feature of the Genevan college was what Jefferson classed as its thoroughly republican bent. However, as he explained to a political ally, the plan's expense and the fact that the Genevan faculty was francophone seemed apt to pose powerful obstacles. Soon enough, Jefferson found himself writing to d'Ivernois to explain the General Assembly's rejection of the proposal.[30] Jefferson listed three reasons for this unfortunate turn of events. First, he said, young Virginians were unprepared for French-language instruction. Second, voters likely would not be happy with the great associated expense. Third, so great an institution was not commensurate with Virginia's relatively slight population. "I should have seen with peculiar satisfaction," Jefferson concluded, "the establishment of such a mass of science in my country," but it was not to be. Soon afterward, he approached President Washington about making the Genevan institution the basis of a national university— to be located in Virginia, as there was not yet a District of Columbia. Washington turned him down too, stressing the francophone factor, though also pointing to the college's political situation in France and to the desirability of drawing a national university's faculty from more than one institution.[31]

Like Washington, Jefferson favored the idea of a national university. From his perch as president of the American Philosophical Society (APS), which he held from March 1797 to 1814, he was involved in awarding a prize to two essayists in an essay contest about a US education system.[32] Both writers envisioned hierarchical systems akin to that contemplated by Jefferson's Bill No. 79 in each state, with a national university atop. Although Jefferson had tried at one point to transform the College of Geneva into an American national university, he never said precisely how that institution ideally would be related to Virginia's state educa- tion system. In light of the fact that he does not seem to have had any role in devising the APS contest and left no writing addressing the subject, we do not know whether Vice President Jefferson thought that ideally there would be one national education system or—more likely—wanted separate state systems and a national university.

As vice president, Jefferson ultimately found himself completely out- side the executive branch policy-making process. Indeed, he became the symbol of opposition to the Federalist Party of President John Adams, his once and future friend. Although he regularly attended sessions of the Senate, his duties as presiding officer left him substantial time for com- piling a manual of parliamentary procedure still fundamental to congres- sional practice, strategizing concerning opposition policy, and engaging in wide-ranging correspondence. Among the matters about which he corresponded was education.

Early in 1800, Jefferson fired off a letter to the prominent English man of letters Joseph Priestley.[33] Jefferson believed Priestley to be of like mind—primarily because he misunderstood Priestley's religious views. He thus felt free to share with Priestley his latest thinking about reform of Virginia's education system. Virginians, Jefferson assured Priestley, "will recieve your ideas with the greatest deference & thankfulness."

Jefferson lamented that William & Mary stood "just well enough endowed to draw out the miserable existence to which a miserable constitution ha[d] doomed it." Besides that, he said, it lay in a sickly part of the Commonwealth. In his first surviving reference to the eventual University of Virginia,[34] he said he hoped to replace it with a centrally located state university "on a plan so broad & liberal & *modern* as to be worth patronizing with the public support" and to draw students from outside Virginia as well as from among Virginians. A fit plan for the university would emphasize practicality. This meant that some of the sciences not much studied at European schools would be included in its curriculum, while some subjects stressed at European institutions (he mentioned "the Oriental learning") would be omitted.

Priestley, Jefferson noted, knew the Americans well. He also knew European educational practices well. Thus, he was uniquely qualified to give Jefferson advice about how the university ought to be organized. Jefferson listed the subjects in which he envisioned having his students instructed—"Botany. Chemistry. Zoology. Anatomy. Surgery. Medicine. Natl. Philosophy. Agriculture. Mathematics. Astronomy. Geology. Geography. Politics. Commerce. History. Ethics. Law. Arts. Fine arts. This list is imperfect because I make it hastily, and because I am unequal to the subject."

Jefferson went on to say that he hoped Priestley would tell him which of these courses could be taught by the same professor and which of them would have to be individual professors' sole areas of expertise, as minimizing the number of professors would help the Old Dominion afford the university. He imagined requiring faculty members "follow no other calling," and he hoped to draw premier instructors from Europe via significant financial inducements; that would not be necessary in succeeding generations, as the university's own graduates succeeded to faculty positions. Jefferson closed the missive by noting that Virginia's leading politicians awaited Priestley's advice. Once they had received it, he forecast, they would move swiftly to begin the project. "They will receive your ideas with the greatest deference & thankfulness," he wrote.

Jefferson wrote Priestley again a few days later.[35] This time he reminded Priestley of Bill No. 79. He also took the opportunity to note that while he had omitted any mention of linguistic study from his first letter, and while he did not anticipate that Greek and Latin would form a key component of the program of study in the university he envisioned, he found boundless enjoyment in the study of Greek and Latin. "I thank on my knees him who directed my early education for having put into my possession this rich source of delight," he gushed, noting that he considered the highest achievements of Greek and Roman writers preeminent in world letters. Not for university students, however, but for the young was study of languages best suited. While their minds did not yet possess the capacity for higher study, they were entirely fit for the memory work of which learning languages was chiefly composed.

In closing his letter, Jefferson tied it to contemporary political goings-on. The Alien and Sedition Acts Crisis seemed to him just ending, and Jefferson begged the immigrant scientist to forgive Americans their "temporary delirium." "The Gothic idea that we are to look backwards instead of forwards for the improvement of the human mind, and to recur to the annals of our ancestors for what is most perfect in government, in religion & in learning, is worthy of those bigots in religion & government, by whom it has been recommended, & whose purposes it would answer, but is not an idea which this country will endure." For Jefferson, his education reforms were of a piece with his political posture, and his opponents tended to recognize it as well: he supported liberalization of education as a prop/outgrowth of liberalized political life, and they opposed it for the same reason.

Priestley took issue with some of Jefferson's ideas.[36] Perhaps most significantly, he attempted to dissuade the vice president from trying to recruit European professors. He would do that only if necessary, Priestley said, because European professors would expect more deference from their pupils than Americans were accustomed to give. Priestley also held that there ought to be two types of post-secondary educational institution, corresponding to our contemporary division between undergraduate and graduate schools. The former would be for potential government officials, the other for budding professionals. Jefferson ultimately rejected these ideas.

His assumption of the presidency in March 1801 put Jefferson in position to influence a different aspect of American educational organization: establishment of the United States Military Academy at West Point, New York.[37] Jefferson's choice as first superintendent reflected the president's goals for the academy. Major Jonathan Williams had no great military accomplishments to his name, and in fact was inexperienced. What he had were a family tie to Benjamin Franklin, with whom he had conducted significant scientific experiments, and a long-standing relationship with Jefferson, who knew him to be politically reliable. This fit him well for a school whose legislative purpose was to prepare members of the army's Corps of Engineers.

Neither Jefferson nor Secretary of War Henry Dearborn gave Williams much guidance at all regarding how the academy was to achieve its assigned task. Although Jefferson added to the list of books and implements Williams told him he judged necessary, Dearborn more than once told him to bear in mind that Congress was in a parsimonious mood. Williams dove into his task energetically, founding the United States Military Philosophical Society, setting up a library which included some books

Williams had inherited from Franklin, and winning Jefferson's assent to have his name used as "Patron."

Williams and Jefferson wanted to relocate the academy to Washington. They hoped that there it would "become a national school of engineering," a type of institution more than one prominent man had said America should establish. Williams also wanted to broaden the school's curriculum to include several other scientific subjects. Jefferson tried in a Special Message to persuade Congress to act on Williams's relocation proposal by noting, "The scale on which the Military Academy at West Point was originally established is become too limited to furnish the number of well-instructed subjects in the different branches of artillery and engineering which the public service calls for."[38] He added that, "The idea suggested by him of removing the institution to this place is also worthy of attention. Besides the advantage of placing it under the immediate eye of the Government, it may render its benefits common to the Naval Department, and will furnish opportunities of selecting on better information the characters most qualified to fulfill the duties which the public service may call for." Ultimately, however, the Williams/Jefferson concept of a national university with a military college joined the ranks of proposals Congress never endorsed. Joel Barlow's proposal for a national university, this time without an engineering college, also won President Jefferson's support, and it too went down to defeat. Jefferson told Barlow that these things simply took time.[39] He hoped for eventual success.

As president, Jefferson filled one other role not often mentioned: that of the first president of the Washington, DC, school board.[40] He assumed the position in August 1805 and accepted reappointment two years later. The board's report on September 19 echoed Jefferson's old Committee of Revisors Bill No. 79 in laying out a plan for a three-tiered education system providing free schooling for the indigent, with "Schools for teaching the rudiments of knowledge necessary to the common purposes of life; a College in which the higher branches may be taught; and a Univer-

sity, in which the highest and most splendid attainments may be acquired."
Like Jefferson's other federal education proposals, this one ran aground
on the shoal of Congress's resistance to funding it. However, DC public
education's day would come.

Jefferson spent all seventeen years of his retirement in Virginia. While he
paid attention to federal politics, and while he occasionally and privately
lent his weight to such causes as government primary and secondary
schools and state constitutional reform, his twilight years would be most
notable for his role in establishing the University of Virginia. He took the
failure to implement his whole educational plan in his lifetime in stride,
saying, "If we cannot do everything at once, let us do one thing at a time."[41]

In the first months of his retirement, Jefferson resisted the urge to re-
enter the political fray. When Governor John Tyler, a boyhood friend,
asked the ex-president to accept election to the House of Delegates and
there advocate Tyler's education program, Jefferson replied that he
had not the energy for it.[42] Tyler sympathized, conceding that the program for which he had called would likely achieve little more success
than efforts to pass Bill No. 79 had achieved a quarter of a century earlier.
Virginians still disliked taxes.

If Jefferson had had his way, however, the entire program laid out in
Bill No. 79 would have been implemented. At its base would have been
the hundreds, or—as he now called them—wards. On April 2, 1816, Jefferson wrote to his close associate (and in-law) Governor Wilson Cary
Nicholas that his wards proposal concerned more than education. Rather,
he thought of it as apt to improve public administration generally. In the
New England states, he said, local organization helped maintain the "order and economy" of government. It also accounted for New Englanders'
"momentum . . . as a nation." (Note: New England was a "nation.") At
about the same time, he explained the matter similarly to Joseph Carrington Cabell. Cabell was destined to play a huge role in Jefferson's
education efforts. In Russia, Jefferson told Cabell, concentration of

power in an autocrat had "destroyed liberty and the rights of man." The response in America should be to "let the national government be entrusted with the defence of the nation, and its foreign and federal relations; the State governments with the civil rights, laws, police, and administration of what concerns the State generally; the counties with the local concerns of the counties, and each ward direct the interests within itself." Ultimately, each man should supervise his farm himself. "By placing under every one what his own eye may superintend, . . . all will be done for the best."

This remains a dream. His university idea is another matter.

To call Jefferson's effort in founding the University of Virginia "herculean" would flatter the first Heraclid. A 1973 Founder's Day address at UVA summarized his work by saying that the former president "had to purchase the land, to plan the grounds and buildings, to supervise the construction, to direct the engagement of professors, to devise the curriculum, and finally to act as the chief executive officer and also as secretary, taking notes, writing the minutes, and compiling voluminous reports for the authorities in Richmond." In the history of American higher education, there has never been anything like it.[43]

At the time of the University of Virginia's founding, no other American university existed. As Yale College's president, the prominent Federalist Timothy Dwight, noted in 1816, America had colleges and seminaries, but no university.[44] Jefferson not only conceived of a university but did everything to bring his conception into being.

The idea of a new university had continued percolating within the Virginia political elite even during Jefferson's presidency. St. George Tucker and Littleton Waller Tazewell, two leading intellectual lights of the Old Dominion, both pondered the notion, Tucker even drawing up a plan.[45] Tazewell wrote to Jefferson at the close of 1804 with news that the Commonwealth might have money to fund their plan (which was much like Jefferson's) and that they contemplated a location in the environs of Charlottesville—Jefferson's hometown. He solicited the older man's advice concerning the basics of establishing a university, including its organization, courses of study, financing, and so on.

Jefferson replied in a lengthy missive shortly after receiving Tazewell's.[46] "Its importance," Jefferson gushed, "induces me to hasten the answer." "No one can be more rejoiced at the information that the legislature of Virginia are likely at length to institute an University on a liberal plan." He went on to lay out the reasons why he favored establishment of a Virginia university.

"Convinced that the people are the only safe depositories of their own liberty, & that they are not safe unless enlightened to a certain degree, I have looked on our present state of liberty as a short-lived possession unless the mass of the people could be informed to a certain degree." Two levels of education were required: universities and local schools. The former "would prepare a few subjects in every State, to whom nature has given minds of the first order," while the latter would equip each other citizen with "such a degree of learning . . . as [would] enable him to read, to judge & to vote understandingly on what is passing." As only one of these two goals seemed attainable at present, "let us receive with contentment what the legislature is now ready to give." Characteristically, Jefferson ended with a prediction that "the other branch will be incorporated into the system at some more favorable moment."

Jefferson next gave Tazewell his opinions about the various matters that had to be addressed before a university could actually commence operation. First was that the General Assembly had to pass an act establishing the institution. This act "should deal in generals only," providing for the university's object, its site, its endowment, and its organization. The object should be stated only generally, as specifics would become outdated rather quickly. "Every one knows," he wrote, "that Oxford, Cambridge, the Sorbonne, etc. are now a century or two behind the science of the age." Best to let the university's visitors be in charge of the school's mission, within general guidelines established by the legislature.

The location should not be specifically stipulated in the law, because then the landholders would have the whip hand in negotiating for sale of land to the purchasing agents. The endowment should be for the visitors to invest, as the value of any particular piece or type of property might decline in value over time. The visitors or some such group should be responsible for choosing replacements for the initial ones chosen by the General Assembly.

The visitors would have to consider several different types of questions. The location, the professors, the types of investments, and the needed buildings would all be identified by them. Jefferson repeated what he had said to Priestley about the need to minimize the number of professors by having each teach as many of the subjects offered as could reasonably be expected. Jefferson told Tazewell that he had both Priestley's and Pierre S. du Pont's thoughts about this matter in written form. He also said that he had Edinburgh's, the Sorbonne's, and Geneva's organizational structures to use for guidance. "From these the Visitors could select the branches useful for the country & how to groupe them. A hasty view of the subject on a former occasion led me to believe 10. professorships would be necessary, but not all immediately. Half a dozen of the most urgent would make a good beginning." He also relayed to Tazewell his idea that while the first recruits to the faculty would require bountiful remuneration, their successors' affection for the school would reduce this need.

Jefferson confessed his lack of expertise regarding investment, saying others would know more. As to the buildings, he counseled against large buildings on the grounds that they "are always ugly, inconvenient, exposed to the accident of fire, and bad in cases of infection. A plain small house for the school & lodging of each professor is best." As if this did not foreshadow the eventual shape of his Academical Village clearly enough, he immediately added that "these connected by covered ways out of which the rooms of the students should open would be best." He thought the number could be increased as the school grew. "In fact," he said, "an University should not be an house but a village. This will much lessen their first expenses."

If the school were begun "on a plan worthy of approbation," Jefferson teased, "I shall have a valuable legacy to leave it." What he meant was his huge private library, "which certainly has not cost less than 15,000 Dollars." Not only were the books valuable, but the purchase of those about America by Jefferson or under his direction from booksellers in five different European countries could never be duplicated.

Not much came of this matter. Still, on February 8, 1810, the Senate passed a House bill creating "The Literary Fund of Virginia."[47] This bill's point was to take the resources to which Tazewell had pointed in his initial letter to Jefferson and devote them to public education—purportedly of the poor. In time, this fund would form the germ of the University of Virginia.

The War of 1812, which ravaged Virginia's Tidewater region and seriously straitened its finances, put education reform on the back burner.[48] In the meantime, however, Jefferson exploited an opportunity to take control of a local school that might be remade into his university. The Virginia General Assembly had chartered Albemarle Academy in 1803, and Jefferson's nephew Peter Carr was president of its foundation. As one historian explained, "Jefferson invited himself to one of Albemarle's board meetings at the Old Stone Tavern [near the courthouse] in Charlottesville in March 1814 and joined the school's trustees."

Soon enough, Jefferson was explaining at length to Carr exactly what he hoped to make of Albemarle Academy—and indeed what form he hoped education in Virginia generally would take.[49] "I promised the trustees," he said, "that I would prepare for them a plan, adapted, in the first instance, to our slender funds, but susceptible of being enlarged, either by their own growth or by accession from other quarters." He then laid out his vision for government schools in Virginia in terms very similar to those we have seen him use in his letters to Priestley and Tazewell on the subject, including his concept of a public university, "either with or without incorporation into . . . William and Mary."

Hinting at his desire ultimately to transform Albemarle Academy into something far grander, Jefferson said Virginians "must ascertain with precision the object of our institution." Having identified the state of learning generally, they could proceed to establish "elementary schools," "general schools," and "professional schools." Here Jefferson seems to have modified the plan reflected in Bill No. 79, for he envisions the third level as entirely professional, with separate courses of study for "the lawyer," "the ecclesiastic," "the physician," "the military man," "the agricultor," and "the gentleman, the architect, the pleasure gardener, painter, and musician." There would also be a catchall "school of technical philosophy" for "the mariner, carpenter, shipwright, pumpmaker, clockmaker, machinist"—in short, skilled workers, who could "learn as much as shall be necessary to pursue their art understandingly, of the sciences of geometry, mechanics, statics, hydrostatics, hydraulics, hydrodynamics, navigation, astronomy, geography, optics, pneumatics, physics, chemistry, natural history, botany, mineralogy, and pharmacy." These men would study their subjects in the evening, after working all day long. Besides that, all students should be taught the rudiments of soldiering and "should be under a standing organization as a military corps," as which they should regularly drill.

The Albemarle Academy, he concluded, should "have nothing to do" with the elementary schools. "The sciences of the second grade are our first object." In the earliest days, the more advanced sciences would be chief among its cares, and the number of instructors to teach them would increase, as would their specialization, as financial means became more abundant. He proposed that the school at first have four professorships: one for ancient and modern languages, belles lettres, rhetoric, and oratory; one for mathematics, physico-mathematics, physics, anatomy, medicine, and theory; one for chemistry, zoology, botany, and mineralogy; and one for philosophy. More practical organizational and financial questions, he said, should be addressed by visitors more competent to the task.

The historian of Jefferson's career as an educational theorist notes that the "ecclesiastic" program made no appearance in subsequent iterations of Jefferson's Albemarle Academy plan.[50] Jefferson also excised the "school of technical philosophy," a rather unwieldy concept, from later descriptions of his vision.

The board of Albemarle Academy accepted Jefferson's proposal in the letter to Carr. Soon enough, Jefferson's allies in the legislature began work on funding the school. Jefferson threw his support behind renaming Albemarle Academy "Central College," though some preferred "Jefferson College."[51] When illness drove Peter Carr from leadership of the school, Jefferson turned to Joseph Carrington Cabell. Cabell, a scion of one of the state's most prominent political dynasties, the owner of its most storied plantation, and a state senator, would become "the main pillar" of legislative effort in behalf of Jefferson's scheme.[52]

Cabell replied that he had not heard of the bill for reorganization of Ablemarle Academy, but would do his best to win passage. He at first hoped his alma mater, William & Mary, would not suffer in the process, but eventually he decided that Jefferson's plan for Central College deserved his support regardless of its impact on William & Mary. With some alterations, "the bill creating Central College became law on February 14, 1816."[53]

Jefferson achieved a political coup with appointment of Central College's initial board of visitors. They included former presidents Jefferson and James Madison, President James Monroe, and state legislators from three counties bordering Albemarle—including Joseph C. Cabell of Nelson County. Never in history has a college had so august a board. Surely the General Assembly must have realized that Jefferson had big plans in mind.[54]

Jefferson sent requests for advice to two prominent architects,

Dr. William Thornton and Benjamin Henry Latrobe.[55] He knew both from their work on the US Capitol. The advice they returned included that the pillars on the pavilions around "the lawn" (as Jefferson now dubbed it) should be round, not the square Jefferson had in mind, and that the north end of the lawn should be dominated by a single building. In time, that would be the famous Jeffersonian Rotunda. Here as in the case of the Declaration of Independence, what is regarded as "Jefferson's" conception actually reflects the contributions of plural heads.

Jefferson laid out the lawn himself, deciding on 255 feet as the north-south length of each of the terraces and 200 feet as the distance between the east and west sides of the lawn. All three members of the Virginia dynasty of Jeffersonian Republican presidents were in attendance as Board of Visitors members when the cornerstone of the first pavilion was laid on October 6, 1817. As Philip A. Bruce, a historian from a Virginia family that has produced several prominent historians, described the scene, "President Monroe applied the square and plumb, the chaplain asked a blessing on the stone, the crowd huzzaed, and the band played 'Hail Columbia.'" A Masonic ceremony was performed, a Masonic grand master gave a speech, and that was it: Central College officially had begun to be built.[56]

Not only did Jefferson now have a "go" signal for the greatest architectural project of his spectacular architectural career, but he at last could also begin to shape the faculty of his school. Among the first men he tried to hire was the notorious religious skeptic Dr. Thomas Cooper.[57]

Cooper had first come to Americans' attention as son-in-law of the eminent Joseph Priestley. During the Alien and Sedition Acts Crisis, he had been imprisoned for expressing banned opinions.[58] This certainly must have won him favor with Jefferson. However, Cooper's religious/scientific opinions—although he called himself a Unitarian, he has been described as "a strict materialist" and was widely considered an atheist—put him in bad odor with Virginians.[59] One scholar classified the attempt to hire Cooper as "a public relations disaster," adding that the political hit Jefferson and his project took in Cooper's behalf is hard to explain, because Jefferson did not want atheism to be taught at UVA.

Jefferson called Cooper "the greatest man in America in the powers of mind and acquired information."[60] Whether that was true, he likely admired Cooper's willingness publicly to buck convention. For example, Cooper did not graduate from Oxford University because he refused to subscribe to the Thirty-nine Articles, the touchstones of Anglican faith.[61] As we have seen, Jefferson disapproved of William & Mary's traditional structure, and proposed to alter it, in part on the ground that professors had to subscribe to the Thirty-nine Articles. His failure to reform his alma mater to his liking helped account for his desire to create Central College. Cooper had subsequently had trouble with multiple employers, including Transylvania College in Kentucky. He told Transylvania, "you will do no good with a clergyman at the head of your institution, you must have a gentleman and a man of the world."

Despite their misgivings, the Board of Visitors accepted Jefferson's request to hire Cooper in March 1819. This facilitated religious Virginians' linking UVA to the French Revolution—an upheaval that, of course, Jefferson had strongly supported. Cooper had publicly denied that fundamental Christian teachings such as the human soul, free will, and eternal punishment even merited consideration. In this, he classed them with still more basic Christian beliefs such as in the Trinity—the Christian definition of God. Cooper's leading critic was a friend of John Hartwell Cocke and Cabell, two members of the Board of Visitors. Though he supported Central College, he opposed Thomas Cooper.

In the end, Cooper decided to stay in South Carolina rather than step into the hornet's nest his critics had stirred up. Jefferson explained this turn of events by saying that Presbyterians "dread the advance of science as witches do the approach of day." As he told Cooper, "The Presbyterian clergy alone, remain bitterly federal and malcontent with their government. They are violent, ambitious of power, and intolerable in politics as in religion. . . . Having a little more monkish learning than the clergy of other sects, they are jealous of the general diffusion of science, and therefore hostile to our seminary."

If this had been true, critics could have thwarted the drive to establish Central College and pushed for primary schools led by ministers. That they did no such thing showed that they did not want to—that, despite Jefferson's assertion to Cooper, people who criticized Cooper were not "hostile to" the project for UVA. They were simply hostile to the idea of paying someone with Cooper's opinions to oversee instruction of their young men.

Meanwhile, Jefferson's plans ran into significant opposition in the House of Delegates. Although Senator Cabell did yeoman's service in the Senate, the House's consideration of these matters came under the guidance of Charles Francis Mercer, chairman of the House Committee on Finance.[62] Mercer pushed to have the university, if there was to be one, put west of Charlottesville, by hook or by crook. Still, his February 1816 resolution marked "the first official sanction for bringing into existence a University of Virginia," as the historian of Jefferson's education reforms put it.

Jefferson responded to this difficulty by drafting his own updated legislative proposal for a general education program. In October 1817, he sent Cabell a revision including nine, rather than the original twenty, grammar schools—thereby substantially reducing the cost of those schools and the cost of sending their best students on to a university.[63] This bill notably included a provision that only the literate should be citizens; Cabell struck that out before introducing the proposal.[64] When Cabell introduced this bill to the Senate in January 1818, Jefferson personally sent the General Assembly an update on Central College's progress. He gave the legislators the hard sell, enumerating several positive traits of the institution—its location, its healthy climate, its possession of significant real estate, the campus's ("Grounds'") layout (which was capable of significant expansion as money became available), the fact that significant funds had already been raised, and the substantial start that had already been made in faculty recruitment, before he presumptuously noted that "if the Legislature [should] think proper to proceed to the establishment of an University, and to adopt for its location the site of the Central College, . . . towards the establishment of such an University, . . . we ourselves shall be ready to deliver over our charge." In other words, if the General Assembly adopted Central College as its future university, the visitors would be happy to sign it over for that purpose. The letter was signed, in order, by (President) Monroe, Madison, Watson, Cocke, Jefferson, and Cabell.[65]

The project did not come to full fruition just yet. In fact, the General Assembly rejected it and two competing plans (one of them Mercer's) before voting to spend $45,000 from the Literary Fund on a school for the poor in each county. Although that bill won the governor's signature on February 21, 1818, Cabell achieved the significant feat of adding an amendment stipulating that $15,000 per year would be set aside from the Literary Fund to help pay for a university. It also said "twenty-four discreet and intelligent persons" should be named to a commission to answer the broad organizational questions involved in setting up a university: location, physical organization, curriculum, number of professors, tasks of each professor, and governmental structure. These twenty-four (one for each state senate district) were to meet in the summer of 1818 at Rockfish Gap in the Blue Ridge Mountains.[66]

Jefferson attended as his senate district's delegate. Three Tidewater commissioners were no-shows. The commission elected Jefferson to preside.[67] One tale has it that Jefferson displayed a cardboard cutout of Virginia with a dot on it, and that he "proved" the dot central to the cutout—and thus to Virginia—by balancing the cutout on a pencil at the dot. The dot was for Charlottesville.[68] In the end, the advocates of putting the university at Staunton or Lexington joined proponents of William & Mary in defeat: Jefferson's scheme won all but five votes when the commission voted.

The commissioners' report clearly reflected Jefferson's priorities.[69] Dated August 4, it began by saying they had convened on August 1 "as the law required, at the tavern, in Rockfish Gap, on the Blue Ridge" and took up their legislative charge. The first matter of business was to select a site for "the 'University of Virginia,'" and they thought "the governing considerations should be the healthiness of the site, the fertility of the neighboring country, and its centrality to the white population of the whole State." These points may seem rather odd, but we should recall that in those days before modern medical science, particular geographic locations—for example, Williamsburg, whose reputation for unhealthiness had led commissioner James Madison as a young man to opt to attend the College of New Jersey at Princeton over Virginia's own College of William & Mary—were thought to be unhealthy, thus to be avoided. The reference to Albemarle's location in the center of Virginia (which still included West Virginia) would have struck its nineteenth-century audience as quite significant. In fact, numerous states, including Virginia, had moved their capitals from their coastal colonial locations (New York, Charleston, Savannah, Jamestown-cum-Williamsburg, and so forth) precisely because it seemed fairer to locate them more or less in states' centers. The report said that it was Albemarle's location that ultimately gave it the advantage over Lexington (home of Washington College, now Washington and Lee University) and Staunton.[70]

In regard to "the second of the duties assigned to them," the board adopted the plan Jefferson had long advocated: it proposed "that [the university] should consist of distinct houses or pavilions, arranged at proper distances on each side of a lawn of a proper breadth, and of indefinite extent, in one direction, at least." It continued by saying that each pavilion should provide accommodations for a professor and his family, besides space for instruction. The pavilions should be connected by dormitories, each large enough for no more than two students. This would promote study without promoting immoral behavior of the kind Jefferson had lamented while he was a student at William & Mary six decades before.

Jefferson imagined that the numbers of pavilions and dormitories could grow as the student body did. Here was one of the plan's chief attractions, along with "security against fire and infection," "comfort to the professors and their families thus insulated," and "retirement to the students." Capping the whole project, as Benjamin H. Latrobe had suggested in July 1817, would be "a building of somewhat more size in the middle of the grounds . . . in which may be rooms for religious worship, under such impartial regulations as the Visitors shall prescribe, for public examinations, for a library, for the schools of music, drawing, and other associated purposes."

In reply to the charges "of reporting 'the branches of learning, which should be taught in the University, and the number and description of the professorships they will require,'" the commissioners first outlined what they believed should be taught in the primary schools. Obviously, the university would not be charged with instruction in basic matters such as the mechanics of writing. Jefferson and company took the opportunity to instruct the legislature on the proper content of an elementary education, the purpose of which was "to give to every citizen the information he needs for the transaction of his own business," besides enabling him to write clearly, to perform basic mathematical calculations, "to improve, by reading, his morals and faculties," to know "his duties to his neighbors and country," and to vote wisely. Thus, the subjects taught in the elementary schools should be "reading, writing and numerical arithmetic, the elements of mensuration, (useful in so many callings,) and the outlines of geography and history."

Beyond the elementary schools, the curriculum's chief goal should be "to form the statesmen, legislators and judges" on whom Virginians would rely. Those men should be taught both civic and international law, besides "a sound spirit of legislation, which, banishing all arbitrary and unnecessary restraint on individual action, shall leave us free to do whatever does not violate the equal rights of another." Products of Virginia's advanced schooling would understand the relationships among the

Commonwealth's three main areas of economic activity—agriculture, manufactures, and commerce—and "give a free scope to the public industry." Prosperity would be optimized, in Jefferson's mind, by setting men free to do as they would, so long as they harmed no other.

Besides that, they should learn "mathematical and physical sciences," and their education should "form them to habits of reflection and correct action," which would make "them examples of virtue to others, and of happiness within themselves."

Jefferson and the commission conceded that some considered education in all these matters impractical—too expensive to be a proper government concern. To buy that argument, however, would mean that Virginians would have to go abroad to pursue advanced education. Fortunately, the legislature's charge to them showed that it was not so parsimonious. Not only was this a hopeful sign for the present generation, but "we should be far, too, from the discouraging persuasion that man is fixed, by the law of his nature, at a given point; this his improvement is a chimera, and the hope delusive of rendering ourselves wiser, happier or better than our forefathers were." If Jefferson was a progressive, his faith lay not in the potential of government for improving the human condition, but in the potential of man to cultivate himself and of science to expand his knowledge, with its psychic and practical ramifications, "not *infinitely*, as some have said, but *indefinitely*." "What but education," he asks, "has advanced us beyond the condition of our indigenous neighbors? And what chains them to their present state of barbarism and wretchedness, but a bigotted veneration for the supposed superlative wisdom of their fathers?"

Next came the organization of professorships on which the commission had agreed. There would be a professor of ancient languages (Latin, Greek, and Hebrew); one of modern languages (French, Spanish, Italian, German, and Anglo-Saxon); one of mathematics (algebra, "fluxions," geometry, and military and naval architecture); one of "physico-mathematics" (mechanics, statics, dynamics, pneumatics, acoustics, optics, astronomy, and geography); one of physics, chemistry, and mineralogy; one of botany and zoology; one of anatomy and medicine; one of government, political economy, the law of nature and nations, history, politics, and law; one of municipal law; and one of ideology, grammar, ethics, rhetoric, belles lettres, and fine arts.

After explaining precisely what some of these professors would teach, the report noted that study of the languages could overwhelm the school with a multitude of small boys. A solution lay ready to hand: establishment of schools for this purpose throughout the Old Dominion. Such schools could take in boys of about ten years old, and their charges could study not only the languages, but also "English grammar, higher branches of numerical arithmetic, the geometry of straight lines and of the circle, the elements of navigation, and geography." Finished products of these institutions would be ready for the university, say "about the fifteenth year of their age."

After a few words about the report's language proposal and its medicine provision, Jefferson turns to the question of religious instruction. "Our [Virginia's] Constitution," he says, "places all sects of religion on an equal footing," and that fact, besides the different sects' mutual jealousies and "the sentiments in the Legislature in favor of freedom of religion," had led the commission to omit any provision for a professor of divinity. The ethics professor will have responsibility for proofs of God's existence, which are related to His role as "the creator, preserver, and supreme ruler of the universe, the author of all the relations of morality, and of the laws of obligation those infer [*sic*]." Besides that, it should be left to future visitors to decide exactly how the various instructional duties will be allocated among professors; the commission's proposal is only that.

During their free time, students at the university should study "the manual exercise, military manœuvres, and tactics generally" frequently. This is the best age for acquisition of such skills. "The arts which embellish life, dancing, music, and drawing; the last more especially, as an important part of military education," ought also to be attended to. These matters will not be charged to university faculty members, however, but "may be left to accessory teachers, who will be paid by the individuals employing them."

In passing, the report said that instruction should be entirely up to the faculty, diet should be up to the students, lodging should be in dormitories, and whether degrees or honorary degrees should be granted ought to be up to the visitors. Government might be on the pattern of father and son (as opposed to the strict corporal type of discipline used in European schools). In a footnote, the commissioners note that "a police exercised by the students themselves, under proper discretion, has been tried with success in some countries" and might be tried at the University of Virginia. In time, the university would indeed opt for its famous honor system—which has a higher reputation among alumni and the public than it does among the faculty. In general, today's undergraduates, less concerned with honor by far than their predecessors in times gone by, commonly shrink from imposing the single sanction: expulsion. Thus, malefactors often skate. In Jefferson's day, this development lay far in the future.

Finally, the report described various gifts of land and other assets offered by proponents of the Lexington, Washington College, and Central College bids for the new university's site. The legal imperfection of the first two was also noted. In regard to Central College's support, saved for last probably to maximize its effect, no such caveat was entered. The commissioners voted 16–3–2 for Central College over Washington College and Staunton. The next day, August 4, 1818, came the commissioners' signatures, which included those not only of Jefferson and Madison, but of Judge Spencer Roane of the state's highest court, former governor William H. Cabell, prominent state politician Archibald Stuart, law professor and judge Creed Taylor, and numerous other worthies. They voted too that Jefferson had presided with "great ability, impartiality, and dignity."[71]

Via some expert political maneuvering, Cabell finally overcame geographic and ideological opposition. The ideological opposition echoed former US senator William Branch Giles's argument earlier in the decade that public schools made no sense: most families could not afford for their children to go off to college for three years, which anyway would have very little practical use for the typical farmer or laborer whose tuition was to be shouldered by the affluent.[72] Followers of Adam Smith in the Legislature, Cabell worriedly told Jefferson, insisted schooling should be privately financed.[73] But the opposition came to naught, and the House's January 19, 1819, vote of 141–28 for the university was followed by a 22–1 vote for it in the Senate six days later.[74]

In the seven years left to him, Jefferson would alternate between urging legislators to support the university and personally handling, or at least supervising, most of the myriad tasks involved in creating Virginia's new school. He felt a particular imperative to complete the task as the Missouri Crisis (1819–1821) impinged upon his consciousness, saying to Cabell that the alternative to establishing a University of Virginia was to see many Virginian youths go to Harvard, which would "return them to us fanatics & tories."[75] He later told Cabell that "the great object of our aim from the beginning, has been to make the establishment the most eminent in the United States, in order to draw to it the youth of every State, but especially of the south and west." Thus, the organizers must aim to hire the best faculty, build the best facilities, and win the best reputation. The school was not to be "another Hampden Sidney or Lexington [that is, Washington College]."[76] Rather, it would be a southern institution to cultivate the True Principles of the Old Republican point of view.[77]

Jefferson took the lead in hiring the first professors, designing the buildings, supervising their construction, and even deciding what books would be in the library. During his tenure as rector, students dined with him at Monticello in rotation.[78] Among those who probably did was the most notable of the earliest students, Edgar Allan Poe. Poe excelled scholastically, though the gambling debts he incurred (more than one historian speculates that this was due to his need for funds) exceeded his capacity to pay. Campus lore in the 1990s, when I was in graduate school at Mr. Jefferson's University, credited Poe with shooting the wooden hands off the face of the Rotunda clock; this, one heard, accounts for the use of metallic hands ever since. Alas, this apocryphal story is likely untrue.

In time, the university become somewhat different from what Jefferson envisioned. Eventually, a chapel was placed between the Rotunda and the main library. Students long ago ceased all to live on the lawn, instead finding accommodations in huge dormitory buildings and off-campus apartments. Professors too have long since moved off-campus. Decades ago, officials responded to students' unwillingness to stay in the small Jeffersonian quarters with their common showers to be reached only by walking outside, including in winter, by making assignment to Jefferson's dormitories an honorific; the next thing one knew, All-American basketball player Ralph Sampson and UVA's leading scholars were living on the lawn. Jefferson might be surprised that the university ceased to be all-white and virtually all-male about half a century ago, though both developments fulfilled his prognostications.

His conception shines through even now. "Mr. Jefferson's University," as everyone there calls it, long ago became the leading university in the South, and it is always atop or near the top of national rankings of public universities. Students hail from all over the world, including many from other states, though the bulk are Virginians—just as Jefferson planned. The chapel is essentially open to anyone, and the Department of Religious Studies treats that topic as a scientific one—even if a Catholic priest and some of the world's leading exponents/practitioners of Tibetan Buddhism are among its professors.

The only one of Jefferson's original buildings no longer standing is his medical amphitheater, where America's first full professor of medicine, Dr. Robley Dunglison, presided from 1825, the year the university opened.[79] Although very ingeniously designed, it proved impossible to aerate adequately, which rendered it unhealthful. Today the university is the site of a substantial teaching hospital much like other such institutions across the country. In its combination of teaching, research, and service to the surrounding population, the hospital is entirely Jeffersonian.

The initial faculty of Mr. Jefferson's University was recruited, in the main, by Francis Walker Gilmer. A son of Jefferson's close friend, the late Dr. George Gilmer, Francis certainly resented his treatment at the hands of the Virginia dynasty. Seeing his brother rejected for a federal judicial post, Francis wrote to that brother, Peachy Gilmer, that in case the situation were reversed and Jefferson had died young leaving several sons, Dr. George Gilmer would have done more for them than Jefferson, Madison, and Monroe ever had for the Gilmer boys.[80] At another point, Francis wrote that he had had dinner in the "sanctum sanctorum" (Monticello) the night before, and if James Monroe—one of Jefferson's dinner guests—was bright enough to be president, anyone could be president.[81] For his part, Jefferson held Gilmer to be "the best-educated subject we have raised since the Revolution."[82] Chosen the university's first law professor by Jefferson over some resistance from other visitors, Gilmer ultimately died before the school opened. One of his brothers eventually served as governor of Georgia, while the Gilmers' brother-in-law William Wirt was long US attorney general.[83]

Gilmer succeeded handsomely in his endeavors to recruit distinguished European men of letters for the university's faculty. That group included men with credentials from some of the leading European schools, including Cambridge University, Trinity College, and England's Society of Apothecaries. The leading historian of the subject notes his disappointment at not finding anyone at the University of Edinburgh willing to relocate to Charlottesville, but given the remoteness of Virginia and the university's remoteness within Virginia, it is hard to see how he could have done better.[84]

In other such schools, Jefferson told Madison, assignment of a textbook was frequently the visitors' job.[85] Due to the great disparity between the university faculty's learning and that of the visitors, on the other hand, Jefferson envisioned leaving it to the faculty unless some problem arose. "But there is one branch in which I think that we are the best judges," he said, "and the branch itself is of that interesting character to our state, and the US. As to make it a duty in us to lay down the principles which are to be taught. It is that of government." Clearly, by "we," he referred to Madison and himself.

Jefferson went on to say that prior to Gilmer's passing, some had thought Gilmer's ideas a bit tinged with the federalism "of the Richmond lawyers," and although he did not believe a word of it, there was always a chance that the political powers that be would impose some such person as UVA's law professor. As a hedge against any such development, he concluded, "I think it a duty to guard against danger by a previous prescription of the texts to be adopted."

Madison replied that there really was no adequate textbook available.[86] Algernon Sidney and John Locke had written works of general applicability "admirably calculated to impress upon young minds the right of Nations to establish their own Governments," but when it came to the immediate problem—the habit of the Supreme Court under John Marshall and other American judges of remaking the US Constitution and state constitutions in the guise of construction—they afforded "no aid." "The Declaration of Independence . . . falls nearly under a like observation." *The Federalist* had not foreseen all the misconstructions that would arise or prevented all of those it had foreseen, and neither political party agreed entirely with the book. The Virginia *Report of 1800*, Madison's great blast against Hamiltonian constitutional excesses in the Washington and Adams administrations, would as a partisan document tend to drive away potential UVA students from non-Republican families. In fact, "the Document is not, on every point, satisfactory to all who belong to the same party." Madison hoped they could make it less imperative upon the law professor that he use the assigned texts, and he added both President Washington's First Inaugural and his Farewell Address to the list. This could solve the problem of partisan appearances. The main thing, however, was that "the most effectual safeguard against heretical intrusions into the School of politics, will be an able & orthodox Professor." The Board of Visitors accepted its august leaders' recommendation on March 4, 1825.[87]

Generally leaving selection of texts to professors was not the only liberal innovation Jefferson made at the University of Virginia. In keeping with his project of replacing the traditional European curriculum with something more practical, he also persuaded the Board of Visitors to adopt a resolution saying it would be up to students to decide for themselves what shape their programs of study would take. It seems this idea came to him when pondering his grandson Francis Eppes's experience at South Carolina's Columbia College.[88] Eppes chafed under the strict assignment of undesired courses, mandatory progression through four successive years with the same entering cohort (as freshmen, sophomores, and so forth), and the mandatory expenditure of four years' time to complete them. Sympathetically, Jefferson wrote that it would be "the fundamental law of our university to leave everyone free to attend whatever branches of instruction he wants, and to decline what he does not want." Jefferson shared his idea with a Harvard professor of his acquaintance, who took up the idea with only limited success.[89] Mr. Jefferson's University stood alone in its curricular liberality for half a century, and to this day no one at the University of Virginia is called "freshman," "junior," or by any such title.

In the eighteenth century, Jefferson, Madison, and other college students had been subjected to extensive requirements of rote memorization. At the University of Virginia, on the other hand, students listened to lectures from faculty members—a far superior system.[90] Rather than reciting what they had memorized, they also from earliest days took written exams—which Yale began to use in 1830 and Harvard adopted as normal in 1857.[91]

Although they once did, UVA students do not undergo military training as part of their curricula.[92] Rather, their state, like the rest, depends on precisely the kind of large military establishment Jefferson feared as an instrument of an American foreign policy very unlike what Jefferson envisioned. This foreign policy, and the sprawling government at Washington, have much to do with the high price of education at the university. So too does the Old Dominion's declining commitment to funding its post-secondary institutions. There is talk at UVA of ceasing to denominate the university a "public" institution, since in 2014 only 5.8 percent of the university's funding came from the Commonwealth, and the trend is downward.[93] That's right, 5.8 percent, which translates to one-seventeenth. The state cut funding for its colleges and universities by over half from 1980 to 2011, and its flagship school was hard hit.[94] Meanwhile, enrollment and expenses actually grew. The shortfall was made up chiefly by private donations, but tuition increased significantly as well. Here is one reason Virginia's college-attending young people tend to leave the university with substantial debt. As we have seen, this amounts to complete abandonment of Jefferson's goal for the brightest young Virginians to have their education financed by the Commonwealth. There are arguments that those who reap the direct benefits of a public university education should pay for that education, but that was not Jefferson's position: he proposed that the University of Virginia's student body should include a large contingent of students on full scholarship, and that none of the Old Dominion's top young people forgo a UVA education due to inability to pay. To the extent that this goal has not been met, Jefferson's dream of rule and leadership by the "natural aristocracy" remains unfulfilled.

Perhaps surprisingly, this is not a novel situation, but can be traced all the way to the university's first cohort of students. On the rolls of the first matriculants one finds the names Randolph, Mason, Lee, Harrison, Marshall, Page, Carter, Cary—all the surnames of the fabled First Families of Virginia who had governed the Old Dominion from its beginning and who played such an outsize role in the United States' early history.[95]

(Jefferson himself was a Randolph on his mother's side.) In fact, through the antebellum era, the University of Virginia remained America's most expensive school.

Also absent from Virginia's educational establishment at Jefferson's death on the fiftieth anniversary of the Declaration of Independence—July 4, 1826—were the lower-level public schools he always said should be the base of the public education pyramid. Governor John Tyler Sr., Senator Joseph Carrington Cabell, Governor Wilson Cary Nicholas, Delegate James Madison, and other sympathetic leaders told him over a period of more than four decades that Virginia's landed elite would not voluntarily pay the taxes necessary to finance the scheme. Only with the coming of Reconstruction, when the indigenous elite's power had been shattered, did Virginia come to have public primary and secondary schools.

A central feature of the University of Virginia's grounds is a large alumni cemetery. There, among beautiful trees and lovely monuments, one can encounter the graves of many young UVA men who died defending their Commonwealth in what Virginians of their day preferred to call the "War Between the States," as well as those of numerous of the university's early faculty members. The huge contribution of Mr. Jefferson's University, and indeed of the Old Dominion, to the Confederate hosts surely resulted in large part from Jefferson's and Madison's success in making their school a hotbed of Jeffersonian Republican constitutionalism. "It is in our Seminary," Jefferson wrote a few months before his death, "that that Vestal flame is to be kept alive. It is thence it is to spread anew over our own and the sister states. If we are true and vigilant in our trust, within a dozen or 20. years, a majority of our own legislature, will be from our school, and many disciples will have carried it's doctrines home with them to their several states, and have leavened thus the whole mass."[96]

Conclusion

Thomas Jefferson is remembered by the general public today chiefly for having been president of the United States. Close behind is his very felicitous expression in 1776 of what several years later were latched onto as appealing ideas. Thus, he is commonly called the author of the Declaration of Independence, and to him are imputed various twentieth- and twenty-first-century ideas about equality. In addition, many people are fascinated by his sex life. Speak to a group about Jefferson, and "Did he or didn't he?" is bound to be asked.

It seems to me that what Jefferson did as a constructive statesman is far more important than is generally recognized. He was the most significant statesman in American history. After describing some of his most important easily achieved reforms, I have undertaken in this book to examine what I take to be the most significant reform programs that run through the entire story of Jefferson's long political career.

Those quick achievements were momentous. The Louisiana Purchase, arguably the most important of his public acts, came to him unexpected and unwanted. The reform of Virginia's land tenures, which meant elimination of the colonial landed aristocracy, was an easy achievement. Moving Virginia's capital from Williamsburg to Richmond came easily too.

The five major themes that form the subjects of this book's five chapters drove him during his entire public career. Though no longer central to American constitutionalism, federalism—the principle of decentralization—always struck Jefferson as essential to popular self-government. He argued forcefully that British colonists in North America were entitled to it, and then he based the Declaration of Independence on it. He insisted in the age of federal constitution writing that it be respected, and once the Articles of Confederation gave way to the US Constitution, he held that the states remained the sovereign players in the political game, the federal government's powers strictly limited. Whether in the highest federal offices or as a private citizen, he held the federal government to this principle until his very end.

Within the Old Dominion, Jefferson argued that freedom of conscience was the first principle of free society. His role in enactment of the Virginia Statute for Religious Freedom, a role that he exaggerated to his friend James Madison's detriment, struck him as his most memorable achievement. Nevermore would Virginians' deepest, most personal commitments be dictated by their government—because some things were too important for government. The Creator, he said, made the mind of man free, and government must respect this fact.

As a citizen of the Republic of Letters, Jefferson found himself defending the Western Hemisphere against the aspersions cast upon it by the greatest of Enlightenment biologists, the comte de Buffon. One score upon which he defended his hemisphere's honor was in relation to the natural endowments of its original inhabitants. Buffon and his biological circle erred outright in insisting that Indians were physically and mentally inferior to Europeans, Jefferson forcefully argued. In fact, Indians were the white man's equal, and they would make fine American citizens; this only seemed unlikely, Jefferson held, because their cultures were at so much ruder a stage of development than the Europeans'. If they could be acculturated, they could become American. Jefferson argued that Indians should be encouraged to farm as white men did. As president, however, he held acquisition of Indian lands a more pressing priority than Indians' incorporation into American society—and thus arguably laid the groundwork for the forced dispossession of Indians east of the Mississippi River undertaken by Jacksonian Democrats within a few years of Jefferson's death.

Jefferson's position regarding black people's future in North America lacked the optimistic thread that ran through his Indian policy—and indeed, his thinking about virtually all public questions. Contrary to popular myth, Jefferson did not passively accept that slavery, despite its apparent inconsistency with his political principles, should continue to exist. However, his scheme for hastening slaves' freedom included their deportation . . . somewhere. Anywhere. They would be freed, and they must be deported. This program of colonization, as it was called, would make both whites and blacks better off, he thought, because whites were irredeemably biased against blacks, and blacks had a gigantic reservoir of reasons to hate whites. Free them here, and cataclysmic violence would follow. If blacks were to enjoy their rights to life, liberty, and the pursuit of happiness—as he insisted God would have them do eventually—they would have to be divorced from whites first. Yet, while his friend Madison headed up the quixotic American Colonization Society and their ally James Monroe eventually gave his presidential imprimatur to the establishment of Liberia as a place to which American freedmen could be sent, Jefferson was mostly smiling passivity on this question. He did scout out foreign lands to which they could be sent early in his presidency, but for the most part, he was all words in regard to colonization.

Contemporary historians have often rebuked Jefferson for not applying himself in his retirement to the task of selling the idea of emancipating the slaves, at least in Virginia. They have tended to take his insistence that this would involve spending political capital he had earmarked for a more politically plausible cause as mere rhetoric covering disinterest in the topic. However, Jefferson also gave this answer to his friend Governor John Tyler when that fellow revolutionary asked the ex-president to return to the General Assembly and support what was likely a futile effort to establish public primary and secondary schools throughout Virginia. No one argues that Jefferson's stated support for public education was a ruse.

In fact, the dear cause for which he carefully husbanded his political resources in those last few years was another component of his plan for public education: establishment of the University of Virginia. Mr. Jefferson's University, as it will forever be known, would be the alternative to the old landed aristocracy. Where formerly that class had given Virginia, and America, a quality of leaders—George Washington, George Mason, George Wythe, Jefferson, Madison, Monroe, Edmund Randolph, John Marshall, Patrick Henry—unique in history, the education system Jefferson envisioned would cull the cream of Virginia's population and prepare it for the top posts in government and in society in a revolutionary way. The University of Virginia would provide the best young men in Virginia, rich and poor, a radically new type of education, an education for republican leadership. Envied for it in Jefferson's day by leaders at Harvard and Yale, UVA was America's first university with the first American professor of medicine, a novel curriculum, novel instructional methods, novel flexibility in course selection, and a planned living arrangement for students and faculty members that would make them not a British-style hierarchy but an "academical village." In short, the place would have reflected Jefferson's personality even if he had not drawn the architectural plans, overseen construction of all the buildings, overseen selection of the faculty members, had his finger in the choice of some classes' textbooks and the library's first holdings, and otherwise put his impress on every element of the university that comes to mind. This genius of republican optimism gave vent to all his hopes in fathering that school.

Thomas Jefferson never wrote a book of political philosophy or explained exactly what he hoped Virginia, or America, would be. Yet, if he had been a pointillist painter, there would be enough dots on his canvas for the viewer to be able to make out a clear image. I hope that in reading this book, you have come to see that image.

Acknowledgments

T his book could not have been written without the support of my agent, Andrew Stuart, and my editor, Michael Flamini. Michael's editorial team at St. Martin's Press made this a markedly better book than I first gave them. Thanks to my colleagues in the Western Connecticut State University Department of History & Non-Western Cultures for various types of help, and for their friendship. Additional thanks go to Western Connecticut State University for a one-semester research sabbatical. The staff of the Connecticut State University libraries, particularly the staff of the Haas Library at Western Connecticut State, provided invaluable assistance. Many thanks, in particular, to our patient, cheerful, professional interlibrary loan technician, Joanne Elpern. Thank you too to students in my various undergraduate and graduate courses on Jeffersonian America/The Early Republic. Thinking through the various problems and themes in the historiography and primary materials of that period with you has shaped this book profoundly.

Special thanks go to four scholars whose close readings of parts of this manuscript helped me greatly in bringing the project to completion. Daniel Dreisbach gave me several suggestions that contributed to making the chapter on Jefferson and freedom of conscience a far better essay than it had been. Annette Gordon-Reed highlighted several flaws in my chapter on colonization; the finished product is better in several places because of her intervention. Bob Paquette's expert reading of that chapter saved me from numerous missteps, large and small.

Then there is Peter S. Onuf. Typically of my treatment of him ever since I first became his mentee in my first year of graduate school at Mr. Jefferson's University, I asked Peter for commentary only on the chapter with which I knew he was apt to disagree. He generously reported that this tack put him in mind of our shouting matches, mostly on the general topic of the chapter in question, long ago. Along with the time I spent as ancient history TA to Elizabeth Meyer, those discussions were the most important parts of my graduate education. He said the memories were happy ones for him too. He remains my model of a scholar, a mentor, and a historian.

When I began this project, Trianna, Marika, and Cyril were fourteen, twelve, and ten. Now Trianna is about to be a junior in college (pre-med, because she's smarter than her dad), Marika is about to start (as an engineering major at UVA, no less, because she is too), and Cyril is nearly as tall as I am. Thank God for them.

Notes

1. Federalism

1 I think particularly of John Marshall, who in *McCulloch v. Maryland* (1819) misleadingly equated the argument that the states created the US Constitution with an argument that the state governments created the US Constitution.

2 The point between the dashes was made by the Stamp Act Congress of 1765 in its famous resolutions. Resolutions of the Continental Congress, October 19, 1765, Avalon Project (Yale University), avalon.law.yale.edu/18th_century /resolu65.asp.

3 Speech of Edmund Randolph, June 24, 1788, *Documentary History of the Ratification of the Constitution*, eds. John P. Kaminski et al. (Madison: State Historical Society of Wisconsin, 1993), 10:1483.

4 Speech of George Nicholas, June 24, 1788, ibid., 1507.

5 James Wilson, State House Yard Speech, October 6, 1787, *Collected Works of James Wilson*, eds. Kermit Hall and Mark David Hall (Indianapolis: Liberty Fund, 2007), 1:171–77, oll.libertyfund.org/titles/2072.

6 Kevin R. C. Gutzman, *Virginia's American Revolution: From Dominion to Republic, 1776–1840* (Lanham, MD: Lexington Books, 2007), 129–30.

7 This paragraph and the next rely on Merrill D. Peterson, *Thomas Jefferson and the New Nation: A Biography* (New York: Oxford University Press, 1970), 35–36.

8   Resolves of the House of Burgesses, May 16, 1769, *Encyclopedia Virginia*, ency-
     clopediavirginia.org/media_player?mets_filename=evr3808mets.xml.
9   "Autobiography," *Thomas Jefferson: Writings*, ed. Merrill D. Peterson (New
     York: Library of America, 1984), 3–101, at 9.
10   Joseph Ellis, *Passionate Sage: The Character and Legacy of John Adams* (New
     York: W. W. Norton, 1993), 64.
11   "A Summary View of the Rights of British America," *Thomas Jefferson: Writings*,
     105–22.
12   For the idea that Jefferson "had envisioned federalism as the desired form of union
     for America" at least as early as "A Summary View," also see David N. Mayer, *The
     Constitutional Thought of Thomas Jefferson* (Charlottesville: University Press of
     Virginia, 1994).
13   For Bland's originality and Jefferson's debt to him, see K[evin] R. Constantine
     Gutzman, "Jefferson's Draft Declaration of Independence, Richard Bland, and
     the Revolutionary Legacy: Giving Credit Where Credit Is Due," *Journal of the
     Historical Society* 1 (2001), 137–54.
14   My favorite account of the imperial crisis and the American Revolution is John R.
     Alden, *A History of the American Revolution* (New York: Da Capo Press, 1989).
     A concise account is Gordon S. Wood, *The American Revolution: A History* (New
     York: Modern Library, 2003).
15   For the relationship among Adams's personality, his politics, and his faith, see
     Ira Stoll, *Samuel Adams: A Life* (New York: Free Press, 2008).
16   This paragraph relies on R. B. Bernstein, *Thomas Jefferson* (New York: Oxford
     University Press, 2003), 22.
17   The distinctions between the constitutional views of American colonists and
     those of Britons are clearly explained in Jack P. Greene, *Peripheries and Center:
     Constitutional Development in the Extended Polities of the British Empire and the
     United States, 1607–1788* (New York: W. W. Norton, 1990).
18   This paragraph relies on Merrill Peterson, *Thomas Jefferson and the New Nation*
     (New York: Oxford University Press, 1970), 78–79.
19   Ibid., 81–82.
20   "Resolutions of Congress on Lord North's Conciliatory Proposal," July 31,
     1775, *Thomas Jefferson: Writings*, 331–35.
21   Kevin R. C. Gutzman, *Virginia's American Revolution: From Dominion to Re-
     public, 1776–1840*, chapter 1.
22   A good biography is Kent J. McGaughy, *Richard Henry Lee of Virginia: A
     Portrait of an American Revolutionary* (Lanham, MD: Rowman & Littlefield,
     2003).

23 Henry Mayer, *A Son of Thunder: Patrick Henry and the American Republic* (Charlottesville: University Press of Virginia, 1991).

24 Douglass Adair, *Fame and the Founding Fathers* (Indianapolis: Liberty Fund, 1998).

25 TJ to Thomas Nelson, May 16, 1776, Founders Online (National Archives), founders.archives.gov/documents/Jefferson/01-01-02-0153.

26 Jefferson's three drafts, George Mason's first draft, the committee revision of Mason's draft, the committee report, and the final Virginia Constitution of 1776 can be found at *The Papers of Thomas Jefferson*, ed. Julian P. Boyd et al. (Princeton, NJ: Princeton University Press, 1950–) (hereafter *PTJ*), 1:337–86.

27 Far the best of the numerous studies is Pauline Maier, *American Scripture: Making the Declaration of Independence* (New York: Alfred A. Knopf, 1997).

28 TJ to William Fleming, July 1, 1776, *PTJ*, 1:411–13, at 412–13.

29 "A Declaration by the Representatives of the United States of America, in General Congress Assembled," *Thomas Jefferson: Writings*, 19–24. This edition includes both the portions of Jefferson's original draft excised by Congress and the portions of the final version added by Congress. My concern is with Jefferson's version.

30 TJ to James Madison, February 8, 1786, *Thomas Jefferson: Writings*, 848–52, at 848–49.

31 For Madison and the constitutional reform effort through the Philadelphia Convention, see Kevin R. C. Gutzman, *James Madison and the Making of America* (New York: St. Martin's Press, 2012; paperback edition with a new introductory essay, St. Martin's Griffin, 2013), chapter 3.

32 For Madison and the ratification campaign, see Kevin R. C. Gutzman, *James Madison and the Making of America*, chapter 4, and Kevin R. C. Gutzman, "James Madison and the Ratification of the Constitution: A Triumph over Adversity," in *A Companion to James Madison and James Monroe*, ed. Stuart Leibiger (Malden, MA: Wiley-Blackwell, 2012), 74–90.

33 Dumas Malone, *Jefferson and the Rights of Man* (Boston: Little, Brown, 1951), 162.

34 TJ to John Adams, August 30, 1787, *Thomas Jefferson: Writings*, 906–09.

35 TJ to William S. Smith, November 13, 1787, *Thomas Jefferson: Writings*, 910–12, at 910–11.

36 TJ to John Adams, November 13, 1787, *Thomas Jefferson: Writings*, 912–14.

37 Dumas Malone, *Jefferson and the Rights of Man*, 165.

38 TJ to James Madison, December 20, 1787, *Thomas Jefferson: Writings*, 914–18.

39   For Madison and ratification, see Kevin R. C. Gutzman, *James Madison and the Making of America*, chapters 4–6.

40   Dumas Malone, *Jefferson and the Rights of Man*, 249.

41   Appendix, Thomas E. Woods Jr., and Kevin R. C. Gutzman, *Who Killed the Constitution? The Federal Government vs. American Liberty from World War I to Barack Obama* (New York: Crown Forum, 2009), 215.

42   The best Hamilton biography, though admiring, is Forrest McDonald, *Alexander Hamilton: A Biography* (New York: W. W. Norton, 1982).

43   Alexander Hamilton to Robert R. Livingston, June 28, 1777, Founders Online (National Archives), founders.archives.gov/documents/Hamilton/01-01-02-0201.

44   Alexander Hamilton, ed. Joanne Freeman (New York: Library of America, 2001). "Report on Public Credit," January 9, 1790, *Alexander Hamilton: Writings*, 531–74.

45   Alexander Hamilton, "Report on a National Bank," December 13, 1790, *Alexander Hamilton: Writings*, 575–612.

46   Alexander Hamilton, "Report on the Subject of Manufactures," December 5, 1791, *Alexander Hamilton: Writings*, 647–734.

47   This account depends on Kevin R. C. Gutzman, *Virginia's American Revolution: From Dominion to Republic, 1776–1840*, 116–17.

48   For Madison's House speech against the Bank Bill, see Kevin R. C. Gutzman, *James Madison and the Making of America*, 256–60.

49   For the attempts to charter a bank under the Articles, see Charles Rappleye, *Robert Morris: Financier of the American Revolution* (New York: Simon & Schuster, 2010).

50   John J. Reardon, *Edmund Randolph: A Biography* (New York: Macmillan, 1975).

51   Contrast Marshall's opinion in *McCulloch v. Maryland* (1819). Marshall expert R. Kent Newmyer says Marshall never cited the ratification conventions in a court opinion. Perhaps this is why. Newmyer to Gutzman, correspondence in possession of author.

52   Speech of George Nicholas, June 24, 1788, *Documentary History of the Ratification of the Constitution*, 10:1507.

53   Kevin R. C. Gutzman, *Virginia's American Revolution: From Dominion to Republic, 1776–1840*, 86.

54   "Opinion on the Constitutionality of a National Bank," February 15, 1791, *Thomas Jefferson: Writings*, 416–21.

55   Alexander Hamilton, "Opinion on the Constitutionality of a National Bank," February 23, 1791, *Alexander Hamilton: Writings*, 613–46.

56   TJ to James Madison, October 1, 1792, and notes, Founders Online (National Archives) founders.archives.gov/documents/Jefferson/01-24-02-0392.

57   This paragraph is based on David N. Mayer, *The Constitutional Thought of Thomas Jefferson*, 198–99.

58   For the Cabell presentment and Iredell's grand jury charge, see TJ to Peregrine Fitzhugh, June 4, 1797, note, Founders Online (National Archives), founders .archives.gov/documents/Jefferson/01-29-02-0328.

59   Draft Petition to the Virginia House of Delegates, no later than August 3, 1797, Founders Online (National Archives), founders.archives.gov/documents/Jefferson /01-29-02-0390-0002. Jefferson's alarm was shared by Virginia's US senator Henry Tazewell. Henry Tazewell to James Madison, June 4, 1797, Founders Online (National Archives), founders.archives.gov/documents/Madison/01-17-02 -0010.

60   Revised Petition to the Virginia House of Delegates, August 7–September 7, 1797, Founders Online (National Archives), founders.archives.gov/documents /Jefferson/01-29-02-0390-0003.

61   TJ to James Monroe, September 7, 1797, Founders Online (National Archives), founders.archives.gov/documents/Jefferson/01-29-02-0416.

62   Editorial Note, TJ to James Madison, August 3, 1797, Founders Online (National Archives), founders.archives.gov/documents/Madison/01-17-02-0023.

63   The only account that considers all of the pertinent evidence is Kevin R. C. Gutzman, *Virginia's American Revolution: From Dominion to Republic, 1776–1840*, chapter 4.

64   Thomas Jefferson to Francis Hopkinson, March 13, 1789, Founders Online (National Archives), founders.archives.gov/documents/Jefferson/01-14-02-0402.

65   Simon P. Newman, *Parades and the Politics of the Street: Festive Culture in the Early American Republic* (Philadelphia: University of Pennsylvania Press, 1997), chapter 4.

66   A good brief account of the Alien and Sedition Acts is found at R. B. Bernstein, *Thomas Jefferson* (New York: Oxford University Press, 2003), 123–24.

67   Kevin R. C. Gutzman, *Virginia's American Revolution: From Dominion to Republic, 1776–1840*, chapter 4. The following account of the Resolutions' background is drawn from this source.

68   "Draft of the Kentucky Resolutions," *Thomas Jefferson: Writings*, 449–56.

69   David N. Mayer, *The Constitutional Thought of Thomas Jefferson*, 199–200.

70   "Virginia Resolutions," December 21, 1798, Founders Online (National Archives), founders.archives.gov/documents/Madison/01-17-02-0128.

71   Adrienne Koch and Harry Ammon, "The Virginia and Kentucky Resolutions:

An Episode in Jefferson's and Madison's Defense of Civil Liberties," *William and Mary Quarterly*, 3d Series, 5 (1948), 147–76.

72 Dumas Malone, *Jefferson and His Time* (6 volumes, Charlottesville: University Press of Virginia, 1948–81); Merrill D. Peterson, *Thomas Jefferson and the New Nation*.

73 Wendell Bird, "Reassessing Responses to the Virginia and Kentucky Resolutions: New Evidence from the Tennessee and Georgia Resolutions and from Other States," *Journal of the Early Republic* 35 (2015), 519–57.

74 TJ to James Madison, August 23, 1799, Founders Online (National Archives), founders.archives.gov/documents/Jefferson/01-31-02-0145.

75 TJ to Wilson Cary Nicholas, September 5, 1799, Founders Online (National Archives), founders.archives.gov/documents/Jefferson/01-31-02-0151; James Madison, The Report of 1800, January 7, 1800, Founders Online (National Archives), founders.archives.gov/documents/Madison/01-17-02-0202.

76 TJ to Edmund Randolph, August 18, 1799, Founders Online (National Archives), founders.archives.gov/documents/Jefferson/01-31-02-0142.

77 For divisions over this question among leading Republicans, see Kevin R. C. Gutzman, *Virginia's American Revolution, 1776–1840*, 117–21.

78 Ibid., chapter 5.

79 First Inaugural Address, March 4, 1801, *Thomas Jefferson: Writings*, 492–96.

80 TJ to John Dickinson, March 6, 1801, *Thomas Jefferson: Writings*, 1084–85, at 1084.

81 TJ to Judge Spencer Roane, September 6, 1819, Founders Online (National Archives), founders.archives.gov/documents/Jefferson/98-01-02-0734; ibid., 1425–28, at 1425.

82 TJ to P. S. du Pont de Nemours, January 18, 1802, ibid., 1099–1101, at 1100.

83 TJ to Abigail Adams, June 13, 1804, Founders Online (National Archives), founders.archives.gov/documents/Adams/99-03-02-1280.

84 Raoul Berger, *Impeachment: The Constitutional Problems* (Cambridge, MA: Harvard University Press, 1973), 224–51.

85 Alexander Hamilton, *The Federalist* No. 79, May 28, 1788, Founders Online (National Archives), founders.archives.gov/documents/Hamilton/01-04-02-0242; TJ to Judge Spencer Roane, September 6, 1819, Founders Online (National Archives), founders.archives.gov/documents/Jefferson/98-01-02-0734.

86 TJ to Abigail Adams, July 22, 1804, Founders Online (National Archives), founders.archives.gov/documents/Adams/99-03-02-1294.

87 TJ to Abigail Adams, September 11, 1804, Founders Online (National Archives), founders.archives.gov/documents/Adams/99-03-02-1317.

88 Far the best account of John Adams in retirement is Joseph Ellis, *Passionate Sage: The Character and Legacy of John Adams* (New York: W. W. Norton, 1993).

89 Leonard W. Levy, *Jefferson and Civil Liberties: The Darker Side* (Lanham, MD: Ivan R. Dee, 1989).

90 Kevin R. C. Gutzman, *James Madison and the Making of America*, 288; Dumas Malone, *Jefferson the President: First Term, 1801–1805* (Boston: Little, Brown, 1970), 296, et seq.

91 This scenario and Jefferson's response are in TJ to John C. Breckinridge, August 12, 1803, *Thomas Jefferson: Writings*, 1136–39.

92 TJ to Dr. Joseph Priestley, January 29, 1804, ibid., 1141–43, at 1142–43.

93 Sixth Annual Message, December 2, 1806, ibid., 524–31, at 529; Eighth Annual Message, November 8, 1808, ibid., 543–49, at 549.

94 Kevin R. C. Gutzman, *James Madison and the Making of America*, 333; James Madison, Veto of Federal Public Works Bill, March 3, 1817, constitution.org /jm/18170303_veto.htm.

95 TJ to the Danbury Baptist Association, January 1, 1802, Founders Online (National Archives), founders.archives.gov/documents/Jefferson/01-36-02 -0152-0006.

96 The following explanation depends in part upon Daniel L. Dreisbach, "A New Perspective on Jefferson's Views on Church-State Relations: The Virginia Statute for Establishing Religious Freedom in Its Legislative Context," *American Journal of Legal History* 35 (1991), 172–204, at 194–96.

97 Second Inaugural Address, March 4, 1805, The Avalon Project (Yale University), avalon.law.yale.edu/19th_century/jefinau2.asp.

98 TJ to (Rev.) Samuel Miller, January 23, 1808, Founders Online (National Archives), founders.archives.gov/documents/Jefferson/99-01-02-7257. Jefferson wrote in response to (Rev.) Samuel Miller to TJ, January 18, 1808, Founders Online (National Archives), founders.archives.gov/documents/Jefferson/99 -01-02-7222.

99 Jean Edward Smith, *John Marshall: Definer of a Nation* (New York: Henry Holt, 1996), 11; Dumas Malone, *Jefferson and His Time: The Sage of Monticello* (Boston: Little, Brown, 1981).

100 The full story of Jefferson and the Tracy manuscripts appears at ibid., 208–12 and 305–07.

101 TJ to A. L. C. Destutt de Tracy, January 26, 1811, *Thomas Jefferson: Writings*, 1241–47.

102 This paragraph is based on TJ to William H. Crawford, June 20, 1816, *The Works of Thomas Jefferson*, ed. Paul Leicester Ford (New York: G.P. Putnam's Sons,

1904–05), 11:536–41, at 538, oll.libertyfund.org/titles/jefferson-the-works-vol-11 -correspondence-and-papers-1808-1816?q=crawford#lf0054-11_head_149.

103   This discussion is drawn from TJ to Joseph C. Cabell, February 2, 1816, Founders Online (National Archives), founders.archives.gov/documents/Jefferson/03 -09-02-0286. Also see TJ to Samuel Kercheval, July 12, 1816, Online Library of Liberty (Liberty Fund), oll.libertyfund.org/titles/808. I am indebted for recognition of the utility of making this point here to Peter S. Onuf.

104   The best Marshall biography—though like all the others, it celebrates its subject, taking the correctness of virtually all of his opinions, judicial and political, for granted—is R. Kent Newmyer, *John Marshall and the Heroic Age of the Supreme Court* (Baton Rouge: Louisiana State University Press, 2001). A general corrective is Kevin R. C. Gutzman, *The Politically Incorrect Guide to the Constitution* (Washington, D.C.: Regnery Publishing, 2007), particularly 75–104. Also see Kevin R. C. Gutzman, *Virginia's American Revolution: From Dominion to Republic, 1776–1840*, chapters 5 and 6; and Kevin R. C. Gutzman, *James Madison and the Making of America*, chapters 3–8.

105   For Jefferson's sentimentalism and attempts to bring his hopes to fruition, see Andrew Burstein, *The Inner Jefferson: Portrait of a Grieving Optimist* (Charlottesville: University Press of Virginia, 1995).

106   Alan Pell Crawford, *Twilight at Monticello: The Final Years of Thomas Jefferson* (New York: Random House, 2008), is a fine account. See also Dumas Malone, *The Sage of Monticello*; and Peter S. Onuf, *Jefferson's Empire: The Language of American Nationhood* (Charlottesville: University Press of Virginia, 2000).

107   Kevin R. C. Gutzman, *James Madison and the Making of America*, 330.

108   An outstanding description of the Bank Case is given in R. Kent Newmyer, *John Marshall and the Heroic Age of the Supreme Court*, 291–302.

109   John Marshall, *McCulloch v. Maryland*, March 6, 1819, *John Marshall: Writings*, ed. Charles F. Hobson (New York: Library of America, 2010), 412–36.

110   William L. Reynolds II, "Luther Martin, Maryland and the Constitution," 47 Md. L. Rev. 291 (1987), digitalcommons.law.umaryland.edu/mlr/vol47/iss1 /35.

111   Edmund S. Morgan, *Inventing the People: The Rise of Popular Sovereignty in England and America* (New York: W. W. Norton, 1988).

112   James Madison, "Report of 1800," *The Papers of James Madison: Congressional Series*, eds. William T. Hutchinson and William M. E. Rachal et al. (Chicago and Charlottesville: University of Chicago Press and University Press of Virginia, 1956–91), 307–50, at 309.

113   The attacks on the Supreme Court's decision, together with Marshall's re-

sponses, are collected in *John Marshall's Defense of McCulloch v. Maryland*, ed. Gerald Gunther (Stanford, CA: Stanford University Press, 1969).

114　The story is told with a strongly pro-Marshall twist in F. Thornton Miller, *Judges and Juries Versus the Law: Virginia's Provincial Legal Perspective, 1783–1828* (Charlottesville: University Press of Virginia, 1994). Even Newmyer says Marshall "probably" violated judicial ethics in relation to *Martin v. Hunter's Lessee*. R. Kent Newmyer, *John Marshall and the Heroic Age of the Supreme Court*, 363.

115　R. Kent Newmyer, *John Marshall and the Heroic Age of the Supreme Court*, 349.

116　Drew McCoy, *The Last of the Fathers: James Madison and the Republican Legacy* (New York: Cambridge University Press, 1989), 95.

117　James Madison to Spencer Roane, September 2, 1819, Founders Online (National Archives), founders.archives.gov/documents/Madison/04-01-02-0455.

118　Spencer Roane to TJ, August 22, 1819, Founders Online (National Archives), founders.archives.gov/documents/Jefferson/98-01-02-0701.

119　TJ to Spencer Roane, September 6, 1819, Founders Online (National Archives), founders.archives.gov/documents/Jefferson/98-01-02-0734.

120　The quotations in this paragraph are in Spencer Roane, "Hampden II," June 15, 1819, *John Marshall's Defense of McCulloch v. Maryland*, 114–24, at 122–23.

121　TJ to Spencer Roane, September 6, 1819, Founders Online (National Archives), founders.archives.gov/documents/Jefferson/98-01-02-0734.

122　Jefferson's disappointment with Republican Supreme Court appointees is documented in Donald G. Morgan, *Justice William Johnson, The First Dissenter: The Career and Constitutional Philosophy of a Jeffersonian Judge* (Columbia: University of South Carolina Press, 1954).

123　Robert J. Brugger, *Beverley Tucker: Heart Over Head in the Old South* (Baltimore: Johns Hopkins University Press, 1978).

124　A recent account is Robert Pierce Forbes, *The Missouri Compromise and Its Aftermath: Slavery and the Meaning of America* (Chapel Hill: University of North Carolina Press, 2007), but see Kevin R. C. Gutzman, "Slavery and the Coming of the Civil War: The Missouri Controversy," review of Robert Pierce Forbes, *The Missouri Compromise and Its Aftermath: Slavery and the Making of America*, at *Civil War Book Review* (Winter 2008), cwbr.com/civilwarbookreview/index.php?q=3900&field=ID&browse=yes&record=full&searching=yes&Submit=Search.

125　Peter S. Onuf, *Jefferson's Empire: The Language of American Nationhood* (Charlottesville: University Press of Virginia, 2000).

126　Dumas Malone, *Jefferson and His Time: The Sage of Monticello*, 310, et seq.

127　For his last years generally, see Alan Pell Crawford, *Twilight at Monticello*.

128 This and the following paragraphs are based on TJ to Albert Gallatin, December 26, 1820, Founders Online (National Archives), founders.archives.gov /documents/Jefferson/98-01-02-1705. President Monroe agreed with Jefferson about the reasons for Missouri agitators' position. In one letter, Monroe, who had voted against ratification of the Constitution in 1788 partly on the basis of northern congressmen's attempt in 1786 to empower Secretary for Foreign Affairs John Jay to trade away access to the Mississippi for access to Spanish ports, confided that some of the authors of that 1786 Yankee gambit were among the leaders of the Missouri exclusionists. James Monroe to TJ, February 7, 1820, Founders Online (National Archives), founders.archives.gov/documents/Jefferson/98-01 -02-1065.

129 Alan Taylor, *The Internal Enemy: Slavery and War in Virginia, 1772–1832* (New York: W. W. Norton, 2013), 404.

130 This "Jeffersonian" metaphor was actually taken by Jefferson from an ancient Greek model. K[evin] R. Constantine Gutzman, "Jefferson's 'Dances With Wolves,'" *Uncommon Sense*, the Newsletter of the Omohundro Institute for Early American History and Culture 119 (Fall 2004), 15.

131 Alan Taylor, *The Internal Enemy: Slavery and War in Virginia, 1772–1832*, 404–09.

132 TJ to Albert Gallatin, December 26, 1820, Founders Online (National Archives), founders.archives.gov/documents/Jefferson/98-01-02-1705.

133 TJ to John Holmes, April 22, 1820, Founders Online (National Archives), founders.archives.gov/documents/Jefferson/98-01-02-1234.

134 For the association, Alan Taylor, *The Internal Enemy, Slavery and War in Virginia, 1772–1832*, 408.

135 Peter S. Onuf, *Statehood and Union: A History of the Northwest Ordinance* (Bloomington: Indiana University Press, 1987).

136 John Taylor, *Tyranny Unmasked* (Indianapolis: Liberty Fund, 1992).

137 John Taylor, *New Views of the Constitution of the United States* (Washington, DC : Regnery Gateway, 2001).

138 TJ to Thomas Ritchie, December 25, 1820, Founders Online (National Archives), founders.archives.gov/documents/Jefferson/98-01-02-1702; John Taylor, *Construction Construed and Constitutions Vindicated* (New York: Da Capo Press, 1970).

139 A good discussion of the book is Garrett Ward Sheldon and C. William Hill Jr., *The Liberal Republicanism of John Taylor of Caroline* (Madison, NJ: Farleigh Dickinson University Press, 2008), chapter 6.

140 Ibid., 145.

141 Dumas Malone, *Jefferson and His Time: The Sage of Monticello*, 316.

142 TJ to John Taylor of Caroline, February 14, 1821, Founders Online (National Archives), founders.archives.gov/documents/Jefferson/98-01-02-1836.

143 John Taylor, *Construction Construed and Constitutions Vindicated*, 194–5.

144 The following quotations are from TJ to Spencer Roane, March 9, 1821, Founders Online (National Archives), founders.archives.gov/documents/Jefferson/98-01-02-1900.

145 TJ to Thomas Ritchie, December 25, 1820, Founders Online (National Archives), founders.archives.gov/documents/Jefferson/98-01-02-1702.

146 Translation courtesy of Claire Albrecht.

147 TJ to William Johnson, June 12, 1823, Founders Online (National Archives), founders.archives.gov/documents/Jefferson/98-01-02-3562.

148 Rex Beach, "Judge Spencer Roane: A Champion of States' Rights" (MA Thesis, University of Virginia, 1941), 88.

149 Donald G. Morgan, *Justice William Johnson: The First Dissenter*, 181–82.

150 Ibid., 184.

151 Ibid., 185.

152 John Quincy Adams, Inaugural Address, The Avalon Project (Yale Law School), avalon.law.yale.edu/19th_century/qadams.asp.

153 John Quincy Adams, First Annual Message, December 6, 1825, Miller Center (University of Virginia), millercenter.org/president/jqadams/speeches/speech-3514.

154 "Draft Declaration and Protest of Virginia 1825, on the Principles of the Constitution of the United States of American, and on the Violations of them," December 1825, The Avalon Project (Yale Law School), avalon.law.yale.edu/19th_century/jeffdecl.asp.

155 Kevin R. C. Gutzman, "Thomas Jefferson's Federalism, 1774–1825," *Modern Age* 53 (2011), 74–80, at 74.

156 Adrienne Koch and Harry Ammon, "The Virginia and Kentucky Resolutions: An Episode in Jefferson's and Madison's Defense of Civil Liberties," *William and Mary Quarterly* 5 (1948), 147–76.

157 For the explicit partisanship, see, for example, ibid., Editors' Note, 145–46. Contrast Kevin R. C. Gutzman, *Virginia's American Revolution: From Dominion to Republic, 1776–1840*, chapter 4. That the same people acted similarly in regard to other areas of Jefferson's life is the subject of Edward L. Ayers and Scott French, "The Strange Career of Thomas Jefferson: Race and Slavery in American Memory, 1943–1993," in *Jeffersonian Legacies*, ed. Peter S. Onuf (Charlottesville: University Press of Virginia, 1993), 418–56, and particularly,

Annette Gordon-Reed, *Thomas Jefferson and Sally Hemings: An American Controversy* (Charlottesville: University Press of Virginia, 1998).

158   James Madison to Thomas Ritchie, December 12, 1825, Founders Online (National Archives), founders.archives.gov/documents/Madison/99-02-02-0591.

159   James Madison to TJ, February 24, 1826, Founders Online (National Archives), founders.archives.gov/documents/Madison/99-02-02-0627.

2. Freedom of Conscience

1   Thanks to Daniel L. Dreisbach for pointing out that "liberty of conscience" captures Jefferson's position more accurately than "religious freedom." Dreisbach email to author, December 1, 2015.

2   I was saved from ascribing too great a significance to the Virginia Statute for Religious Freedom by Daniel L. Dreisbach, "A New Perspective on Jefferson's Views on Church-State Relations: The Virginia Statute for Establishing Religious Freedom in its Legislative Context," *American Journal of Legal History* 35 (1991), 172–204.

3   Rhys Isaac, *The Transformation of Virginia, 1740–1790* (Chapel Hill: University of North Carolina Press, 1999).

4   "Notes on Locke and Shaftesbury" and "Notes on Episcopacy," *The Papers of Thomas Jefferson*, ed. Julian P. Boyd et al. (Princeton, NJ: Princeton University Press, 1950–) (hereafter *PTJ*), 1:544–53.

5   "William Small," Thomas Jefferson Foundation, Inc., monticello.org/site/jefferson/william-small.

6   "Editorial Note: Notes and Proceedings on Discontinuing the Establishment of the Church of England," Founders Online (National Archives), founders.archives.gov/?q=Ancestor%3ATSJN-01-01-02-0222&s=1511311111&r=1 (from *PTJ*, 1:525–29).

7   TJ to Benjamin Rush, January 16, 1811, Founders Online (National Archives), founders.archives.gov/documents/Jefferson/03-03-02-0231 ("trinity").

8   "First Draft by Jefferson," Before June 13, 1776, *PTJ*, 1:337–45.

9   Kevin R. C. Gutzman, *James Madison and the Making of America* (New York: St. Martin's Press, 2012).

10   "Autobiography," *Thomas Jefferson: Writings*, ed. Merrill D. Peterson (New York: Library of America, 1984), 3–101.

11   "A Memorandum (Services to My Country)," c. 1800, *Thomas Jefferson: Writings*, 702–04, at 702.

12   Ibid.

13 Rhys Isaac, *The Transformation of Virginia* (New York: W. W. Norton, 1988); "Notes and Proceedings on Discontinuing the Establishment of the Church of England," Editorial Note, *PTJ*, 1:525–29, at 525. The latter is the chief source of the following account, except where otherwise noted.

14 "Autobiography," 34.

15 "The Revisal of the Laws," Editorial Note, *PTJ*, 2:305–24, at 305.

16 "Autobiography," 38.

17 "The Revisal of the Laws," Editorial Note, *PTJ*, 2:305–24, at 308–09.

18 *PTJ*, 2:531–42, plus notes at 542–43.

19 *PTJ*, 2:545–47, notes at 547–53.

20 James Madison to TJ, January 22, 1786, Founders Online (National Archives), founders.archives.gov/documents/Madison/01-08-02-0249.

21 "Autobiography," 40.

22 *PTJ*, 2:553–54, notes at 554–55.

23 *PTJ*, 2:555, notes at 555–56.

24 *PTJ*, 2:556.

25 *PTJ*, 2:558–59, 559–61.

26 *PTJ*, 2:589–90.

27 *PTJ*, 2:638.

28 *PTJ*, 2:119n.

29 For the story of the book's conception and execution, see Thomas Jefferson, *Notes on the State of Virginia*, ed. William Peden (Chapel Hill: University of North Carolina Press, 1982), xii–xvii.

30 *Notes on the State of Virginia*, 157–61.

31 Kevin R. C. Gutzman, *James Madison and the Making of America* (paperback edition, New York: St. Martin's Griffin, 2013), Introduction.

32 Ibid.

33 Dumas Malone, *Jefferson the Virginian* (Boston: Little, Brown, 1948), 279.

34 Martin E. Marty, "The Virginia Statute Two Hundred Years Later," in *The Virginia Statute for Religious Freedom: Its Evolution and Consequences in American History* (New York: Cambridge University Press, 1988), 1–21, at 9.

35 Thomas E. Buckley, S.J., "The Political Theology of Thomas Jefferson," in *The Virginia Statute for Religious Freedom: Its Evolution and Consequences in American History*, 75–107, at 76–77.

36 Ibid., for this point and the following quotation.

37 For Jefferson's understanding of the Tenth Amendment principle and federal government religious observances, also see TJ to (Rev.) Samuel Miller, January 23, 1808, Founders Online (National Archives), founders.archives.gov

/documents/Jefferson/99-01-02-7257. Thanks to Daniel L. Dreisbach for this reference.

38 Daniel L. Dreisbach, *Thomas Jefferson and the Wall of Separation Between Church and State* (New York: New York University Press, 2002), 22.

39 The "Danbury" Baptists actually comprised "twenty-six churches, most of them in the Connecticut Valley, stretching from Suffield to Middletown and including several as far west as Amenia, New York." Daniel L. Dreisbach, *Thomas Jefferson and the Wall of Separation Between Church and State*, 21.

40 For the letter's didactic purpose, see TJ to Attorney General Levi Lincoln, January 1, 1802, in John Ragosta, *Religious Liberty: Jefferson's Legacy, America's Creed* (Charlottesville: University of Virginia Press, 2013), 232–33.

41 Daniel L. Dreisbach, *Thomas Jefferson and the Wall of Separation Between Church and State*, 19.

42 TJ to Messrs. Nehemiah Dodge and Others, a Committee of the Danbury Baptist Association, in the State of Connecticut, January 1, 1802, *Thomas Jefferson: Writings*, 510.

43 TJ to Attorney General Levi Lincoln, January 1, 1802, in John Ragosta, *Religious Freedom: Jefferson's Legacy, America's Creed*, 232–33.

44 Postmaster General Gideon Granger to TJ, December 31, 1801, in John Ragosta, *Religious Freedom: Jefferson's Legacy, America's Creed*, 233.

3. Colonization

1 TJ to Samuel Kercheval, July 12, 1816, *Thomas Jefferson: Writings*, ed. Merrill D. Peterson (New York: Library of America, 1984), 1395–1403, oll.libertyfund.org/titles/jefferson-the-works-vol-12-correspondence-and-papers-1816-1826.

2 Neil Vigdor, "Democrats drop Thomas Jefferson and Andrew Jackson names from annual fundraising dinner," *CT Post*, July 23, 2015, www.ctpost.com/news/article/Democrats-drop-Thomas-Jefferson-and-Andrew-6400544.php.

3 Jo Mannies, "Jefferson and Jackson removed as namesakes for Missouri Democratic Party's biggest annual event," St. Louis Public Radio, July 12, 2015, news.stlpublicradio.org/post/jefferson-and-jackson-removed-namesakes-missouri-democratic-partys-biggest-annual-event.

4 Paul Finkelman, "'Treason Against the Hopes of the World': Thomas Jefferson and Slavery," *Slavery and the Founders: Race and Liberty in the Age of Jefferson* (2nd ed., Armonk, NY: M.E. Sharpe, 2001), 129–62, quotation at 129. For Washington, see Henry Wiencek, *An Imperfect God: George Washington, His Slaves, and the Creation of America* (New York: Farrar, Straus, 2003); for

Randolph, Russell Kirk, *John Randolph of Roanoke* (4th ed.; Indianapolis: Liberty Fund, 1997); for Carter, Andrew Levy, *The First Emancipator: The Forgotten Story of Robert Carter, the Founding Father Who Freed His Slaves* (New York: Random House, 2005).

5 William W. Freehling, "The Founding Fathers and Slavery," *American Historical Review* 77 (1972), 81–93; and William W. Freehling, *The Reintegration of American History: Slavery and the Civil War* (New York: Oxford University Press, 1994), 12–33.

6 Joseph Ellis, *American Sphinx: The Character of Thomas Jefferson* (New York: Vintage Books, 1996).

7 Andrew Burstein, *The Inner Jefferson: Portrait of a Grieving Optimist* (Charlottesville: University Press of Virginia, 1995).

8 Annette Gordon-Reed, *Thomas Jefferson and Sally Hemings: An American Controversy* (Charlottesville: University Press of Virginia, 1997).

9 Scot A. French and Edward L. Ayers, "The Strange Career of Thomas Jefferson: Race and Slavery in American Memory, 1943–1993," in Peter S. Onuf, ed., *Jeffersonian Legacies* (Charlottesville: University Press of Virginia, 1993), 418–45.

10 Eugene A. Foster et al., "Jefferson fathered slave's last child," *Nature* 396 (November 5, 1998), 27–28. "Almost conclusively" because although the idea had never been seriously floated before November 1998, it is possible that some other male Jefferson fathered the Hemings offspring in question.

11 Here and throughout, I use the term "African-American" only in reference to free black Americans. Slaves, Virginians decided at the very beginning of their republican experiment, were not Americans. They were, in Jefferson's conception, a captive nation. For Virginians, see Kevin R. C. Gutzman, *Virginia's American Revolution: From Dominion to Republic, 1776–1840* (Lanham, MD: Lexington Books, 2007), chapter 1.

12 Jefferson's friendship with Bland and Bland's effect on Jefferson's most significant act are recounted in K[evin] R. Constantine Gutzman, "Jefferson's Draft Declaration of Independence, Richard Bland, and the Revolutionary Legacy: Giving Credit Where Credit Is Due," *Journal of the Historical Society* 1 (2001), 137–54. For Bland generally, Brent Tarter, "Richard Bland (1710–1776)," *Dictionary of Virginia Biography*, in *Encyclopedia Virginia*, EncyclopediaVirginia.org/Bland_Richard_1710-1776.

13 Frank L. Dewey, *Thomas Jefferson: LAWYER* (Charlottesville: University Press of Virginia, 1986), 88.

14 John Chester Miller, *The Wolf by the Ears: Thomas Jefferson and Slavery* (New York: The Free Press, 1977), 5–6.

15 "Draft of Instructions to the Virginia Delegates in the Continental Congress (MS Text of *A Summary View*, &c.)," July 1774, *The Papers of Thomas Jefferson*, ed. Julian P. Boyd et al. (Princeton, NJ: Princeton University Press, 1950–) (hereafter *PTJ*), 1:121–35.

16 For Jefferson's role, Editorial Note, *PTJ*, 1:187–92.

17 "Jefferson's Composition Draft," *PTJ*, 1:193–98.

18 "Resolutions of the Virginia Convention Calling for Independence," *PTJ*, 1:220–21. Far the best account of the Declaration of Independence is Pauline Maier, *American Scripture: Making the Declaration of Independence* (New York: Knopf, 1997).

19 "Resolution of Independence, Moved by R.H. Lee for the Virginia Delegation," June 7, 1776, *PTJ*, 1:298.

20 "Notes of Proceedings in the Continental Congress," June 7–August 1, 1776, *PTJ*, 1:309–27, at 313. The congressional editing process is described at 314–19.

21 For Jefferson's intention that the Declaration be presented orally, see Jay Fliegelman, *Declaring Independence: Jefferson, Natural Language, and the Culture of Performance* (Redwood City, CA: Stanford University Press, 1993).

22 Pauline Maier, *American Scripture: Making the Declaration of Independence*.

23 TJ to Richard Henry Lee, July 8, 1776, *PTJ*, 1:455–56.

24 As in Richard Henry Lee to TJ, July 21, 1776, *PTJ*, 1:471, and Edmund Pendleton to TJ, August 10, 1776, *PTJ*, 1:488–91.

25 TJ to Thomas Nelson, May 16, 1776, *PTJ*, 1:292–93.

26 "Editorial Note," "First Draft by Jefferson," "Second Draft by Jefferson," and "Third Draft by Jefferson," June 1776–Before June 13, 1776, *PTJ*, 1:329–65.

27 George Wythe to TJ, July 27, 1776, *PTJ*, 1:476–77.

28 "Editorial Note: The Revisal of the Laws, 1776–1786," *PTJ*, 2:305–24, at 313.

29 Ibid., 320.

30 Ibid., 470–73. Statements in my text about the final law depend upon the extensive editorial notes at 472–73.

31 Bruce Chadwick, *I Am Murdered: George Wythe, Thomas Jefferson, and the Killing That Shocked a New Nation* (Hoboken, NJ: Wiley, 2009).

32 *PTJ*, 2:475–76 provides the texts of these bills and notes describing the history of their amendment and adoption.

33 *Notes on the State of Virginia*, ed. William Peden (Chapel Hill: University of North Carolina Press, 1982).

34 Ibid., xii.

35 Ibid., n. 1.

36   Most prominent by far of these mischaracterizations is Winthrop D. Jordan, *White Over Black: American Attitudes Toward the Negro, 1550–1812* (Baltimore: Penguin Books, 1968), 433. See also Paul Finkelman, *Slavery and the Founders: Race and Liberty in the Age of Jefferson*, 160.

37   Paul Finkelman, *Defending Slavery: Proslavery Thought in the Old South: A Brief History with Documents* (New York: Bedford/St. Martin's, 2003), 20.

38   *Notes on the State of Virginia*, 162–63.

39   Charles A. Miller, *Ship of State: The Nautical Metaphors of Thomas Jefferson* . . . (Lanham, MD: University Press of America, 2003).

40   Peter S. Onuf, " 'To Declare Them a Free and Independent People': Race, Slavery, and National Identity in Jefferson's Thought," *Journal of the Early Republic* 18 (1998), 1–46, at 2.

41   *Notes on the State of Virginia*, 130–49.

42   Peter S. Onuf, " 'To Declare Them a Free and Independent People': Race, Slavery, and National Identity in Jefferson's Thought," 3.

43   John Taylor of Caroline, *Arator*, ed. M.E. Bradford (Indianapolis: Liberty Fund, 1977), 123.

44   Ibid.

45   Ibid., 125.

46   Ibid., 124.

47   Peter Thompson, " 'I have known': Thomas Jefferson, Experience, and *Notes on the State of Virginia*," *A Companion to Thomas Jefferson*, ed. Francis D. Cogliano (Chichester, UK: Blackwell Publishing, Ltd., 2012), 60–73, at 61.

48   Andrew Burstein, *The Inner Jefferson: Portrait of a Grieving Optimist*.

49   TJ to Nicholas Lewis, December 19, 1786, Founders Online (National Archives), founders.archives.gov/documents/Jefferson/01-10-02-0466.

50   TJ to Jean-Nicolas Démeunier, June 26, 1786, Founders Online (National Archives), founders.archives.gov/documents/Jefferson/01-10-02-0001-0006.

51   Winthrop D. Jordan, *White Over Black: American Attitudes Toward the Negro, 1550–1812*, 450, n. 37 (Banneker as first black employee); Benjamin Banneker to TJ, August 19, 1791, Founders Online (National Archives), founders.archives.gov /documents/Jefferson/01-22-02-0049.

52   TJ to Benjamin Banneker, August 30, 1791, Founders Online (National Archives), founders.archives.gov/documents/Jefferson/01-22-02-0091.

53   TJ to Condorcet, August 30, 1791, Founders Online (National Archives), founders.archives.gov/documents/Jefferson/01-22-02-0092.

54   Winthrop D. Jordan, *White Over Black: American Attitudes Toward the Negro, 1550–1812*, 452.

55 TJ to Abbé Grégoire, February 25, 1809, Founders Online (National Archives), founders.archives.gov/documents/Jefferson/99-01-02-9893.

56 TJ to Joel Barlow, October 8, 1809, Founders Online (National Archives), founders.archives.gov/documents/Jefferson/03-01-02-0461.

57 Winthrop D. Jordan, *White Over Black: American Attitudes Toward the Negro, 1550–1812*, 450.

58 Benjamin Banneker to TJ, August 19, 1791, Founders Online (National Archives), founders.archives.gov/documents/Jefferson/01-22-02-0049.

59 Peter H. Wood, *Black Majority: Negroes in Colonial South Carolina from 1670 Through the Stono Rebellion* (New York: W. W. Norton, 1974).

60 David Goldfield, *America Aflame: How the Civil War Created a Nation* (paper, New York: Bloomsbury Press, 2012).

61 The most compelling—nay, unforgettable—account of the Haitian Revolution, based largely on research in primary materials, is Madison Smartt Bell, *All Souls' Rising* (New York: Penguin Books, 1996).

62 See Governor James Monroe's comments on the Haitian Revolution's effect and "any mischief resulting from it," Douglas Egerton, *Gabriel's Rebellion: The Virginia Slave Conspiracies of 1800 and 1802* (Chapel Hill: University of North Carolina Press, 1993).

63 Don E. Fehrenbacher and Ward M. McAfee, *The Slaveholding Republic: An Account of the United States Government's Relations to Slavery* (New York: Oxford University Press, 2001), 112.

64 Voltaire, pseudonym of François-Marie Arouet, *Candide* (1759). The full quotation is "dans ce pays-ci, il est bon de tuer de temps en temps un amiral pour encourager les autres" ("in this country, it is good to kill from time to time an admiral to encourage the others"). Voltaire here spoofs the execution of a British admiral for poor performance early in the Seven Years' War.

65 Don E. Fehrenbacher and Ward M. McAfee, *The Slaveholding Republic: An Account of the United States Government's Relations to Slavery*, 113–14.

66 Robert Pleasants to TJ, June 1, 1796, Founders Online (National Archives), founders.archives.gov/documents/Jefferson/01-29-02-0084.

67 TJ to Robert Pleasants, August 27, 1796, Founders Online (National Archives), founders.archives.gov/documents/Jefferson/01-29-02-0135. This document shows that Paul Finkelman erred in saying that, "Jefferson . . . opposed . . . black education." Paul Finkelman, *Slavery and the Founders: Race and Liberty in the Age of Jefferson*, 192.

68 *The Revolution of 1800: Democracy, Race, and the New Republic*, ed. James J.

Horn, Jan Ellen Lewis, and Peter S. Onuf (Charlottesville: University of Virginia Press, 2002).

69 Douglas R. Egerton, *Gabriel's Rebellion: The Virginia Slave Conspiracies of 1800 and 1802.*

70 James Monroe to TJ, June 15, 1801, Founders Online (National Archives), founders.archives.gov/documents/Jefferson/01-34-02-0274.

71 TJ to James Monroe, November 24, 1801, Founders Online (National Archives), founders.archives.gov/documents/Jefferson/01-35-02-0550.

72 Joshua D. Rothman, *Notorious in the Neighborhood: Sex and Families Across the Color Line in Virginia, 1787–1861* (Chapel Hill: University of North Carolina Press, 2003), 12–13.

73 Ibid., 13.

74 For Jeffersonian ideas of nature and separate varieties of humans, see Daniel J. Boorstin, *The Lost World of Thomas Jefferson* (Chicago: University of Chicago Press, 1993), 57–108.

75 Monroe, as president 1817–1825, would play a key role in excluding slavery from much of the Louisiana Purchase Territory, which Jefferson obtained from France in 1803. He also sponsored the establishment of the West African state of Liberia, whose purpose was to serve as the Jeffersonian "receptacle of the blacks transported into this hemisphere." Robert Pierce Forbes, *The Missouri Compromise and Its Aftermath: Slavery and the Meaning of America* (Chapel Hill: University of North Carolina Press, 2007); Harry Ammon, *James Monroe: The Quest for National Identity* (Charlottesville: University Press of Virginia, 1990), 523.

76 Winthrop D. Jordan, *White Over Black: American Attitudes Toward the Negro, 1550–1812*, 475–78.

77 TJ to Rufus King, July 13, 1802, Founders Online (National Archives), founders.archives.gov/documents/Jefferson/01-38-02-0052.

78 Don E. Fehrenbacher and Ward M. McAfee, *The Slaveholding Republic: An Account of the United States Government's Relations to Slavery*, 113.

79 Sixth Annual Message, December 2, 1806, The American Presidency Project, www.presidency.ucsb.edu/ws/?pid=29448.

80 Paul Finkelman, *Slavery and the Founders: Race and Liberty in the Age of Jefferson*, 151.

81 Quotations and background in this paragraph come from the missive and notes at John Lynch to TJ, December 25, 1810, Founders Online (National Archives), founders.archives.gov/documents/Jefferson/03-03-02-0196.

82   TJ to John Lynch, January 21, 1811, Founders Online (National Archives), founders.archives.gov/documents/Jefferson/03-03-02-0243.

83   Suzanne Cooper Guasco, *Confronting Slavery: Edward Coles and the Rise of Antislavery Politics in Nineteenth-Century America* (DeKalb: Northern Illinois University Press, 2013), 255, n. 52.

84   Quotations in this and the next paragraph are from Edward Coles to TJ, July 31, 1814, Founders Online (National Archives), founders.archives.gov/documents/Jefferson/03-07-02-0374.

85   TJ to Edward Coles, August 25, 1814, Founders Online (National Archives), founders.archives.gov/documents/Jefferson/03-07-02-0439.

86   Suzanne Cooper Guasco, *Confronting Slavery: Edward Coles and the Rise of Antislavery Politics in Nineteenth-Century America*, passim.

87   The mural and the story are found at "Future Governor Edward Coles Freeing His Slaves While Enroute [sic] to Illinois 1819," *Encyclopedia Virginia,* encyclopediavirginia.org/media_player?mets_filename=evr7069mets.xml.

88   Kevin R. C. Gutzman, *James Madison and the Making of America* (New York: St. Martin's Press, 2012), 356–57.

89   My thanks to Annette Gordon-Reed for pointing out that I should address this question. Thanks to Robert Paquette for the constitutional point.

90   This paragraph is based on John Chester Miller, *The Wolf by the Ears: Thomas Jefferson and Slavery*, 256.

91   Alan Taylor, *The Internal Enemy: Slavery and War in Virginia, 1772–1832* (New York: W. W. Norton, 2013), 408.

92   For the Roane and Giles quotations, ibid., 407.

93   US Senate president pro tempore James Barbour was one. Noble E. Cunningham Jr., *The Presidency of James Monroe* (Lawrence: University Press of Kansas, 1996), 103.

94   Kevin R. C. Gutzman, *James Madison and the Making of America.*

95   TJ to Jared Sparks, February 4, 1824, Founders Online (National Archives), founders.archives.gov/documents/Jefferson/98-01-02-4020.

96   William Short to TJ, January 11, 1826, Founders Online (National Archives), founders.archives.gov/documents/Jefferson/98-01-02-5826.

97   Winthrop D. Jordan, *White Over Black: American Attitudes Toward the Negro, 1550–1812*, 467–69.

98   The leading work is Annette Gordon-Reed, *Thomas Jefferson and Sally Hemings: An American Controversy*. See also Eugene A. Foster et al., "Jefferson fathered slave's last child," *Nature* 396 (November 5, 1998), 27–28, which explains the DNA evidence concerning one line of Hemings's descendants.

4. Assimilation

1   James W. Ceaser, *Reconstructing America: The Symbol of America in Modern Thought* (New Haven: Yale University Press, 1997). The Jefferson-related material is principally at 17–53.

2   Douglas L. Wilson, "Jefferson and the Republic of Letters," *Jeffersonian Legacies* (Charlottesville: University Press of Virginia, 1993), 50–76.

3   James W. Ceaser, *Reconstructing America*, 29.

4   Ibid., 28.

5   Ibid., 28.

6   Ibid., 29.

7   Bernard W. Sheehan, *Seeds of Extinction: Jeffersonian Philanthropy and the American Indian* (Chapel Hill: University of North Carolina Press, 1973), 71–72.

8   *Notes on the State of Virginia*, ed. William Peden (Chapel Hill: University of North Carolina Press, 1982), 26–72. That the Frenchman had not asked that question is noted at Peter Thompson, "'I have known': Thomas Jefferson, Experience, and *Notes on the State of Virginia*," *A Companion to Thomas Jefferson*, ed. Francis Cogliano (Chichester, UK: Blackwell Publishing, Ltd., 2012), 60–73, at 62.

9   Ibid., 58 ff.

10 For the significance of the Logan speech, Anthony F. C. Wallace, *Jefferson and the Indians: The Tragic Fate of the First Americans* (Cambridge, MA: Harvard University Press, 1999).

11 James W. Ceaser, *Reconstructing America*.

12 The following discussion is based on *Notes on the State of Virginia*, 97–100.

13 Ibid., n. 8 at 281. See also Anthony F. C. Wallace, *Jefferson and the Indians*, 92.

14 Jefferson's discussion of the Indians' languages is at ibid., 100–02.

15 Ibid., 150–54. The relevant portion is at 151.

16 In the second of the Declaration's four sections, Jefferson says of King George III that "He . . . has endeavoured to bring on the inhabitants of our frontiers, the merciless Indian Savages, whose known rule of warfare, is an undistinguished destruction of all ages, sexes and conditions."

17 Roy Harvey Pearce, quoted in Anthony F. C. Wallace, *Jefferson and the Indians*, 95. The following description of Jefferson's views is drawn from ibid., 95–96.

18 TJ to Marquis de Chastellux, June 7, 1785, *Thomas Jefferson: Writings*, ed. Merrill D. Peterson (New York: Library of America, 1984), 799–802, at 801.

19 Anthony F. C. Wallace, *Jefferson and the Indians*, chapter 5.

20   Ibid., 333–34.

21   A recent study vindicating Jefferson's appraisal of Hamilton (and reaching similar conclusions regarding John Adams, James Iredell, James Wilson, and others), though without ever mentioning that it vindicates Jefferson, is Eric Nelson, *The Royalist Revolution: Monarchy and the American Founding* (Cambridge, MA: Harvard University Press, 2014). The points about Jefferson's response to Hamilton come from Anthony F. C. Wallace, *Jefferson and the Indians*, 178, 180.

22   Robert J. Miller, *Native America, Discovered and Conquered: Thomas Jefferson, Lewis & Clark, and Manifest Destiny* (Westport, CT: Praeger, 2006), 85–86.

23   The following discussion depends on Robert J. Miller, *Native America, Discovered and Conquered*; quotations at 20, 63–64.

24   Ibid., 65.

25   Ibid., 65–66.

26   Ibid., 85, has Jefferson saying, "I believe the Indian, then, to be, in body and mind, equal to the white man."

27   Kevin R. C. Gutzman, *James Madison and the Making of America* (New York: St. Martin's Press, 2012), 289–91.

28   A readable account is Stephen Ambrose, *Undaunted Courage: Meriwether Lewis, Thomas Jefferson and the Opening of the American West* (New York: Simon & Schuster, 1996).

29   Ibid., 278.

30   Robert J. Miller, *Native America, Discovered and Conquered*, 105.

31   Deep disappointment at the fate of the lexicons Lewis and Clark had compiled is revealed in TJ to Dr. Benjamin S. Barton, September 21, 1809, Founders Online (National Archives), founders.archives.gov/documents/Jefferson/03-01-02-0430.

32   Robert J. Miller, *Native America, Discovered and Conquered*, 112–14.

33   Ibid., 87–88.

34   Anthony F. C. Wallace, *Jefferson and the Indians*, 220–21.

35   Ibid., 96.

36   TJ to the Chiefs of the Cherokee Nation, January 10, 1806, *Thomas Jefferson: Writings*, 561–63.

37   Anthony F. C. Wallace, *Jefferson and the Indians*, 221.

38   Ibid., 224.

39   Ibid., 239.

40   Ibid., 239.

41   Second Inaugural Address, *Thomas Jefferson: Writings*, 518–23, at 520.

5. Mr. Jefferson's University

1 This chapter is strongly influenced throughout by Jennings L. Wagoner Jr., *Jefferson and Education* (Charlottesville, VA: Thomas Jefferson Foundation, 2004). Also see "Bibliographic Essay," in Cameron Addis, *Jefferson's Vision for Education, 1760–1845* (New York: Peter Lang, 2003), 153–62.

2 Merrill D. Peterson, *Thomas Jefferson and the New Nation* (New York: Oxford University Press, 1970), 962.

3 M. Andrew Holowchak, *Thomas Jefferson's Philosophy of Education: A Utopian Dream* (New York: Routledge, 2014), 7.

4 Ibid., 8.

5 Edmund Pendleton to TJ, July 22, 1776, *The Papers of Thomas Jefferson*, ed. Julian P. Boyd et al. (Princeton, NJ: Princeton University Press, 1950–) (hereafter *PTJ*), 1:471–72, at 472.

6 "A Bill for the More General Diffusion of Knowledge," *PTJ*, 2:526–33.

7 Ibid., n. at 534.

8 John Locke, *An Essay Concerning Human Understanding* (New York: Oxford University Press, 1979).

9 TJ to Nathaniel Burwell, *Thomas Jefferson: Writings* ed. Merrill D. Peterson (New York: Library of America, 1984), 1411–13.

10 Robert Pleasants to TJ, June 1, 1796, Founders Online (National Archives), founders.archives.gov/documents/Jefferson/01-29-02-0084.

11 TJ to Robert Pleasants, August 27, 1796, Founders Online (National Archives), founders.archives.gov/documents/Jefferson/01-29-02-0135.

12 *PTJ*, 2:534, n.

13 Samuel Stanhope Smith to TJ, March [?] 1779, Founders Online (National Archives), founders.archives.gov/documents/Jefferson/01-02-02-0094.

14 This paragraph depends on Cameron Addis, *Jefferson's Vision for Education, 1760–1845*, 10.

15 For the story of the project, see "Introduction," *Notes on the State of Virginia*, ed. William Peden (Chapel Hill: University of North Carolina Press, 1954), xi–xxv.

16 The chapter is at ibid., 130–49, and the section on Bill No. 79 is at 147–49.

17 Robert Orvis Woodburn, "An Historical Investigation of the Opposition to Jefferson's Educational Proposals in the Commonwealth of Virginia" (Ph.D. dissertation, American University, 1974).

18 James Madison to TJ, Founders Online (National Archives), founders.archives.gov/documents/Madison/01-09-02-0096.

19 For Norfolk, Cameron Addis, *Jefferson's Vision for Education, 1760–1845*, 16.

20 *PTJ*, 2:535–42, with nn. at 542–43.

21 "Autobiography," *Thomas Jefferson: Writings*, 3–101, at 43.

22 "The Indian School at William & Mary," William & Mary website, wm.edu /about/history/historiccampus/indianschool/, accessed May 31, 2016.

23 Robert Orvis Woodburn, "An Historical Investigation of the Opposition to Jefferson's Educational Proposals in the Commonwealth of Virginia," 51.

24 "Autobiography," *Thomas Jefferson: Writings*, 3–101, at 43.

25 *PTJ*, 2:542–43, n.

26 *PTJ*, 2:544, n. at 2:544–45.

27 Ibid., n.

28 Cameron Addis, "Jefferson and Education," *A Companion to Thomas Jefferson*, ed. Francis Cogliano (Chichester, UK: Blackwell Publishing, Ltd.), 547–73, at, 560.

29 TJ to Wilson Cary Nicholas, November 23, 1794, Founders Online (National Archives), founders.archives.gov/documents/Jefferson/01-28-02-0151.

30 TJ to François d'Ivernois, February 6, 1795, Founders Online (National Archives), founders.archives.gov/documents/Jefferson/01-28-02-0196.

31 Jennings L. Wagoner Jr., *Jefferson and Education* (Charlottesville, Virginia: Thomas Jefferson Foundation, 2004), 49.

32 Ibid., 49–51.

33 TJ to Joseph Priestley, January 18, 1800, Founders Online (National Archives), founders.archives.gov/documents/Jefferson/01-31-02-0275.

34 Cameron Addis, *Jefferson's Vision for Education, 1760–1845*, 30.

35 TJ to Joseph Priestley, January 27, 1800, Founders Online (National Archives), founders.archives.gov/documents/Jefferson/01-31-02-0289.

36 Adam R. Nelson, "The Perceived Dangers of Study Abroad, 1780–1800: Nationalism, Internationalism, and the Origins of the American University," *The Founding Fathers, Education, and "The Great Contest": The American Philosophical Society Prize of 1797*, ed. Benjamin Justice (New York: Palgrave Macmillan, 2013), 190.

37 The following account draws largely on Jennings L. Wagoner Jr., *Jefferson and Education*, 56–66.

38 Special Message to the Senate and House of Representatives, March 18, 1808, The American Presidency Project (University of California, Santa Barbara), presidency.ucsb.edu/ws/?pid=65764.

39 TJ to Joel Barlow, December 10, 1807, Founders Online (National Archives), founders.archives.gov/documents/Jefferson/99-01-02-6952.

40 Jennings L. Wagoner Jr., *Jefferson and Education*, 69–70, gives a summary

account. For the appointment, TJ to Robert Brent, August 14, 1805, Founders Online (National Archives), founders.archives.gov/documents/Jefferson/99-01-02 -2240; for the reappointment, see TJ to Robert Brent, September 19, 1807, Founders Online (National Archives), founders.archives.gov/documents/Jefferson/99 -01-02-6400.

41 Merrill D. Peterson, *Thomas Jefferson and the New Nation*, 983.

42 Kevin R. C. Gutzman, *Virginia's American Revolution: From Dominion to Republic, 1776–1840*, 150–54.

43 Virginius Dabney, *Mr. Jefferson's University: A History* (Charlottesville: University Press of Virginia, 1981), 2.

44 Virginius Dabney, *Mr. Jefferson's University: A History*, xiii.

45 Jennings L. Wagoner Jr., *Jefferson and Education*, 73. For Tucker, see Phillip Hamilton, *The Making and Unmaking of a Revolutionary Family: The Tuckers of Virginia, 1752–1830* (Charlottesville: University of Virginia Press, 2008); for Tazewell, see Norma Lois Peterson, *Littleton Waller Tazewell* (Charlottesville: University Press of Virginia, 1983). Tazewell and his father Henry are the only father-son US Senate president pro tempore tandem in American history, and the older Tazewell was a close friend of Jefferson's. The younger, meanwhile, was an intellectual eminence besides a prominent politician.

46 TJ to Littleton Waller Tazewell, January 5, 1805, *Thomas Jefferson: Writings*, 1149–53. This letter "was the genesis of Jefferson's plan for the University of Virginia." Merrill D. Peterson, *Thomas Jefferson and the New Nation*, 964.

47 Jennings L. Wagoner Jr., *Jefferson and Education*, 75.

48 For the War of 1812 in Virginia, see Alan Taylor, *The Internal Enemy: Slavery and War in Virginia, 1772–1832* (New York: W. W. Norton, 2013); for the rest of this paragraph, Cameron Addis, *Jefferson's Vision for Education, 1760–1845*, 30–31.

49 TJ to Peter Carr, September 7, 1814, *Thomas Jefferson: Writings*, 1346–52.

50 Jennings L. Wagoner Jr., *Jefferson and Education*, 87.

51 Ibid., 87–88.

52 For Cabell's background, see Phillip Hamilton, *The Making and Unmaking of a Revolutionary Family: The Tuckers of Virginia, 1752–1830*; for his personal life, see especially Alan Taylor, *The Internal Enemy: Slavery and War in Virginia, 1772–1832*; for his cooperation with Jefferson on the UVA project, see Dumas Malone, *The Sage of Monticello* (New York: Little, Brown, 1981), and Alan Pell Crawford, *Twilight at Monticello: The Final Years of Thomas Jefferson* (New York: Random House, 2008); besides Jennings L. Wagoner Jr., *Jefferson and Education*.

The letter mentioned in this paragraph is TJ to Joseph C. Cabell, January 5, 1815, Founders Online (National Archives), founders.archives.gov/documents /Jefferson/03-08-02-0156.

53　Jennings L. Wagoner Jr., *Jefferson and Education*, 89–91, quotation at 91.

54　Ibid., 91–92.

55　Ibid., 97–98.

56　Ibid., 100, 102.

57　Ibid., 102–03.

58　Peter Charles Hoffer, *The Free Press Crisis of 1800: Thomas Cooper's Trial for Seditious Libel* (Lawrence: University Press of Kansas, 2011).

59　For "atheist" and "strict materialist," see Cameron Addis, *Jefferson's Vision for Education, 1760–1845,* 83.

60　Merrill D. Peterson, *Thomas Jefferson and the New Nation,* 977.

61　My account of Cooper's career is based on Cameron Addis, *Jefferson's Vision for Education,* 83–86.

62　Jennings L. Wagoner Jr., *Jefferson and Education,* 104, et seq. Quotation in this paragraph at 105.

63　Ibid., 109. See Jefferson's "A Bill for Establishing a System of Public Education," as introduced by Senator Joseph C. Cabell in January 1818, at search.lib .virginia.edu/catalog/uva-lib:1002925/view#openLayer/uva-lib:867009/3756 /2644/0/1/0.

64　Jennings L. Wagoner Jr., *Jefferson and Education,* 129.

65　Visitors of Central College to the Speaker of the House of Delegates, January 6, 1818, Early history of the University of Virginia : as contained in the letters of Thomas Jefferson and Joseph C. Cabell, hitherto unpublished; with an appendix, consisting of Mr. Jefferson's bill for a complete system of education and other illustrative documents; and an introduction, comprising a brief historical sketch of the university, and a biographical notice of Joseph C. Cabell (hereafter *J-CC* for *Jefferson-Cabell Correspondence*), ed. Nathaniel F. Cabell (Richmond, VA. : J. W. Randolph, 1856), babel.hathitrust.org/cgi/pt?id=njp .32101068145802;view=1up;seq=448.

66　Jennings L. Wagoner Jr., *Jefferson and Education,* 110–11.

67　Ibid., 116.

68　Rex Bowman and Carlos Santos, *Rot, Riot, and Rebellion: Mr. Jefferson's Struggle to Save the University that Changed America* (Charlottesville: University of Virginia Press, 2013), 28.

69　"Report of the Commissioners for the University of Virginia," August 4, 1818, *Thomas Jefferson: Writings,* 457–73.

70 For Jefferson's careful explanation to the other commissioners that Albemarle County lay near the geographic center of Virginia's white population, see Jennings L. Wagoner Jr., *Jefferson and Education*, 117–18. For his elaboration of the point, see TJ to Joseph Carrington Cabell, January 1, 1819, Founders Online (National Archives), founders.archives.gov/documents/Jefferson/98-01-02 -0001.

71 Jennings L. Wagoner Jr., *Jefferson and Education*, 118.

72 Kevin R. C. Gutzman, *Virginia's American Revolution: From Dominion to Republic, 1776–1840*, 156.

73 Jennings L. Wagoner Jr., *Jefferson and Education*, 120.

74 Ibid., 121.

75 TJ to Joseph C. Cabell, January 22, 1820, Online Library of Liberty, *The Works of Thomas Jefferson*, 12:154–56, at 155, oll.libertyfund.org/titles/jefferson-the -works-vol-12-correspondence-and-papers-1816-1826?q=joseph+c.+cabell #lf0054-12_head_034.

76 TJ to Joseph C. Cabell, December 28, 1822, Founders Online (National Archives), founders.archives.gov/documents/Jefferson/98-01-02-3238.

77 Merrill D. Peterson, *Thomas Jefferson and the New Nation*, 981, uses the term "Old Republicanism." For that perspective generally, see Norman Risjord, *The Old Republicans: Southern Conservatism in the Age of Jefferson* (New York: Columbia University Press, 1965); Robert Dawidoff, *The Education of John Randolph* (New York: W. W. Norton, 1979); and Henry Simms, *The Life of John Taylor* (Richmond, VA: William Byrd Press, 1932).

78 This paragraph comes from Virginius Dabney, *Mr. Jefferson's University: A History*, 8. Also see Rex Bowman and Carlos Santos, *Rot, Riot, and Rebellion*, chapter 5, "Tales of Horror."

79 Cameron Addis, *Jefferson's Vision for Education, 1760–1845*, 116, 117.

80 Peachy Gilmer Papers, Virginia Historical Society.

81 Francis Walker Gilmer Letterbooks, The University of Virginia.

82 Virginius Dabney, *Mr. Jefferson's University: A History*, 6.

83 John Gilmer Speed, *The Gilmers in America* (New York: printed for private distribution, 1897), books.google.com/books?id=8YlBAAAAYAAJ&printsec =frontcover&source=gbs_ge_summary_r&cad=0#v=onepage&q&f=false, tells the whole family story. For Wirt, see Anya Jabour, *Marriage in the Early Republic: Elizabeth and William Wirt and the Companionate Ideal* (Baltimore: Johns Hopkins University Press, 2002).

84 Jennings L. Wagoner Jr., *Jefferson and Education*, 135.

85 This discussion relies on TJ to James Madison, February 1, 1825, Founders

Online (National Archives), founders.archives.gov/documents/Jefferson/98-01 -02-4929.

86   James Madison to TJ, February 8, 1825, Founders Online (National Archives), founders.archives.gov/documents/Jefferson/98-01-02-4946.

87   Jennings L. Wagoner Jr., *Jefferson and Education*, 138.

88   This paragraph is based on Merrill D. Peterson, *Thomas Jefferson and the New Nation*, 975.

89   TJ to George Ticknor, July 16, 1823, Founders Online (National Archives), founders.archives.gov/documents/Jefferson/98-01-02-3639; Rex Bowman and Carlos Santos, *Rot, Riot, and Rebellion*, 43.

90   Cameron Addis, *Jefferson's Vision for Education, 1760–1845*, 115.

91   Rex Bowman and Carlos Santos, *Rot, Riot, and Rebellion*, 44.

92   Ibid., 122.

93   Mary Ellen Flannery, "Due to State Budget Cuts, Public Colleges and Universities Now Less 'Public' Than Ever," neaToday, May 8, 2014, neatoday.org/2014 /05/08/due-to-state-budget-cuts-public-colleges-and-universities-less-public -than-ever/.

94   Thomas G. Mortenson, "State Funding: A Race to the Bottom," American Council on Education, Winter 2012, acenet.edu/the-presidency/columns-and -features/Pages/state-funding-a-race-to-the-bottom.aspx.

95   This paragraph relies on Cameron Addis, *Jefferson's Vision for Education, 1760– 1845*, 115.

96   TJ to James Madison, February 17, 1826, Founders Online (National Archives), founders.archives.gov/documents/Madison/99-02-02-0625.

Index